Contemporary Turkey in Conflict

Ethnicity, Islam and Politics

Tahir Abbas

D1407495

EDINBURGH
University Press

For Yalina

Edinburgh University Press is one of the leading university presses in the UK. We publish academic books and journals in our selected subject areas across the humanities and social sciences, combining cutting-edge scholarship with high editorial and production values to produce academic works of lasting importance. For more information visit our website: edinburghuniversitypress.com

© Tahir Abbas, 2017

Edinburgh University Press Ltd
The Tun – Holyrood Road
12 (2f) Jackson's Entry
Edinburgh EH8 8PJ

Typeset in 11/15 Adobe Garamond by
Servis Filmsetting Ltd, Stockport, Cheshire,
and printed and bound in Great Britain by
CPI Group (UK) Ltd, Croydon CR0 4YY

A CIP record for this book is available from the British Library

ISBN 978 1 4744 1798 3 (hardback)
ISBN 978 1 4744 1799 0 (paperback)
ISBN 978 1 4744 1800 3 (webready PDF)
ISBN 978 1 4744 1801 0 (epub)

The right of Tahir Abbas to be identified as author of this work has been asserted in accordance with the Copyright, Designs and Patents Act 1988 and the Copyright and Related Rights Regulations 2003 (SI No. 2498)

Contents

Figures and Tables

Preface

Turkey is a nation beset with contradictions. At the turn of the twenty-first century, in just one decade, it transformed from a country caught up in a financial crisis into a successful G20 economy. The stance that Turkey takes in amalgamating Islam, capitalism and democracy remains of significant interest to Middle East and Western European nations currently undergoing their own social, political, economic and cultural challenges. Yet, Turkey is in a precarious regional position compared to its neighbours. In 2015 the economy of Greece was on the brink of collapse, a situation that risked the stability of the entire Eurozone. Since 2011 Syria has spiralled into chaos because of an 'Arab Spring' quagmire that resists resolution. A matter made worse by the emergence of Islamic State, the instability in Syria is not only threatening the entire region but it also affects Western Europe in relation to both questions of terrorism and the refugee crisis. In Turkey the 'Kurdish issue' has re-emerged with great vigour. Rising wealth inequalities, regional disparities, internal intolerance towards minorities and a weakening Turkish lira remain all-important issues. In early 2016 it seems that the country's immediate future is uncertain. Only through implementing sound economic policy and the delicate balance of interethnic relations and religio-cultural inclusivity can Turkey now achieve the success that its people rightly deserve.

In 1997 a 'postmodern' *coup d'état* occurred when the Turkish military issued a memorandum and the Necmettin Erbakan government resigned without suspension of the constitution. It was alleged Erbakan was instituting Islamism at the time. The coup led to immense political and economic instability, and eventually brought on the Turkish financial crisis of 2000–1. In that same year, Recep Tayyip Erdoğan and his close acolytes formed the Justice and Development Party (AKP) after the collapse of the Turkish economy. In 2002 the AKP ran for election, winning 34 per cent of the vote and forming a majority government. The AKP thrived partly because of the sheer political and economic leadership vacuum that had engulfed the nation at the time. Since taking power in 2002 the AKP has increased its majority in each subsequent election, including in November 2015 after that same year's June election resulted in a hung parliament. Erdoğan has been at the helm of the AKP from the outset. He effortlessly won the 2014 presidential election, when he could no longer remain in office as prime minister due to constitutional rules. In transforming the institutions of society, combined with a neo-liberal economic individualism that has operated through a majoritarian nationalist zeal, Erdoğan and the AKP have configured Turkey into a determined administration after many years in the doldrums. Erdoğan achieves this partly by maintaining an air of authority comparable to the Ottomans and perhaps even Atatürk. Yet, at the same time, the AKP has pursued a neo-liberal economic and political agenda that has narrowly defined 'Turkishness' (ethnically, religiously and culturally). Before the AKP took power the secular Kemalist elite maintained firm control over the people of Turkey. Throughout the generations these elites periodically used excessive force. By the late 1980s and early 1990s the secularist-Kemalists lost their once established status, increasingly replaced by the Islamists. The third AKP victory in 2011 cemented the party's position as the supreme authority over many institutions of society (that is, military, judiciary, media and education), with little or no effective opposition. Immediately after the June 2015 general election confidence dropped and, with the realistic possibility of coalition government, the party's future was unclear. A period of instability ensued, when Islamic State terrorist attacks targeted indigenous populations. Following a campaign that concentrated on protecting Turkey 'from its enemies', the AKP achieved an outright win in November 2015. There has been no period of normalisation and reconciliation since then, leading to even greater authoritarianism combined with insecurity and growing political violence. It invariably sustains Erdoğan and the AKP in power, but presents no clear path forward in relation to government. For Turkey in the twenty-first century, the story of its development has been all about one man: Erdoğan. Progress has come to the country, but there are also many issues. Can Turkey maintain its role on the global stage? How will it balance the eastern–western, European–Islamic, modern–traditional and inward-looking–outward-looking issues that it endures? Is it possible to create a society that fulfils the anticipations of both its Islamic Sufi heritage and the European ideal?

Since the time of the Ottomans, the centre-periphery dynamic has compounded social relations in Turkey. It produces class, race and religious distinctions associated directly with the means of ownership of production, distribution and exchange combined with the accumulation of physical, social and cultural capital in the hands of elite urbanites. Historically these elites were secular and Kemalist in origin. In the 1990s a shift to conservative and religious groups (Islamists) followed, dominating not just aspects of the economy, but also media and politics. As the contest continues for economic, political and cultural stability, there is one group, the Kurds, representing approximately one-fifth of the population, who continue to suffer disproportionately. Given the sensitivities around the 'Kurdish issue' in Turkey, they have the most to gain and the most to lose from any peace process, and from the current opening up of society and Turkey's emergence from a major financial crisis. In June 2015 the Peoples' Democratic Party (HDP) gained eighty seats in parliament, preventing the AKP from forming a majority government. Under its leader Selahattin Demirtaş, the HDP ran again in November when the party was willing to form a coalition government. In spite of this, the situation changed again in the November 2015 election, where the HDP forfeited twenty seats. This happened largely due to the influence of the AKP, which stoked up fears of the enduring conflict between Turks and Kurds that has plagued the modern nation. This strategy did most damage to the Kurds, a community already facing the consequences of historical political and cultural marginalisation. Since the inception of the Turkish republic, the Kurds have routinely faced isolation. The ongoing theme has been misrecognition, attributed to their lack of 'Turkishness', as defined by the centre at the expense of the periphery. In the 1930s the modern republic rendered a significant part of the population illiterate by changing the character, content and importance of the Turkish language as a means of recognition by the state literally overnight. As the secular elites concentrated the wealth, power and authority at the centre, those at the margins, including other groups such as Alevis, Jewish and Christian minorities, faced increasing marginalisation. It was in the late 1970s that the Kurdistan Workers' Party (PKK) formed – since classified as a terrorist organisation by the state and the EU. From 1984 there has been violent conflict between the PKK and the Turkish state, with as many as 50,000 people losing their lives, mostly Kurdish. In 2012 the PKK and the Turkish government announced a formal cessation of violence. The Peace and Democratic Party (BDP), formed in 2008, evolved into the HDP in 2014. In the November 2015 election the HDP became the third party in Turkish politics, relegating the Nationalist Movement Party (MHP) to fourth place. A few short years ago it would have been unimaginable for a Kurdish party to win sixty seats in parliament. However, there was also an acute sense that Turkey was on the edge of disaster, with ongoing fighting against the PKK in the south-east, the government bombing Kurdish targets, and with an ever-greater clampdown on dissenting voices in the media, including the seizure of İpek Medya Grubu (a large conglomerate that includes mining and media) days before the November 2015 election. Erdoğan's vociferous outcry against 'Academics for Peace', intellectuals in Turkey who signed a petition in January 2016 to draw attention to the implications of the fighting in the south-east, led to the arrest of scores of university professors, some of whom are currently facing trial for 'treason'. While opening up the media through deregulation at one level, the AKP has also used its powers to shut down dissenting voices. At the same time, the domestic intelligence and policing services are firmly in the grip of what has lately become a security state. Using the threat of terrorism won an election for the AKP, but if his aspirations are too narrow and inward-looking, Erdoğan runs the risk of ostracisation at home and within the region.

The AKP began a new Kurdish–Turkish peace process in 2012, but by 2015 the party had changed tack. It started to leverage the conflict, alluding to the idea of 'saving the nation from its enemies', as Kemalists had done in years gone by. In various constituencies, AKP candidates in 2015 actively sought to problematise the struggle for recognition among Kurds. This approach also created unease among some Kurds who eventually switched back to the AKP, distancing themselves from the conflict and its associated negative politics. The AKP routinely demonised the PKK to draw irreducible parallels between it and the HDP. To emphasise its point further, the AKP concentrated on the need to protect Turkey 'from its enemies', evoking a sense of hyper-nationalism among majority ethnic Turks. The gamble helped to win back Kurdish votes lost to the HDP in June and nationalist votes ordinarily cast for the MHP, which has suffered the most in recent elections. The AKP altered its strategy since the June 2015 election, and kept close to party lines, winning back some votes gained by the HDP and MHP. Ultimately, the AKP achieved a decisive victory in November 2015. With 317 seats, Erdoğan's party formed a majority government with 49.5 per cent of the vote, fifty-nine more seats than in June, and with an 8.6 per cent swing. In the June 2015 elections the popularity of the AKP had plunged from 49 per cent to 41 per cent of the national vote. This was mainly due to the emergence of the HDP, which took eighty seats. Many of the HDP voters were previously pro-AKP but Kurds lost confidence in the AKP after the Kobanî incident of 2014. Turkish forces backed off from saving the town from Islamic State, three miles south of the Turkish border in Syria. As the Kurds in Turkey began to show agitation, clashes between Turkish military forces and the PKK resumed, leading to Turkish planes bombing Hakkâri. Between the June and November 2015 elections Turkey suffered three separate terrorist attacks in quick succession. In each case most of the victims were Kurdish. The Diyarbakır bombing in early June 2015 killed four people. The Suruç bombing in July 2015 took thirty-three lives. Then the Ankara bombing on 10 October, in the nation's capital city, killed 102 people, most of them young. The third attack happened just three weeks before the election in November 2015. Again, several of the victims were Kurdish. Ironically, two of the attacks struck Kurdish groups who were taking part in peace rallies aimed at building relations between Kurds and Turks, which was especially important after the peace process that had spectacularly broken down the year before. In four further terrorist incidents in three months, the first in January 2016; a suicide bomber killed thirteen foreign visitors to Sultanahmet, Istanbul's tourist heartland. The incident severely affected tourism, which was precisely the intention. Less than one month later, in February 2016, a car bomb placed outside military barracks in Ankara killed twenty-eight people, with scores injured. In early March a second car bomb in Ankara killed thirty-seven. A radical wing of the PKK, known as the TAK (Kurdistan Freedom Falcons), claimed responsibility for these early 2016 attacks on Ankara. Less than a week later four people died in a suicide bomb attack on Istanbul's busiest thoroughfare, popular with Turks and tourists alike, Istiklal Caddesi.

The question now is what happens next. There are a number of reasons to be optimistic, but also cause to be gloomy. Erdoğan has set his sights on a presidency with executive powers, but while this creates a sense of stability for half of the population loyal to the AKP, his Turkey will be ideological with a post-Islamist outlook. Post-Islamist refers to the ability to move beyond notions of Islamism, which suggests a desire for an Islamic state: a caliphate of sorts. Post-Islamists have realised that there can be no Islamist solution to politics without acceptance of non-theological abstractions of Islamic principles, including equality, human rights and secularism. This approach could take forward a confident stance on the wider Middle East and the Muslim world in general. However, Turkey has clearly become a deeply polarised society, with stark differences between secular and conservative political and ideological orientations, as well as deep religious and cultural schisms between liberals and those of a more religious orientation. Mass political violence, terrorism and social unrest are not new to Turkey, as the Gezi Park events of 2013 demonstrated. Arguably, Erdoğan's goal is to stamp a permanent legacy into the narrative of Turkey by remaining the elected president, potentially with greater executive powers in 2023, when Turkey celebrates the centenary of the founding of the modern secular republic. He has positioned himself and his party as the rightful heirs of Turkey. While democracy is certainly compatible with Islam, unfettered capitalism is not. Meanwhile, democratisation remains incomplete in Turkey, a nation of believers who are familiar with authoritarianism. Nevertheless, other issues have also arisen in the last two years which should be of significant concern to a much-besieged Turkey. Rising from the ashes of the Iraq war, Islamic State presents a worrying development for Turkey, especially when combined with the situation in Syria and the seeming inability of global actors to respond. Foreign fighters come from all over the world to join Islamic State in Syria, most of them travelling via Turkey. In addition, the Syrian refugee situation has produced an increasingly xenophobic, orientalist and Islamophobic attitude in Europe that has caused a distinct shift to the political right, especially in Central Europe. Germany has taken a bold stance on accepting refugees but has also found itself caught in a bind. With hundreds of German-born Turks and indigenous German converts in Islamic State, there is a sense of impending doom as Syrians and other Muslim refugees enter the country to seek asylum. The flow of 'threatening' Muslims into and out of Turkey has caused a great deal of consternation among political elites and media opinion-formers in the West. Democracy is rarely perfect, perhaps even less so in the Middle East.

The central hypothesis of the study is that despite all the developments to its economy, society and politics in the twenty-first century, Turkey is unable to shake off the lure of authoritarianism. The result is a struggle to define national identity in times of crisis, causing Turkey to regress into hyper-ethnic monocultural nationalism, even where Islamism has replaced Kemalism as Turkey's dominant political hegemony. To illustrate how ethnicity, Islam and politics intersect in Turkey today, this book explores issues of ethnic intolerance, social capital and political trust, the 'Kurdish issue' and the Gezi Park events. Research for this study contains primary data collected in the form of ethnographic observations and in-depth interviews with a range of community members across various locations in Turkey. Extensive statistical modelling of large data sets available from the European Social Survey (ESS), namely the survey responses from Turkey in 2004 and 2008, generated a dynamic overview of ethnic, religious and political relations in Turkey. Analysis of the ESS found that majority ethnic Turks remain intolerant of others. Kurdish nationalism is on the rise, while social capital is strengthening between conservative Muslims, who are more likely to demonstrate political trust than others. Meanwhile, qualitative research suggested that wide sections of society have been feeling a sense of betrayal that reached boiling point during the Gezi Park disturbances in 2013. This study charts the position of Turkey in the twenty-first century and the dominant political and cultural hegemony of the AKP. It explores the nature of Turkey's political, economic and social development. It examines how notions of ethnic nationalism transpire in an era of rapid globalisation. The research explores issues ranging from the AKP–Hizmet tension to the Kurdish issue, from late Ottoman history to the recent Gezi Park events, and from the situation of the ethnic and religious minorities to centre-periphery relations. The book presents a series of vignettes on the tensions, ambiguities and inconsistences that face a nation experiencing rapid transformation in an era of internationalisation. In essence, the study explains how post-Islamism and post-Kemalism intersect with processes of neo-liberalism, globalisation and democratisation. As the 'Kurdish issue' lingers as *the* primary ethnic relations conundrum, this book is a perspective on Turkey in the twenty-first century, with an eye on the lingering impacts of twentieth-century history and politics. Tensions between diverse groups in Turkey are as problematic as they were in the 1980s. Those who wrote off Erdoğan, concentrating on his authoritarianism and his iron rule over the state, were premature. There is no doubt that the AKP is fully behind him, backed with a mandate from the population to carry on what it began in 2002. Going forward, Turkey remains unpredictable, but always fascinating. In exploring a country of myriad issues, with tremendous historical and contextual challenges, certain intellectual questions will undoubtedly remain unfulfilled. Moreover, many scholars write from positions that often contain narrow ontological and epistemological biases. It reinforces existing modes of domination and subordination, whether these authors are insiders or outsiders.

While there are countless academic studies on Turkey, they originate from perspectives within political science, sociology, anthropology, history and theology. Few, if any, usefully combine these fields into a single social science analysis of the country, one conducted by a scholar operating within the country. This book aims to do precisely that. As a social researcher specialising in ethnic relations and social conflict, I aspire to learn from the experiences of those who are often the most marginalised. My aim is to tell the story of societies from the bottom up. This approach facilitates an understanding of the workings of wider society, to help increase tolerance, improve equality, build social cohesion, influence social policy and promote a sense of civic national identity that is both inclusive and purposive for the greater good. This is *my* ideological perspective.

Acknowledgements

I would like to thank Fatih University for providing me with the time and space to complete my work to satisfaction. I would especially like to thank scholars and friends, Charles Allen Scarboro, Joshua Hendrick, Ferhat Kentel, Yusuf Sarfati, Berdal Aral, Mohammed Bakari, Latif Tas, Berdal Aral, Tugrul Keskin, Rainer Brömer, Zeynep Yalçın Ökten, Talip Küçükcan, Nuri Tinaz, Ali Murat Yel, Michelangelo Guida and Bruce Lawrence for their valuable insights, my extended conversations with them during the course of my research and writing, and their camaraderie.

I thank the editors of the following journals for reproduction of aspects of the papers, 'The effect of ethno-national conflict on Kurdish families in south-east Turkey' in *Terrorism and Political Violence* (with I. H. Yigit) and 'Scenes from Gezi Park', in *City* (with I. H. Yigit). I am extremely indebted to a true young scholar and a faithful friend, Ismail Hakki Yigit. His assistance in helping with the data collection process and in translating the interview data for these papers was invaluable. We both suffered for this research. In carrying out our interviews with families with members in the PKK, we had to move from house to house in the very early hours of the morning in order to avoid unnecessary attention from the local security forces. Our participants were also wary of spies and informants. When the car could not travel any further, we trudged from house to house in three feet of snow, in temperatures of −14 degrees centigrade. In exploring the Gezi Park events, we endured the fury of the police forces who launched a massive offensive to clear the park on the same day we were carrying out our study. We endured the irritating effects of CS gas and pepper spray shooting out of the water cannon that had caught us in a pincer movement on Istiklal Caddesi. We did this because we wanted to get to the heart of the story, and we surely did. I am also very grateful to Nabil Khattab for his statistical modelling of European Social Survey data based on sampling carried out in Turkey in the 2004 and 2008 waves of the survey.

In the time I spent researching for this book, I travelled across vast swathes of Turkey and explored various aspects of secular and religious life. I discovered much about this complex, rich and diverse nation. While the politics of Turkey is as tumultuous as one can envision anywhere in the world, the striking splendour of the vast geography of an immense territory and its heritage is to behold. I am also grateful for invitations to New York, Rabat, Algiers, Islamabad and Jakarta, as well as universities, think tanks and policy centres all over Turkey to deliver lectures and talks based on my research for this book. I am indebted to my generous hosts for opportunities to undertake visiting fellowships at universities all over the world. At New York University, Leiden University, Hebrew University in Jerusalem, International Islamic University in Islamabad to the Graduate School of the State Islamic University in Jakarta, I was able to take advantage of the immense intellectual resources on offer and to ruminate on the topics of political Islam and Muslim identity politics with diverse students and faculty.

I would like to thank Nicola Ramsey of Edinburgh University Press for her ongoing interest in my research on Islam and politics. I would also like to thank Yusuf Sarfati for his constructive suggestions and finally, yet importantly, Samantha North for her careful copy-editing of my final manuscript. Any errors that remain are of my own making.

TA
Istanbul, Turkey
20 March 2016

Chronology

1984	PKK launched first attack on Turkish Armed Forces
1989	Turgut Özal became eighth president of Turkey
1993	President Özal died in mysterious circumstances
1996	Necmettin Erbakan elected prime minister in coalition government
1994	Recep Tayyip Erdoğan elected mayor of Istanbul
1997	Military memorandum
1998	Erdoğan jailed for reading Islamic poem in Siirt
1998–9	Fethullah Gülen went to the US in self-imposed exile
2000	Collapse of the Turkish government
2002	AKP won election and formed government
2011	AKP won third successive general election with an increased vote
2014	Erdoğan elected president, Ahmet Davutoğlu appointed prime minister
2015	AKP failed to secure June election win, snap election called
2015	Suruç bombing killed thirty-three in June, Ankara bombings killed 102 in October
2015	AKP returned to power with greater majority in November
2016	Islamic State suicide attack killed thirteen tourists in Sultanahmet, twelve were German

1

Setting the Scene

Located in the centre of the world, Turkey is a fascinating nation with an immense history and culture. It is, however, full of contrasts and contradictions. Over the last two decades there has been considerable interest in the economic, political and cultural developments in Turkey, with a great deal written about the country and its people as they have emerged out of periods of crises in the late 1990s. Yet, there has been no single attempt to understand the intersections of ethnicity, Islam and politics across the nation. This book aims to do precisely that. It focuses on change and continuity since the beginning of the twenty-first century, at a time when Turkey has advanced in numerous directions but has also regressed in others. These developments affirm a perpetual state of conflict at the heart of Turkish society, which has undergone an array of transformations since the collapse of the Ottoman Empire at the beginning of the twentieth century. They also raise new challenges in today's globalising world.

By 2010 Turkey had become a global society, confident of its economic and political position regionally and globally. Rising living standards and aspirations helped to cement the bonds within and between the middle classes of society. Since then there have also been periods of economic instability and political unrest that have also generated questions about social capital and political trust. What have been the implications for the practice of Islam at the level of ordinary Turkish society, from vast swathes of Anatolia to the cultural centre of Istanbul? How has this arisen within the framework of globalisation as experienced during the first fifteen years of the twenty-first century? How much of the authoritarian centralised secular past of the Kemalist period remains present in dominant politics today? What is the nature of intergroup relations, and how have certain bonds advanced the wider sociological and political changes affecting Turkey? Why do modes of conflict persist in spite of the desire to improve social cohesion and build social trust? These and other questions provide an opening to further the discussions in the book based on original research. This introductory chapter provides the setting for what follows, describing a historical, cultural and political overview of the Turkish case.

A Brief History of the Turks

Throughout history, the land that is now Turkey has been home to diverse civilisations, ethnicities and religions. They range from the Persians, Hittites, Greeks, Romans and Seljuk Turks, all the way to the Ottomans. This diversity has made Turkey one of the most fascinating countries in the world. Many see modern Turkey as the 'bridge of civilisations', where various communities have intermixed with each other over time – sharing values, customs and traditions that still linger in today's society. From this rich history, modern Turkey is conceptualised as an ongoing process of nation-building and social cohesion. Today, the internationalisation of capital, labour, political principles and cultural aspirations have led to the interconnectedness of diverse people in assorted ways. Globalisation has affected Turkey in crucial directions, and it will continue to do so in the light of numerous ongoing developments, both domestic and international (Park 2012).

The 'Turkic' origins of Turkey go right back to the heartlands of Central Asia, the 'Turko Mongol heritage . . . and their precursors in Asia' (Findley 2005: 5). Modern Turkey personifies groups of people shifting westwards, leaving a trail of Turkic groups eventually scattered across the lands from modern-day Turkey to parts of Inner Mongolia. When thinking about ethnic diversity in Turkey, it is clear that 'Turks' are a category consisting of groups of diverse cultural, linguistic, racial and religious heritage that have continuously shaped Istanbul and the large cities of Anatolia. Nevertheless, there is a fundamental thread that connects historical Turkey to its modern day incarnation: the religion of Islam, first introduced into parts of Anatolia by the Abbasids during the eighth century. Further expansion of Islam in the region came under the Seljuks during the late eleventh century. With the arrival of Turkic migrants who had adopted Sufi leanings inspired by the Safaviyya order of Sheikh Safi-ad-din Ardabili (1252–1334), who was a

Kurdish mystic. These Turks followed the Shafi'i *madhab* (doctrine). In the formalisation of the Ottoman Empire at the end of the fifteenth century, Ottoman Turks adopted the Hanafi *madhab*. Social and cultural relations in contemporary Turkey are characterised through a cultural celebration of Ottomanism and Sunni Islam. This memory echoes in aspects of contemporary Turkish culture that relate back to the formation of the empire. Islam transcended existing tribal, ethnic and linguistic borders through a process of organic expansion. Islam is a diverse religion that flourishes through hybridism with existing cultural forms. Although Islam in Turkey has undergone various transformations over the course of the millennia, modern Turkey has embraced its Islamic heritage as well as its pan-Turkic historical development. This is most noticeable in how the current ruling party, the Justice and Development Party (AKP), has projected a particular vision of Turkey in the everyday vernacular of politics and culture.

One of the specific contributions of this book is the analysis of the rise and dominance of the AKP during the first part of the twenty-first century. At the time of writing, it appears the AKP will remain influential for some time. This is largely due to lack of a credible opposition, but it is also a result of how the AKP has cemented its position through policies of development, democracy and political Islam. The AKP has instrumentalised a political and economic formula to help Turkey recover from economic depression at the end of the twentieth century. Today the nation has become a major regional power; this is the primary reason that the AKP remains popular. Any attempt to understand today's Turkey, therefore, cannot ignore the country's situation before the arrival of Islam, nor can it overlook specific forms of ethno-religious and ethno-cultural nationalism, which have characterised the twentieth century in particular.

Islamic National Identity under the AKP

In recent periods the AKP has mobilised certain Islamic values as part of its political project, and projected these values onto the public sphere. The Gezi Park disturbances in the summer of 2013 demonstrated growing levels of dissatisfaction towards the AKP among different elements of Turkish society. This was partly a function of class and social mobility issues, but there were also major concerns related to a series of ideological battles between the 'old

Kemalism' and the 'new Islamism'. The former refers to the distinctly secular notion of cultural Turkishness that was elitist and centralist. The latter refers to the rise of pious conservative Muslims who possessed both wealth and political power. Questions about the character of an Islamic national identity in Turkey are also associated with how modernity, capitalism, neo-liberalism and Islam have coalesced in Turkey. Neo-liberalism refers to laissez faire economics, deregulation of financial policy, a focus on individual opportunity rather than collective effort and the promotion of market solutions to deliver public services. It leads to all sorts of additional conflicts over identity and belonging, and about modes of political participation in contemporary society. Much of this is also associated with how the constructions of 'East' and 'West' are conceptualised in Turkey, as well as how Islamic and European history is conceived and understood.

Over the ages, Turkey has become a bridge for cultural interaction, but modes of conflict and demonisation of 'the other' have also existed. In the shift from a Christian to a Muslim society, perceptions of East and West became blurred and indistinct. During the last decade of the twentieth century, the 'war on terror' catapulted the intersection between Islam and Christianity to new levels of discussion. Ignorance and aggression were present on all sides. As a member of NATO and a key figure in the Organisation of Islamic Cooperation (OIC), Turkey has held a critical position in the global 'war on terror'. Many feared that the arrival of the AKP in 2002 would lead to the Islamisation, or the re-Islamisation, of Turkish society and politics. At the time such impressions seemed unclear, but the AKP soon began to flex its Islamist muscles. During the first decade of the twenty-first century, Turkey was looking to the West with confidence, engaging in strong economic activity and developing significant trading relations with Europe, as well as maintaining efforts on the EU engagement process. In 2016 Turkey is looking towards the East for equivalent economic interactions, while improving commercial relations with parts of the Middle East, Central Asia, and as far afield as India and China (Ozgulu 2008).

Several issues emerge when conceptualising religious and political identity in Turkey. Since its rise to power in 2002 the AKP has won three consecutive election victories. After a hung parliament in June 2015, it returned to government with just under 50 per cent of the national vote in November

2015, each decisive victory resulting in an increased share of the vote. This political formula appeals to most of the population. The AKP seemed to flourish progressively until the Gezi Park events occurred in 2013. Hakan Yavuz (2009) argues that Recep Tayyip Erdoğan's popular mandate consists of a threefold dynamic: family, Ottomanism and piety. Contrary to common belief, conservatism dominates the ideology of the AKP rather than political Islamism: 'Conservatism in Turkey is more a social attitude than a political one' (Yavuz 2009: 94). Hence, Erdoğan's popularity rests on a mixture of postmodernity and the combination of traditional values regarding family and community. For example, commerce, technology, finance and globalisation are vital constituents of the political project, but the importance of the family for building communities persists to a large degree. An Islamic value system permeates this conservatism, found mainly within the realms of rural areas and smaller towns. The AKP deploys compelling symbols associated with Islam, including direct references to specific Islamic teachings. Still, divisions transpire between how the party faithful adhere to the character of localised Islamism and how the AKP itself perpetuates a system of national conservatism.

The importance of family is emphasised, while a patriarchal understanding of the roles of men and women in Turkey persists in the background, with women often consigned to traditional roles. Men share the dominant public space in terms of politics, community and the formation of a national identity. Romanticised Ottomanism is a celebration of the past successes of a pan-Turkic mode of being, revived through the appeal of a national public discourse, but also through how Turkey projects itself to the rest of the world. As such, '[t]here is a deep feeling of nostalgia towards the Ottoman and even Seljuk periods. Reconstruction of Ottoman identity has been at work for the last three decades and has recently been articulated in art, literature, cuisine and politics' (ibid. 95). Individual claims to religion determine piety, but articulated at the community level, with Islam as the anchor in this creation of a community-orientated philosophy. Such an approach helps to create loyalty, which is idealised as a conservative political project, which has bottom-up characterisation. Grass-roots supporters, and communities throughout the land, hold together precious various constructions of a revered Islam and its applications for community and national identity.

According to Yavuz (2009), the AKP has eliminated Islamism from its political project. The party's national citizenship model encourages individuality and freedom that comes with certain responsibilities associated with being a modern Muslim Turk. It allows the AKP to capture a wide-ranging population, which has improved the range of economic opportunities for all sections of society: from the proletariat to the bourgeoisie, the small business holder to the international conglomerate, the secular to the conservative. Economic neo-liberalism is encouraged and facilitated by the state, generating an inclusive mode of economic wellbeing and participatory democracy.

Religious Revisionism

The stance of the AKP is important in understanding Islam in Turkey, and in particular, the situation of Islam in politics, but there remains a risk of underestimating wider factors in this process. Islamism, understood as the role Islam plays in politics, is important to consider, but the most remarkable dynamic is that of conservatism. The Gülen movement, or Hizmet (meaning 'service'), has been described as one of the most influential Islamist organisations in Turkey, but it achieves its success through conservatism rather than Islamism. Hizmet has made influential gains in the economic sphere (Hendrick 2013) and in civil society (Ebaugh 2009), but its impact on the political process is often exaggerated, both internally and externally. Ali Çarkoğlu and Ersin Kalaycıoğlu (2009: 141) argue that right-conservatism is a function of 'long-term socio-political modernization, industrialization, the more recent increased pace of social mobilization, and contemporary regional turbulences caused by the changes that have been taking place in the international system since the end of the Cold War'. The movement of populations to the centre explains a great deal, as groups are attracted by economic and labour market opportunities given various advances to industrialisation and globalisation. In addition, the Turkish economy has opened up to foreign investment. This move has stimulated the growth of industry and commerce, while creating employment in various sectors, particularly the service and financial sectors, both of which have grown over the last two decades. As the state increased public investment in numerous social infrastructures, including housing, roads, health, education and the civil service, it also created prospects for a new professional middle class, many of whom are also pious Muslims. The economic opportunities afforded to these Muslim groups gave them increased visibility and eventually confidence in the public sphere, bringing their conservatism to the fore.

Given wider developments, the centre-periphery dynamic in Turkey, originated by Şerif Mardin (1973), requires enhancement. The existing theory integrates a dialectic between so-called 'Islam as a popular religion' and a so-called 'secularism' (or *laiklik*). There have been wider changes to Turkey's economy and society, experienced over the last two decades. Thus, a rudimentary Islam versus secularism dichotomy is no longer sufficient to understand Turkish politics and society. The shift towards conservatism underpinned by economic expansionism and globalisation offers a more robust explanation. Moreover, the AKP is politically conservative compared with several of the Islamic organisations popular among the masses, urban and rural, poor and middle-class, including growing Salafi (literalist) movements. Historically, the centre-periphery dualism model carried substantial weight, particularly by the end of the Ottoman Empire, where an elitist and centralist authority viewed the periphery as a backward or even miscreant marginal entity. The centre maintained a degree of authority and control over the periphery by keeping it marginalised and excluded. The centre held on to power through its model of 'Turkishness', specifically in the light of a vigorously enforced secular republic model. Presently, far greater economic, political and social synergy emerges between the centre and the periphery. The conceptualisation of a diverse multireligious Turkey remains ideational. Rather, Turkey has taken a path from territorial–civic to ethno-conservative nationalism. The latter creates ongoing tensions between the Kemalist–secularists and the pan-Turkic Islamists, where religion combined with nationalism and Islam is the dividing line between these two camps. The AKP promotes Islam to the individual and in society as a whole. In doing so, it takes forward nationalism to a new level of conservatism (Uzer 2011).

When Kemalism was at its height, Islam separated into two parts. One part, understood as a type of Turkish Islam that was individual, was rational and national. The other, recognised as political, backward-looking and influenced by outside ethnic forces, namely the Arabs, was a variety of reactionary Islam. The move towards multiparty politics changed this dichotomous perspective. No longer were the ruling elite able to emphasise its sole authority over a specific form of Turkish Islam that characterised the entire nation. Instead, the multiparty political system opened up to different opinions and narratives, challenging the existing dominant political order. The ruling elite reacted by initiating an even narrower centrally-defined notion of Turkish Islam as representing good versus evil (Azak 2010). Overlooked and mis-recognised were the implications of the centre-periphery dualism. The major-ity of the population performed Islam quite differently from the elites at the centre. This dichotomy led to an anti-capitalist movement in the shape of a progressive Islamism. It helped to capture the imagination of Turks outside of the larger urban centres. Kemalism was a direct reproduction of Western capitalism and modernisation, including the authoritarian republi-canism characterising nations in the West, in particular France. Specifically, the function of religion was minimised, perceived as unnecessary for the construction of a new Turkey, despite centuries of Islamic influence across Ottoman territories and the region in general.

Kemalism represented a fundamental departure from the past because it offered a different political paradigm, one without any roots in Turkey's history. It did so at the expense of restricting Islam in the public sphere. It created an opportunity for Islamic scholars to produce a direct critique of Western capitalism and modernisation as well as Kemalism. As forward-facing Kemalism began to erode in the face of globalisation, a new configura-tion of Islamic intellectualism in Turkey arose. It surpassed existing ideas of an Islamic revivalism by embracing modernity and even secularism. In any event, this mode of progressive Islamism did not originate new ways of thinking about Islam, democracy, capitalism or globalisation. Rather, it has maintained the classical Islamic perspective, which continues to be popular in society, especially among the ruling conservative political elite of the present time. Turkish Islamic 'intellectuals are not original ideologues or deep philosophers. Instead, they are contributing to the rejuvenation of Islamic awareness within the society, and they have been very effective in this.' (Karasipahi 2009: 197).

Hizmet and Turkish Islam Reconsidered

In the West, various Muslim intellectuals labour vigorously to develop origi-nal thinking on the study of Islam. Scholars such as Tariq Ramadan, Seyyed

Hossein Nasr and Nasr Hamid Abu Zaid are some of the more notable. Muslim intellectuals have not surfaced in the same vein in Turkey. Rather, they transpire as public intellectuals whose role is to raise awareness of classic Islamic thinking and practice. Said Nursi, who witnessed the end of the Ottoman Empire followed by the formation of the secular republic period, is one of the best known and most followed among an array of Turkish Islamic intellectuals. Nursi 'tried to rejuvenate Islam and its values in an age of crisis against the rising values of positivism and materialism and secularism. Essentially, he fought against materialism and irreligiousness' (ibid. 188–9). His was a reaction to the supposed ungodliness of Kemalism during the first half of the twentieth century. Nursi emphasised the importance of science and technology as an end in itself, but also the value of appreciating the full benefits of Islamic thinking and philosophy. He nevertheless maintained a critique of Western philosophy and life, which he recognised as having reached their peak, coming to a point of decadence and backwardness, ultimately subverting the rules of the Qur'an. In essence, Nursi was a humanist and a revivalist, but also a pragmatist and an inspirational thinker whose deliberations spawned a generation of progressive Islamists in Turkey. These scholars continue to rouse a growing population of pious believers steadfast to the core of the Qur'an's religious teachings. They also aim to be worldly in their aspirations as enlightened human beings (Vahide 2005).

Analysts and thinkers recognise the undertaking inspired by Fethullah Gülen as a movement possessing the characteristics of other formal social movements that have a political ethos. Followers of Gülen prefer the term Hizmet. Use of this term takes attention away from Gülen himself and from the focus on the movement as a social or political entity. It prevents falling into the trap of providing Gülen with mythical cult status, given how Turkey is prone to eulogising its leaders since the appearance of Kemalism. During the last two decades, through various means, Hizmet has made tremendous efforts to spread a 'dialogue of civilisations' across the globe. It has done so largely through exchange and interaction, but also through education and enterprise. The creation of more than 2,000 high schools, especially in the US, Central Asia and sub-Saharan Africa has been an important development and entrepreneurial opportunity. It provides the few young people who can afford it with a valuable educational experience that would otherwise have been unattainable. This education encompasses a wide range of pedagogical and educational content, attracting upwardly mobile groups. Combined with promotion of Turkish language and culture, Hizmet attempts to create a framework in which 'progressive conservative Turkish Islam' is able to counter the negative effects of Islamophobia and xenophobia characterising Muslim experiences, especially in the West, and underdevelopment issues, mainly in the East.

There are detailed academic texts on Fethullah Gülen (Ebaugh 2009; Hendrick 2013; Yavuz 2013). Suffice to say, his moral philosophy, ethical guidelines and historiography of Islam have attracted a growing body of committed Muslims inside Turkey, which commentators suggest could be as many as six million followers, members and activists. An increasing number outside the country have also learned of the apparent positives associated with bottom-up community-orientated Islam developed from this experience, which *de jure* is apolitical but *de facto* has political impacts. Emerging in greater strength and force in the last two decades in particular, until recently Hizmet captured the essence of an existential Islamic experience, which for countless Turks was subdued during the suppressive phases of secularism, historically limiting Islam in public life. Gülenist philosophy taps into the cultural fabric of a Sufi-orientated Islamic perspective on humanity, which is unflinching yet unassuming at the same time. Hizmet has gained popularity partly because of its ability to reach into various aspects of Turkish life, including education, social welfare model, and civil society in general, as well as through economic activity and cultural influence. This uncomplicated Islamic ideological force reaches out to every man, woman and child across the nation. Turkish Sufi-inspired social movements seek to impart greater meaning into the lives of everyday people. Individuals and groups desire values informing not just the material or the organisational, but also the spiritual and the cultural. Hizmet has filled a gap that grew under late Kemalism.

Numerous kinds of Islamic *tariqah* (Sufi orders) exist across the world. They all have their traditions rooted in ethno-national and sectarian essentialisms, but Hizmet aims to displace such instincts and replace them with an extra-national dimension. One specific element of the work of Hizmet is a focus on dialogue and coexistence. It is also a bid to reach out to others in civilisation-building. It encourages the move away from underdevelopment and dependency towards development and independency, achieved through knowledge and research based on an Islamic ideological framework. The work of Hizmet is an effort to reach the pinnacle of human existence by removing obstacles, processes and the means preventing the achievement of such outcomes. The internationalisation of Hizmet further appeals as part of its attempts to eradicate inequalities, barriers, faithlessness, discrimination and corruption in all of its guises. To achieve its desired outcomes, humility and justice are important drivers in determining the essence of humankind. In the process, Hizmet seeks to challenge the deleterious outcomes of post-enlightenment European rationalism, and the subsequent global divisions that emerge as functions of individualism, consumerism and immediate gratification. The ethical, moral, psychological, cultural, intercultural and scientific basis of the aspirations behind Hizmet have allowed it to achieve success through the realisation of defining principles in thought and, crucially, through action.

Theologically, underpinned by Turkic–Sufi theology through the writings of Said Nursi, Hizmet is also culturally orientated in promoting a sense of Turkishness. Since 2002 the significant emergence of the 'Islamic bourgeois' has helped the country to become one of the strongest economies in the Muslim world and one of the most stable polities in the Middle East. Turkey has advanced through a growing body of upwardly mobile groups wishing to retain aspects of their cultural, spiritual and theological heritage. These groups form an advanced network of like-minded people, who share the same aspirations for the future of Turkey. Classical Islam inspires Hizmet, but it is also an economic and socially orientated project aspiring to be both inclusive and outward-looking.

Sufism in Politics, Politics in Sufism

Since the 1960s the work of Gülen and his followers have articulated cohesion and connectivity within Turkey. The organisation branched out to establish a host of educational institutions across the world, emphasising learning, science and technology as ways to empower the Muslim psyche and build relations with others. In 1994 the Journalists and Writers Foundation (JWF) launched itself at an event in Istanbul, with Gülen as its honorary president. The JWF aimed to raise awareness of Hizmet activities in order to promote dialogue and inter-civilisation exchange. The image of tolerance and coexistence was in direct contrast to the general perception of Islam and Muslims at the time, and more recently, one that focuses on extremism and fundamentalism. The Islamism espoused here is between conservatism and nationalism, which characterises Turkey. The concept of Hizmet promulgated in this milieu is the interplay between Islam and nationalism in Turkey (Bilici 2005). The 9/11 attacks provided a new awareness of Islam across the world, but it was by constructing associations between Islam and terrorism. Hizmet achieved global notoriety by challenging the concept of the 'clash of civilisations'. It aimed to do so by concentrating on dialogue and coexistence (Weller and Yilmaz 2012).

After Nursi's death various factions appeared, some as a response to 1970s communism, while others moved towards a conservative nationalism that emerged after the establishment of the National Order Party (NOP) in 1970. Gülen and his followers split into one camp, basing themselves in the city of Izmir. Several diverse Nur movements appeared in this period, but Hizmet is by far the most significant in size and impact. The movement promoted reconceptualisation of the Ottoman past, as well as the projection of a resilient Turkish state at its core. 'Gülen's followers are much more organized than any other Islamic group in Turkey . . . It is the project of a Muslim society with a powerful state. The Ottoman state is the prototype for this project' (ibid. 10). This vision cannot be realised without incorporating modernity into the movement. Gülen and his followers are thus pragmatists, realists and internationalists. Since the 'postmodern coup' of 1997 (a memorandum issued by the military to dissolve the government of Necmettin Erbakan of the Welfare Party, triggering his resignation and the suspension of the constitution), the movement embraced pluralism, human rights and democracy. Nevertheless, forced into exile soon after the coup, it did not have a positive outcome for Gülen himself. Nevertheless, he remained popular among a body of people, from his devoted followers to international scholars of Islam.

In the light of the events of 9/11, Hizmet has played a crucial role in bridging Islam, democracy and globalisation, when a focus on Muslims as extremists and radicals has become dominant within popular discourses. Hizmet is also popular in parts of Western Europe, namely in locations where Turkish Muslim minorities are found in large numbers, for example in the Netherlands and Germany (Yildiz and Verkuyten 2012). Even so, a number of key criticisms of Hizmet persist, some of which have become urgent due to ongoing assessments of the schools created by the movement across the world, especially in the US and in parts of Europe. Moreover, a lack of intellectual independence ensues; indeed, the only dominant figure is Gülen himself. Perceived as hierarchical, centralised and elitist, Hizmet underemphasises Kurdish matters. An adequate representation of women is not found, whether in publications or in taking an active role in the functioning of the organisation, especially at senior levels. While women are indeed at the forefront of the organisation, and others argue their role is also important behind the scenes, the position of women remains unclear. The other hefty criticism against the organisation is that its goals indoctrinate young Muslims with specific understandings of Islam, as well as using the schools to proselytise Islamic teachings. For David Tittensor (2012: 174), this criticism amounts to: '[c]onsidering that what the Gülen movement is allegedly doing is not so different from its Christian counterparts, it appears that the accusations are most likely fuelled by politicking, prejudice and simple bigotry'. Because of the events of 9/11, and Hizmet's immense resources and outreach capacity, glib prejudices often lie behind many of the criticisms levelled at the movement.

In Turkey, Hizmet has not merely attempted to broaden an approach towards Islam within nationalism, but it has also established various interconnected organs in education, finance and international commerce, all of which have local and global impacts. Though civil society is emphasised, the wider market economy aspects of the movement set it apart from others and contribute to its financial assets. A gradual bottom-up, people-orientated project seeking to build society from below does not shape the movement's discourse. Rather, it is a way to support the existing mechanisms and operations of the state, simultaneously building Turkish Islamic nationalism: 'Gülen's appeal to tolerance, in particular, should be considered, not in terms of the question of democracy, but with reference to state/society relations and the role of Islam in it' (Başkan 2005: 851). There are specific types of resistance that arise among those who view Hizmet with suspicion at worst and with disdain at best. Allegedly, Gülen's memoirs demonstrate less tolerance and openness to differences in society, particularly leftists and communists in the 1960s and

1970s. They are quite the opposite of public statements Gülen has made since the 1990s. In the modern period the movement in Turkey suffers from a closed structure, and the *abiler* (elder brothers) exist entirely for the purposes of supporting the needs of men. Compliance to the proselytisation of Gülen arises, where followers adhere to instructions without critical inquiry or even the ability to respond with alternative suggestions or solutions.

Erol Gulay (2007: 56) argues that Hizmet is a variation of Sufism. Spiritualism, mysticism, piety and the development of the inner self is the primary concern, 'where Gülen's teachings represent a synthesis between scripturalism and experientialism'. In operating within society rather than outside, the movement supports the Turkish modernisation project. Thus:

> [I]n a broad sense then, Gülen's community arises to reject the Kemalist equation of modernization with westernization. As the Kemalist revolution once tried to 'Turkify' Islam and cultural identity, the Gülen community tries to Islamize modernity and national identity by promoting religious values and practices culled from Islam's 'golden age'. (ibid. 59)

The use of Sufism to inspire education and technological advancement, the market economy and working within the parameters of the state constitute Hizmet as a post-Islamist nationalist movement, employing spirituality and objective rational scientific learning. Its schools across the world represent specific methods of educational investment in the future of Turkey. For the petit bourgeois, middle class and urban Muslims in Turkey benefiting from increased economic opportunity and social mobility, such schools provide a useful platform.

It is important to focus on the dynamics of how an Islamic identity in politics is constructed and realised in Turkey. Various commentators and observers, both inside and outside of Turkey, opine much. On the other hand, a great deal about Hizmet is misunderstood and unarticulated. Other so-called Islamist organisations are also of interest in Turkey, but none has the high profile or the exposure of Hizmet. It continues to act as a useful test case for understandings of civil society organisations with a religious ethos, and their impact on a local, national and global scale. Yet, a range of criticisms are levelled at the movement, some of which focus on the impression that it is male-dominated, hierarchical, lacks transparency and is purely ideological.

Critics pour scorn on the movement and view it as political because of how it attempts to place individuals into the institutions of society. Traditional and conservative Muslims argue they find positivity in taking part in an organisation that supports their entire social, economic and cultural outlook. Hizmet is never far from controversy. It faces extensive resistance among specific Turkish groups who claim its goals and aspirations are overtly political. Opposition ultimately compelled Fethullah Gülen to go into self-exile in the US, where he remains today. Gülen's situation worsened in the light of the 'graft probe', an extensive corruption scandal that began on 17 December 2013. The beginning of 2014 saw a severe freeze in the once-positive relations between Hizmet and the AKP, which had originally characterised their respective mutually reinforcing growth (see Chapter 7).

The 'Kurdish Issue' Defined

No social and political analysis of Turkey would be complete without including the so-called 'Kurdish issue'. To appreciate the core questions in this formidable debate, it is important to understand the historical dimensions and the ongoing political impacts. Indeed, Kurdish presence in the area that is today called Turkey predates that of the Turks themselves. Moreover, the Kurdish language is of a completely different origin from Turkish, being Indo-European, and closely related to Persian.

After the Great War vast territories were included in the geopolitical rationalisation of the Ottoman Empire. Communities were ethnically, linguistically and religiously diverse in description and organisation. European imperial processes divided the Kurdish communities that straddled four adjoining nations: Turkey, Iran, Syria and Iraq. The Kurds in the south-east region of Anatolia were convinced that the British would support their quest for national ethnic and cultural recognition. Such aspirations were premature. The British did not wish for a united Kurdistan. They had greater ambitions, which were to affect the political and economic situation in Persia (Iran after 1935) (Eskander 2000). While Kurdish nationalism in Turkey became a twentieth-century phenomenon, a wider historical precedent existed regarding claims of Kurdish ethnic identity during the Ottoman Empire (see Chapter 2). Indeed, the end of the Great War in 1918 changed the geographical and political landscape in this part of the world. Today's

Turkey contains the largest Kurdish communities across the Middle East. This is where the most serious concerns around the recognition of Kurdish identity in the region persist (Yavuz 1998).

In many senses, the 'de-Turkification' of Turkish integration policy would restrict the legitimate demands of Kurdish ethno-nationalism. Most commentators and analysts suggest that the Kurdish situation in Turkey consists of demands for recognition, equality, status and justice denied thus far. The repressive policies of the Turkish state have created the conditions for ethnic conflict, which has become a cyclical process of forced assimilation, resistance and accommodation. This, coupled with vilification, demonisation and exclusion, has resulted in further confrontation in a perennial cycle of violence and conflict, which recently witnessed signs of resolution in 2013, but descended back into chaos in 2015. The process has also transfigured Kurdish groups into racialised groups, first occurring at the end of a forced assimilation period when the ethnic category of 'Kurdish' obtained a degree of salience on its own (Ergin 2014). According to Zeki Sarigil (2010), reducing exclusion and marginalisation in the form of limited economic opportunity for social mobility are the primary factors in improving integration.

The ethno-national consciousness of Kurdish communities aligns not just with the formation of the Turkish Republic, but also with Iraq and Syria. Kurdish groups have found themselves as separate entities in an otherwise connected geographical territory. At the outset, Mustafa Kemal Atatürk assured Kurdish communities that they would enjoy all their communal rights under the new republic. Atatürk abandoned these promises. What followed were a series of ruthless suppressions of armed uprisings emanating from Kurdish ethnic nationalism, which continued until Atatürk's death in 1938. Some analysts have blamed the present-day malaise squarely on Atatürk and his proclamations regarding the establishment of the Turkish Republic (Mango 1999). From this situation Kurdish communities throughout the region have resisted assimilation, but none more so than in Turkey. The process of the emergence of the republic and the philosophies of ethnic Turkishness has created the conditions for this conflict.

In the 1960s a leftist strand evolved in Turkish politics. It created the opportunity for Kurdish groups who, until then, were tribalistic with respect to the materialisation of a Kurdish national identity. Endeavours made by the

Turkish state to quash these efforts led to further radicalisation of Kurdish groups. The Kurdistan Workers' Party (PKK), established in the late 1970s, commenced violent militaristic confrontation in 1984. Resistance persisted until 1999, when Abdullah Öcalan, one of the founding members of the PKK and its undisputed leader since its foundation, was captured and imprisoned on İmralı Island, where he remains to this day. Turkish military activities against Kurds during the 1980s and 1990s strengthened the resolve of Kurdish groups to maintain their ethnic and national identity. Since the beginning of the conflict against the PKK there has been 'silencing and detention of journalists and political activists, covert assassinations, torture and scorched-earth policies that have emptied around 3000 Kurdish villages of the inhabitants' (Park 2012: 83). Despite efforts to bring about a permanent reconciliation, over 50,000 lives have been lost on all sides, but mostly Kurdish (Heper 2007).

Part the success of the PKK in maintaining a hold on the Kurds in Turkey, compared with other Kurdish ethno-national populist projects in region, is the allusion to a glorious historic past reiterated through the myth of Newroz. The legend of Newroz tells of the overthrow of the Assyrian King Dehak by a rebellion headed by 'Kawa the Blacksmith (Kawayi Hesinkar) [who] on 21 March 612 BC led an uprising by the Medes and defeated the Assyrian Empire, killed Dehak and liberated the Medes – the ancestors of Kurds – from long-suffering oppression and tyranny' (Gunes 2013: 254). Kurdish communities celebrate Newroz every year on this day in March. The event is also embracing the coming of spring and the New Year according to Persian tradition. It therefore carries both political and cultural undertones. In Turkey's south-eastern cities there are often violent clashes between the Turkish police and Kurdish youth, such are the underlying simmering tensions between them.

Awakening the Kurdish Consciousness

The Turkish state has attempted to determine a peaceful solution to the ethnic and national conflict with the Kurds but with limited success. The Özal era repealed the ban on the use of Kurdish language in everyday life that began at the time of the military coup of 1980. Even so, by the end of the 1990s, Turkish elites had little interest in determining a solution to the so-called 'Kurdish issue'. The EU-integration process, reignited in the early 2000s by the AKP, has somewhat opened up the opportunity again, as Turkey's candidature depends partly on its ability to resolve its internal human rights problems. In 2009, Erdogan, as prime minister, made a definitive statement in his address to the nation on 28 August, known as the 'Kurdish opening'. It created consternation among specific Kemalist groups in Turkey who opposed the development. The opening did not stop clashes between Kurdish militant groups and the Turkish army. In March 2013 PKK leader Abdullah Öcalan delivered a recorded speech promising the end of confrontations and the start of a definitive peace process. It led to a sustained truce. In 2014 the AKP permitted the teaching of the Kurdish language in private schools. In 2015 the pro-Kurdish Peoples' Democratic Party (HDP) entered parliament and, in many ways, the 2015 election was indeed the story of the formal arrival of the Kurds in the political process. By the end of 2015 and in early 2016 violent clashes between the Turkish armed forces and the PKK in the south-east of Turkey, in the Hakkâri and Şırnak provinces in particular, escalated to new levels. Once again, it rendered peace a distant dream.

While internal drivers inside Turkey have strained to encourage a settlement to a long-running conflict, it is also important to consider a range of European and wider international actors whose influence cannot be underestimated. Despite a range of occasional positive developments, Turkey has yet to come to terms with its past human rights violations affecting Armenians, Alevis and Kurds (see Chapters 2 and 3). It is a variety of 'majoritarian conservatism', defined as 'promoting uncritical and conservative-nationalist interpretations of the past that have popular appeal to ensure ongoing political support and boost a particular conception of collective belonging' that seems to prevail (Bakiner 2013: 692). The 'Kurdish Spring' created opportunities for Kurdish groups across the Middle East where populations are concentrated, principally in Iraq. It is unambiguous how matters will pan out in Turkey (Gunter 2013), when the popular imagination associates 'terrorism' and 'separation' with the 'Kurdish question' (Gunes 2012). It is no coincidence that Kurds in Turkey have lower levels of political trust in domestic institutions and higher levels of political trust in international institutions compared with ethnic Turks (Karakoç 2013) (see Chapter 6).

A focus on nationalism on both sides is perhaps a deterrent to any long-term solution to the 'Kurdish issue'. Instead, a multicultural proposition involving respect, mutual recognition and appreciation serves as a useful way forward. In 1984 the PKK took up armed struggle, but resistance among Kurdish groups goes back much further, from throughout Ottoman history to the beginning of the republic. A recognition-based multiculturalism may well provide a significant opportunity in a framework where various sides adhere to a preconceived notion of inclusive nationalism. Mutual recognition of central universal values needs grounding. The dominant norms of the majority ethnic groups need to be mollified. Within its boundaries, Turkey has always been historically less keen to identify with Muslim groups who consider themselves as separate ethnic categories. A mutual recognition and acceptance of universal values could lay the foundations for a lasting polity within a diverse multicultural society (Ozkirimli 2014). Soner Çağaptay (2006: 161) argues Turkish nationalism takes an assimilationist approach towards all Muslim groups in the country, but '[w]hile many of these people have already willingly and successfully assimilated, Turkey cannot comprehend why it is difficult for the others to merge into the nation'. The distinction between 'Islam as a religion and Islam as an identity' (ibid. 162) further problematises the situation. Turkish nationalism also disparages Christians and Jews, still viewed as outsiders within.

There are disenfranchised, marginalised, excluded and racialised Kurdish groups in the urban centres of the large cities and towns of Anatolia and in Istanbul. Limited economic activity in the south-east region of Turkey is unsurprising given the nature of the conflict. Many of these Kurds have left Turkey as refugees to go to Iraq, Iran and Syria. Extensive internal migration to Kurdish majority towns such as Diyarbakir and Mardin has also occurred. Ironically, Istanbul is the most populated Kurdish city anywhere in the world. Countless Kurds have also turned to Western Europe to seek asylum and safe haven. It has fuelled the diasporic transnationalism of Kurdish identity politics in unimaginable ways. Until 2015 pro-Kurdish groups, excluded from the political process due to being unable to pass the 10 per cent electoral threshold, even though fairly and freely elected, have found a new voice. Turkey's Europeanisation process has created opportunities to recognise human rights violations. Turkey continues to remain belligerent towards its

Kurdish communities in the eastern territories, and in the major towns and cities across Anatolia.

Structure of the Book

Having set the scene and provided a background to the primary Islamic, ethnic and political conflicts now facing Turkey, Chapter 2 provides a historical analysis of how the Ottomans in the past and postmodern Turkey historically realised religious plurality and monoculturalism. It explores how a diverse empire transformed into a monocultural, mono-religious and secular republic with particular emphasis on authoritarian nationalism and a devotion to the founding father of modern Turkey, Mustafa Kemal Atatürk. This period in history created many tensions for ethnic groups, in particular the Kurds. It also established dedicated centralised elites who maintained power and privileged position through an often brutal reinforcement of the secular republican model. Later, as the economy opened up to neo-liberalism, groups historically deemed as the backward tribal provinces, became the source from which the new 'Islamic bourgeois' were able to boost the economy from the 1990s onwards, turning Turkey into a global and regional economic and political player. Presently, globalisation characterises the relations between different minority and majority groups, as well as the cosmopolitanism of Istanbul and other large cities across the country.

Chapter 3 attempts to understand intolerance towards minorities in Turkey through secondary analysis of data from the European Social Survey. This chapter analyses how minority and majority groups relate to each other, and explores the sources of difference between them. Ironically, despite various labels of Kemalism and Islamism, Turks remain loyal to the national flag, including certain Kurdish groups, despite the challenges they face. It would seem that allegiance to a variety of nationalism, which oscillates between ethnic and civic, is a powerful force in uniting the people of Turkey. The data analysis questions and examines the way religion operates in this regard. In addition, a case study explores ethnic intolerance in Turkey. An analysis of the central Istanbul area of Tarlabaşı, currently the site of the poorest, marginalised and most culturally diverse groups in Turkey is a case in point. Marginalised groups have suffered the debilitating impact of the ethnic gentrification agenda and the neo-liberal policies of urbanisation. This reality suggests that the policy of neo-liberalism has trumped the desire to protect and preserve aspects of the historical and ethnic heritage of Istanbul. This is indicative of a wider process of normalising Turkish national identity in the pursuit of economic and political power. There remains, however, concern over the character of the urban sphere and the willingness to compromise selected memories, which undermines the need to uphold or enhance cultural and ethnic tolerance and coexistence.

Chapter 4 is an ethnographic study conducted in the town of Yüksekova in January 2013. In-depth interviews and observations carried out with families who had one or many of their members in the PKK revealed important insights. The study took months to arrange, in order to achieve the level of trust and confidence needed. The research demonstrated how Kurdish groups in Yüksekova understood the conflict, experienced the realities of the harsh treatment they faced, explained how their young children were persuaded to join the PKK, and how they coped as families locked in a deadly conflict zone. The only Turkish actors that Kurdish groups engaged with were the police, the medical staff at their local hospitals, the security services operating in the area and teachers who taught Kurdish children in Turkish. Trapped in cycles of poverty, alienation and marginalisation, these particular Kurdish communities faced the brunt of the conflict. Immense levels of interest in the workings of the PKK in the mountains surrounding the outer areas of south-east Turkey persists (Marcus 2009), but there is paltry attention paid to families in local towns in this region.

Chapter 5 explores how the new Islamic bourgeois and its political guise, the AKP, have replaced the declining frontiers of the old Kemalist power structures. Tensions between the old and the new erupted during the summer of 2013 in the form of the Gezi Park protests. This uprising symbolised a resistance movement that spread everywhere across Turkey. For commentators at the time, the dominant perspective was confrontation, not between Kemalism and Islamism, but between an authoritarian leader and a diverse body of people, including the young, old, religious, non-religious, urban and middle class. These groups felt subjugated to a cultural and economic upheaval that they were compelled to resist. The Gezi protests began as a public response to the violent police eviction of environmentalists and protesters wishing to preserve the vestiges of green space in a central area of

Istanbul. It eventually became a national outcry. On 15 June 2013 police returned to remove the protesters in Gezi Park. On this day, interviews with young people from diverse backgrounds, representing all the political colours of Turkish society revealed an assortment of opinion. They reflected intransigent Kemalists, pro-Kurdish groups, the secular mothers who held hands and the young volunteers who assisted medical staff. In-depth interviews with respondents helped to understand the diversity and similarity of opinion held by different interest groups. Their remarks echoed ongoing trends in the reshaping and reformation of social capital and political trust among a widening Turkey.

In Chapter 6, the focus moves to politics at a general level. Vast studies exist on the area of social capital and political trust, particularly in Western economies. Yet, few discuss the Middle East or Turkey specifically. Utilising data from the European Social Survey, Chapter 6 questions how different configurations of social capital affect political trust and how patterns diverge according to ethnicity, class and religiosity. As Turkey expands its global outlook, there are questions about the Europeanisation process. Despite the efforts made by Turkey to enter the EU, the vast majority of Turks remain hostile to the idea, although Europe is still Turkey's biggest trading partner. The independent variables of ethnicity, religiosity, education, class and gender are also important in helping to understand social capital and political trust.

In conclusion, Chapter 7 argues that Turkey has undergone rapid transformations in the last two decades or so, but many are still unfolding. Turkey has moved on from its old centralised ethnic nationalism model to one of cosmopolitan civic nationalism. It is now purposive and dedicated to the idea of maintaining a progressive national image across the world and, returning to celebrate historical success in homage to the Ottomans, emphasising the Muslim-ness of a Muslim nation. This new Muslim-ness diverges from the old, but it is not without enemies within the state. The last bastions of secular Kemalism are no longer able to keep their hold on elite educational institutions. Mollified are the media, judiciary and the military. Since the Kemalist era Turkey has found it difficult to hold together as a nation given the deep contradictions beneath the surface. Three *coups d'état* are evidence enough of this. As paradoxes become resolved, not only does Turkey strengthen from the inside but also preserves its image from the outside. In spite of this, in the current climate, accusations of authoritarianism chime louder than ever among the population at large. The 'Kurdish issue' is in utter disarray. Intolerance towards minorities is resistant to change. In addition, the emergence of Islamic State and a significant refugee crisis has created further challenges for a nation already grappling with internal problems. The future of Turkey will be centred on social cohesion, economic stability and political inclusiveness. It will also need to find the balance between how a political and civil Islam coheres with the will of a diverse nation.

2

Historicising Pluralism and Monoculturalism

Is Turkish history imaginable as various episodes of monoculturalism and religious pluralism, from the early Ottoman period to the present day? To answer this question, it is necessary to establish the boundaries of categories. In broad terms, religious pluralism refers to communities containing diverse religious groups, where interethnic relations are porous. Monoculturalism refers to a single dominant cultural framework in which a society operates, and where ethnic relations are delimited. From the Ottoman Empire to the modern Turkish Republic, through to postmodern Turkey, these epochs of history differ from each other based on (1) claims of truth and (2) the recognition of ethnic, cultural and religious differences in society. This chapter offers a theoretical analysis of these periods in Turkish history and politics, along with the nature of the ethno-cultural and sociopolitical interconnections between them. The aim is to explain how Turkish social and political history is categorised through the lens of pluralism and monoculturalism. The analysis presents a retrospective study of diversity in Turkish society to help recognise the various abstract, theoretical and empirical intersections. It also offers a perspective on implications for the political and cultural future of the nation. In a climate of conflict, division and political ambiguity there is a need to move beyond understanding different minority communities as discrete objects. Rather, they share common philosophies incorporating shared approaches to the establishment of an inclusive national culture and the dialogue necessary to achieve it.

Thus, the purpose of this chapter is not only to articulate conceptualisations of religious pluralism and monoculturalism operationalised in Turkey in a retrospective historical context, but also to look ahead. It is an attempt to discern an original way to think about Turkish history in the transformation of a multi-ethnic empire into a monocultural republic, then finally into a rapidly transforming postmodern nation in a global age. The analysis contributes to a growing understanding of how diversity shapes the experience of a nation in transition. This discussion of experiences in Turkey can help sociologists, political theorists and philosophers to appreciate the historical as well as the contemporary character of Turkish society.

Determining a Chronology

Three chronological sections are vital to consider, each relating to specific periods of sociohistorical analysis. In the premodern period, the Ottoman Empire maintained a firm grip on ethno-cultural and religious differences. It did so by displaying a general acceptance and respect for various ethnic and religious differences living under its rule. This understanding came from Islam as the governing system of the empire, although it also had practical social, political and economic ramifications. The claim of an absolute Islamic truth did not mean subjugation or disrespect towards various minorities. To be more precise, this particular Islamic and social perspective led to a largely balanced multireligious and multi-ethnic system during the Ottoman Empire.

The Ottoman system began to dissolve as the Western world rose as a competitor to the Ottoman Empire and the influence of Europeanisation took root in matters of governance. These events led to the second historical period of interest. With growing economic and political power emerging in the West, the spread of authoritarian nationalist ideals eventually caused the dissolution of the Ottoman Empire. When the populations of the empire separated from the centre, the founding fathers of the Turkish Republic acted in accordance with mainstream European modernisation models of the time. A new republic based on the discourse of the idea of a modern state was established. The diverse social fabric was 'monoculturalised' abruptly and aggressively. This new regime snubbed diversity and religious differences. An imagined monoculture placed groups into an invented society. State ideology, for the purposes of the state, negated the space that minorities had established during the Ottoman period. For many years, Kemalist ideology felt bound to eradicate differences and to enforce absolutism. Yet, in reality, differences did not disappear, and various group characteristics based on ethnicity, religion and culture persisted. Dominant modernisation theory, together with the development of international law and human rights, produced more questions than answers. It meant that the new republic was largely ineffective in attempting to convert diverse groups into a single set of 'moderns'. As such, ethnic differences suppressed since the founding of the Turkish Republic in 1923 resurfaced in society over time. The third phase came when the Turkish Republic underwent further change in the postmodern period, which began in the 1980s and took shape after the Cold War ended. Critical objectivity challenged the arbitrary rules of state institutions. In this way, the monocultural structure of society broke down and an intercultural appreciation began to prevail in its place (Shah 2010).

Comprehending Turkish history in this way provides a distinctive approach to understanding events, in particular by applying well-established concepts in sociological thinking to an (near) Eastern model of social, ethnic, cultural and political experience. In the process, scholars of both 'Eastern' and 'Western' societies are able to reflect on the wider historical and contemporary sociopolitical dynamics of Turkey. These ideas have benefited from a rereading of the theories of religious pluralism and monoculturalism in Turkey. The analytical framework relies on a Turkish historical appraisal combined with a Westernised sociological comprehension: an amalgamation of Orientalist and Occidentalist discourse analysis. The consolidation of these two temporal fields allows the integration of classic historical and contemporary sociological and methodological perspectives. This cross-fertilisation process subsequently advanced knowledge, understanding and function (Heper 2000).

Ottoman Class Structure and the Millet System

A specific challenge for the Ottomans was how to provide stability across a wide territory covering three continents, where myriad ethnic and religious divisions existed. To achieve stability the Ottomans established the 'millet system' to encourage peaceful coexistence within diversity. The term 'millet' had a different connotation from 'nation', even if it literally meant 'nation'. The millet system materialised out of the foundations laid down by the Umayyads and Abbasids. For the Ottomans, millets referred to communities, distinct not according to ethnic characteristics, but according to their belief systems, divided into communities along religious affiliations. They had the opportunity to rule their own affairs according to their own creeds. Millets dictated rules and regulations for themselves, not only in matters of religion, but also in other aspects of social and cultural life. As such, they enjoyed relative autonomy and protection under the Ottoman Empire (Aral 2004). Millets were loyal to Ottoman rule, and the Ottoman centre recognised their differences. Ottoman rule sustained peace and stability within diversity. Thus, millets did not perceive any need to rebel against the system. Through a reciprocal arrangement between the centre and the periphery, the Ottoman multireligious system operated effectively (Mardin 1962).

Islam formed the basis of life for Muslim communities living under Ottoman rule. Importantly, it was also the belief system of the sovereign power. To that extent, Islam was the most significant constituent in a method that maintained pluralism within the Ottoman system. Islam was not only a religion that rendered its believers a distinct community living together with other communities, but also the underlying motivation for tolerating the beliefs and cultures of others. Islam requires the faithful to respect the People of the Book, but the Ottomans were tolerant only of believers, that is, Christians and Jews, and less so of Shi'ism. Islamic rule was strengthened by another diktat in Islam that 'there is no compulsion in religion', meaning that it was forbidden to force Islam upon others. The Ottoman state used Islamic law as the system of governance. There was no forced conversion for minority religious groups. These Islamic principles governed the conduct of state affairs regarding all groups. The Ottoman system continued the Islamic tradition inherited from the early Islamic states. As a result, the Ottomans were tolerant of other religions and cultures through a worldview shaped by faith, belief and practice.

Perhaps the Ottomans were more open-minded towards the Jews because they did not dominate any of the lands that the Ottomans had captured. This does not explain why Ottoman rulers were tolerant of different communities even after gaining power over some of them, however. The Ottomans chose not to eradicate differences, but, rather, to accept them. Religious beliefs that prevented forcibly assimilating others or converting them to Islam was at the heart of this approach. Moreover, the Islamic perspective encompassed characteristics of every part of life, including science, language and law (Şentürk 2010). Complex worldviews made it possible for differences to coexist without violating the rights of others. This Islamic society was diverse, with undefined layers within porous borders (Mardin 2005). Ottoman rule gave various cultures space to live according to the norms and values associated with the groups. Nevertheless, it is erroneous to claim that the system supported equal opportunities, as liberal ideology suggests. Moreover, what is understood from the term 'equality' has changed from premodern to modern times. Thus, under Ottoman authority, the rules governing belief systems regulated the norms of social structure. Here, different creeds had the right of religious freedom in equal terms with culture. The millets managed a system of coexistence as distinct communities in accordance with the belief systems to which they belonged. Nevertheless, this method of equal toleration was restricted for non-Muslim communities, while Muslims received higher standards of living and greater opportunity to reach state offices. There was a strict status order in the Ottoman Empire in which a dichotomous cultural structure existed – one was 'high palace culture' and the other was 'folk culture'. For many who belonged to rural culture, attainment of higher social positions at the centre of power was difficult. In this regard the Muslim rural community was no more privileged than non-Muslims were. Thus, the centre treated ordinary Muslim and non-Muslim communities as equally different. Traditionalist 'folk Islam' and other belief systems were both outside of the domains of 'high palace culture'.

The Ottoman example indicates extensive support of religious pluralism. Ottoman millets enjoyed relative autonomy as distinct communities, but they also had a particular awareness and a steadfast appreciation of wider Ottoman society norms and values (Gawrych 1983). Through this multireligious system, Ottoman rule managed the diversity of its subjects without interfering in the religious affairs of different communities (Joppke 1996). The Ottoman millets were the realisation of a multireligious society through a system of cultural coexistence. Different religions and cultures were recognised, and given opportunities to express themselves and exist without significant restraint.

Age of Modernity

Ottoman rule established a social and cultural environment in which different religious and ethnic groups coexisted in a diverse multilayered society, but where boundaries were undefined. Identifying as an Ottoman meant sharing a similar social fabric developed through the contribution of differences found within the empire. Decentralisation characterised the Ottoman Empire, where every minority community managed its own affairs (Calhoun 1993). Decentralisation differentiated the Ottoman system from a state system, the latter operating through modernisation to create uniformity in society. This made the Ottoman Empire multireligious, with multiple layers of self-consciousness, identity and loyalty (Çağaptay 2006).

Comparing the success of the Ottomans with modernity is not straightforward. Political and economic status defines the modern Western European experience. Rather, Ottoman accomplishment rested on its nature as a distinct region holding together a range of different millets. Ottoman supremacy withered away because of the appearance of the West as a rising power in the international arena, as well as weaknesses that emerged from within the empire itself. The inadaptability of empires, including the Ottoman Empire, to maintain technological and sociopolitical advancement was instrumental in their decline in the global political and economic context. Modern conceptualisations of the state, citizenship and nationhood took precedence. This reconfiguration spread across the globe, affecting non-'Westerners' in the process. Imposed over the whole world, by means of force, was the imprint of modernity, as in the case of colonialism or by incentivising 'Easterners' to mimic the 'Western' model. The hegemonic discourse of the West strengthened the modernisation project, enabling it to maintain authority through material superiority, with an ideology that solidified this advantage. During this period, Ottoman rulers turned to the West and began to import the Western worldview into their empire. Reforms known as Tanzimat (1839–) brought Ottoman culture and social life into line with European values in relation to modernity, secularism and rationalism. Further reforms appeared through legislation enacted in 1856.

The empire introduced a contemporary understanding of citizenship that prevented non-Muslim separatists from gaining credence. To achieve its goals, Ottoman elites increased central authority in the provinces in an attempt to integrate groups further politically, defining and fostering a centrally demarcated system of cultural pluralism. The empire adopted Ottomanism as a political ideology to keep its multireligious structure intact, and to prevent its dissolution. Prohibited from affiliation to traditional ties, each individual, regardless of ethnicity or religion, was an equal citizen with direct loyalty to the state. '[T]his state ideology reflected the government's attempt to inculcate in every subject Ottoman patriotism directed toward the Empire and its ruling dynasty' (Gawrych 1983: 522). Removed was the secular character of citizenship, with religious affiliation, once the basis for identification of the Ottomans, no longer the principle of equality before the new secular law. With the state restricting religion in social life, language emerged as the nucleus in the establishment of national identities – 'the political elite sought to linguistically homogenise the nation' (Bayar 2011: 125).

Because Ottoman rule did not follow assimilationist policies concerning minorities, communities were able to maintain their cultural values. Millets in the Ottoman Empire, now deprived of their former identities as members of a religious community, gave meaning to their citizenry through language. Such developments were just one segment of the modernisation process through which modern state formation came into existence. Freed from traditional religious ties, shared language symbolised and developed the new bonds within modernity. Language had been a matter of voluntary personal choice with minimal political significance in Anatolia. Religion became a matter of personal preference with limited political consequences, but language use had the power to include or exclude groups. This new secular view challenged the millet system and, consequently, various groups wished to establish separate states. The shift from religion to ethnicity to language as the central mechanism of group identity was realised. This took place through a system that morphed into considering members of society not as part of a single community containing diversity but as individuals in society.

Collapse of the Ottoman Empire

The Ottomans held the empire together as long as possible, but their partial attempts at reform, combined with external threats posed by the rapidly advancing European nation states against which they could not directly complete, led to its unavoidable demise. Not only was this due to the inadequacy of Ottoman reforms, but also because the restructuring itself became the motivation for millets struggling against separation from the empire.

The secular character of these changes separated individuals from traditional systems of identification, forcing people to ascribe meaning to their lives through the bond of ethnicity (Özoğlu 2004). Nationality, equality and fraternity, without distinguishing between religious affiliations, weakened the hold of religion. In turn, this secular orientation demanded re-evaluation of the spirit of Ottoman society and culture. Moreover, the empire disbanded not merely based on ideological shifts but also due to the economic situation. Because of successive wartime defeats, Ottoman rulers had to cede territory to various foreign powers. Millets separated from the centre of the empire. Material deprivation resulted for these groups as the economic situation of the empire worsened. It served as the root for collective struggle and the basis for social conflict, in particular for the Kurds. Different communities lost their trust in Ottoman rule as economic hardship set in. Class struggle combined with ethnic and cultural identification.

Various adversities led to tensions between Muslims and non-Muslims. The latter became scapegoats because of their aspirations for separation. The situation further aggravated the distress among different communities, leading to closure within ethnicity. This also occurred among non-Muslims who once held important positions within the core of the empire. The result was the drawing of even stricter lines of separation between communities. For centuries a material basis, alongside Islamic ideology, played a major role in the success of Ottoman rule. Economic, political and social opportunity satisfied the demands of different communities as they enjoyed the tolerance of the empire. Western influences regarding state ideology and modernity, and the comparative superiority of the West in material power, however, ended the age of classical Eastern empires, including the Ottoman Empire. Because of wider regional interests, the Ottomans established important political ties with key figures in Kurdistan, encouraging them to ally with the Ottomans rather than the Persians. Through a lens of Sunni Islam, the millet system created a sense of loyalty to the empire. While this helped the Ottomans at some level, concerns affecting minority religious communities emerged. Jews and Muslims were wealthier than their Christian counterparts. When resistance movements occurred to challenge the emerging social and economic divisions, various systems of repression targeted Christian groups. Christians maintained their position 'ultimately based on acceptance of the political dominance of the majority, or, at least, of the symbols thereof' (Tezcan 2012: 165). On the other hand, their visibility added to their vulnerability.

The Ottomans ruled over huge territories, spanning a variety of continents, geographies and ethnicities. Over two centuries, Western nation states projected nationalism rooted in a far longer period of historical development. Analysing the Ottoman Empire as multi-ethnic and multireligious is complex and difficult when 'loyalty to the ultimate political authority had little to do with one's national belonging, and the term "nation" meant quite different things' (ibid. 159). Diversity, as understood in the Ottoman historical past, had particular idiosyncratic characteristics related to religion, culture and tribe. In urban settings professionals of various backgrounds worked with each other as interdependent agents in a bustling economy. Certain niches had comparative advantages; for example, Christians were involved in wine production or swine farming, rejected by Muslims because of religious connotations. In other settings, such religious distinctions did not matter in the context of collective class interests. Both Christian and Muslim had class position and class status as their common bond. Thus, class structure, with ethnic and religious differences operating within it, is as an important factor in determining the relations between communities.

Ultimately, during the seventeenth century, many Christian and Jewish merchants entered the ruling class. As Islam took on the role of maintaining a national collective identity, Ottoman society became characterised by relations between rulers and the population through groups operating as subjects within millets. Through this social, economic and political formation, the Ottoman system was able to maintain an element of cohesion, providing opportunities for mobility and interdependence in relation to class interests. As European powers gained strength, outside interests exploited Christian religious identity markers. It helped to destabilise Ottoman society and added to the internal problems encountered during the middle of the nineteenth century as the Ottomans sought solutions in modernisation.

Modernisation over Religion

The Ottomans faced many difficulties in realising their plans for democratisation, modernisation and industrialisation, seen as the hallmarks of European national political projects that characterised experiences in Britain, France and Prussia. In many senses, the Ottomans were unable to compete with rising European powers economically, politically or militarily. A particular turning point came with restrictions placed upon the transport of goods beyond the empire's immediate borders. The British were marked in their ability to exploit these Ottoman capitulations. It gave 'a legal framework for British economic imperialism, deprived Ottomans of economic autonomy, and thereby detached the Empire from the European concert of nations' (Goffman 2002: 234). The Ottomans were in a precarious position when their empire effectively became a dependency of the British Empire. This also made the Ottoman territories more susceptible to colonisation. By the middle of the nineteenth century the Europeans were no longer fearful of the Ottomans, and regarded the empire as territory ripe for exploitation.

The transformation from empire to nation state was full of violence and conflict, despite the importance of the heritage of various religious groups, and the tolerance practised for many centuries. In the early twentieth century hostility towards the Greeks and the Armenians arose, leading to annihilation of whole communities. The 'Greeks in the 1820s, Syrian and Lebanese Christians in the 1860s, Bulgarians in 1876, and the Armenians of Zeytun in 1862' all experienced extensive animosity (Barkey 2008: 278). The events of the early 1910s have caused great concern over questions about the 'Armenian genocide'. This was an uncomfortable episode in Ottoman history, and it remains a sensitive discussion point today among the political elite and wider Turkish society (see Chapter 3). Turkish explanations focus on the threat of an apparent Armenian alliance with the Russians, combined with internal ethnic nationalism, in particular among the Young Turks' leaders. These Young Turks were 'trying to secure a lasting place for the Empire, while operating in an environment that was inherently unstable and insecure, and where mobilizing nationalist identity and centralisation was effected within the already transformed network structure of the Empire' (ibid. 278). The changing relations were largely a function of economic transformation of the Ottoman Empire and the increasing importance of trade with Europe, until then somewhat neglected. Growing economic and social divisions led to antagonisms based on religious and ethnic differences that deepened under the pressures of insecurity. The intensity of competition, while the Ottoman state looked further inwards, simply exacerbated the problem rather than containing it.

The Young Turks acquired power under the slogan of 'Liberty, Equality, Fraternity and Justice'. They were determined to create a parliamentary democracy, complete with a meritocratic bureaucracy. 'They stood for a new fraternal Ottoman identity, united against European intervention in the affairs of the Empire. They spoke of a free press and of virtually unlimited individual liberties. Very little of this came to pass' (Hanioğlu 2008: 151). Ingrained in the fabric of Turkish society were the denial of the Armenian genocide and the repression of Kurdish identity, with its scorched-earth policy. Although today's AKP government has attempted to recognise past indiscretions, it has not changed position on the subject of apologising or accepting the veracity of history (Üngör 2011). Turkey has begun to come to terms with its past, but this is conflated with majoritarian conservatism, which is the dominant political paradigm in the context of the AKP's attitude to Turkey's past, present and future (Bakiner 2013).

The Turkish Republic in the Modern Era

Following the break up of the Ottoman Empire, groups encompassing Anatolia included the Turks, Kurds, Greeks and Armenians. Other ethnic minorities included Georgians, Bosnians, Albanians, Arabs, Circassians, Jews and Syrians. Based on the dominant ideological stream of thought, the founders of the Turkish Republic took state formation for granted, contrary to the multireligious characteristics of the Ottoman Empire; that is, the Turkish Republic determined a theory of the state based on a monocultural understanding of nation, language and history. Remnants of non-Muslim communities living under Ottoman rule were recognised and their rights were guaranteed by the Treaty of Lausanne (1923), but the Armenians and the Greeks were effectively expelled altogether, and 'Turkey was declared as a Western, non-sectarian, republican-liberal democracy' (Smooha 2008: 429). The proclamation of the new republic neglected to consider that the demography of Anatolia did not constitute a single ethnic entity. Kurds were the foremost group affected by this change (Mousseau 2012), not granted equivalent rights to non-Muslims and not classified as a minority group. Inherited from the Ottomans was the traditional system of categorising groups based on religion rather than ethnic background. Kurds were part of the global Muslim community, hence not considered a minority group. Even so, the aggressive assimilationist policies of the Turkish Republic during its violent struggle to prove itself as a unitary state were exposed in its stance towards the Kurds. Time, space, memory and territory were fundamental factors in determining the make-up of this ethno-nationalist project (Öktem 2004).

In responding to the challenges of ethnic discrimination, Kurds maintained their adherence to Islam, as they had done during the Ottoman Empire. Groups exposed to suppression by the state did not adopt a secular understanding regarding the role of religion in the public sphere. Enacted was a peculiar version of Turkish secularism. Here the state did not detach itself from religion, contrary to the discourse of the republic as a state unrestricted from the interference of religion. Instead, the state took control of religion, claiming it was for the purposes of the state. Through this process, state elites created 'proper enlightened Muslims' who were loyal to authority but not so religious to the extent of, for example, wishing for an Islamic state rather than the newly established secular system. In this imagination of a secular state, various authoritative implementations succeeded one another, in many cases backed by severe coercion. Leaders attempted to alter society through deliberate social engineering, a process where individuals were homogenised through the discourse of citizenship. It resulted in territorial centralisation and consolidation, which went together with cultural standardisation. In this homogenisation process, the discourse of Westernisation was legitimised as a tool of the Turkish elite, first in the establishment of their rule as unquestionable, and then by enforcement of their positions through it. To attain this goal, the elite regarded both religious and ethnic differences as unacceptable.

The foremost threat to the achievement of the 'civilising mission' behind the Westernisation project was religion. For Turkey, the primary risk to the formation of the new state was ethnic differences. For the Kemalist ruling elite, religious and ethnic minorities were singled out as imminent dangers to the established republic. Mounting nationalist aspirations caused the implementation of radical laws to maintain the status quo, ranging from new dress codes to the adoption of a completely new alphabet. The leadership weakened the relative position of religion compared to its significance during Ottoman rule, and nationalism subdued, and, to an extent, assimilated ethnic differences (Akman 2004). The prerequisite for the existence of the nation was shared language. Opposition to linguistic variation was the primary means used by the Kemalist elite to remodel the nation in order to fit the idea of the state. Authoritarian nationalism achieved its objective by proscribing or denying the existence of languages other than Turkish, together with the cultures they reproduced. Modern Turkish became the official language of the new regime as the personality cult of Atatürk developed quasi-mystical overtones (Jenkins 2003). Kemalism became a form of classical authoritarianism that replaced religion as the dominant discourse (Mateescu 2006; Karaveli 2010). Through Western-style adjustments the Kemalist revolution moulded a society based on nationalism and secularism. It suppressed the differences of ethnicity and religion. The former tenet affected the Kurds, while the latter concerned Alevis and non-Muslims.

Enforced Kemalism

Through a top-down democratisation project, the Turkish Republic established the disposition of an authoritarian administration in light of the predicaments of liberalisation politics. Kemalist ideology took a firm hold and established an authoritarian state in the power vacuum left by the dissolution of the Ottoman Empire. The pursuit of change did not occur from the bottom up. In its place, 'enlightened' state elites implemented all decisions affecting the lives of so-called 'backward' populations. The discourse of the republic was to establish democracy, but in reality this new state displayed dictatorial characteristics. The political rhetoric of security was used to maintain control, compelling many to believe that the threat of danger was always looming from outside. Kemalist ideology maintained its hegemony through the conceptualisation of presumed enemies who stood against the security of the state (Öncü 2003). The reconfiguration of the 'constitutive other' was a tool used by the Kemalist select few to politicise both religion and ethnicity. Treatment of the 'other' in this way aggrandised the established powers, thereby legitimising the domination of Kemalist ideology and the subordination of differences. Along with the containment of religious groups, the Kemalist regime also targeted different ethnicities. In this context, simply belonging to a particular minority community problematised ethnic and religious identities, more often than not perceived as a security threat that combined exclusion with denial of the existence of those differences.

The dominant cultural and political hegemony instrumentalised ethnic and religious differences while proscribing the assertion of ethnic or religious identity. These two concerns remain unresolved in Turkey (Aral 1997). Yet, in spite of its discourse, the Turkish Republic was unable to achieve an effective democratic state. Conflicts were unresolved or dealt with by impositions. Tensions because of ethnicity and religion became the target of politicisation by dividing society into polarised camps – variously defined as 'modernists'–'backward', 'secularists'–'Islamists', 'Kemalists'–'fundamentalists' or even 'nationalists'–'separatists' according to the period. Demarcating politics through the constitutive other was a way for elite actors to direct the debate in Turkey. Elites maintained the status quo by describing themselves as 'the guardians of the regime'. The idea of safeguarding the republic was the driving force behind the three military *coups d'état* that Turkey experienced between 1960 and 1980.

To reinforce this Kemalism, the education system transmitted state ideology. Trained as teachers, lawyers or public officials, supporters of the ideology entered society as loyal and devoted secularists (Keyman and Kanci 2011). In support of this dominant Kemalist ideological framework, these individuals and groups saw themselves as the guardians of the regime against the 'backward' beliefs of opposing others. The 'civilising mission' appeared to be the exemplar but also a burden on the shoulders of those supporting the 'backwards' in becoming 'civilised' through a process of ethnic and religious discrimination. Elitism sustained the reproduction of state ideology, which reproduced itself in socio-economic terms and through advanced networked relations among the privileged. Elitism penetrated the system and became an indispensable part of its operation. State ideology was immune from criticism or any attempts to transform it. In every new generation, state chiefs replicated their Kemalist hegemony in Turkish politics and society. Bureaucratic and military structures established a cult status that perpetuated elitism, but they also encouraged the widening of inequalities between the advantaged few and the rest of society.

Reform had a formidable effect on the urban elite of Turkey. It was less successful at penetrating rural areas where the vast majority of the population resided. The practice of 'traditional Islam' continued in these locations with little change, where cultural and linguistic differences persevere to this day. Contrary to the imagination of the elite, which became 'modern' through the Westernisation project of the Turkish Republic, the modernisation project affected the few, not the whole of society. The belief in the wider imagined ambitions of the Westernisation project was that religion would eventually become less significant as modernisation theory envisioned. Moreover, ethnic differences would lose their credibility, as state theory perceived. The fallacy of the modernisation project, the limited imagination of the Turkish secular state and the inefficient implementation of this theory by Turkish elites meant that neither religion nor ethnicity lost their value in the eyes of the many. Reluctant obedience to the arbitrary rules of the state ensued until the time came when groups started to voice their demands.

Kemalists ardently defended their rules and regulations, but by introducing sustained disproportionality to the Anatolian region, the Turkish Republic was unable to deliver a stable democracy. The founders of the republic used Western states as role models for their new secular society, which constituted a one-nation approach. To achieve this, the state implemented various laws, in most cases reinforced by military power. These laws suppressed individuals opposed to the expectations of dominant state actors, but they were not internalised by groups. Rather, many stood up against them. Through these laws, the state intended to influence every aspect of people's lives. Thus, from the very moment of the establishment of the republic, strife between the Kemalists and the wider population emerged. Since then, it has become a dominant force within Turkish politics. For example, 'homegrown' radicalisation, particularly among 'militant' Kurdish factions, is a phenomenon that has emerged because of the enforcement of a regressive monocultural politico-ideological project carried out by the Turkish Republic (Laçiner and Bal 2004). Kurds and traditional Muslims wanting to live according to the diktats of Islam were the primary targets of these drastic edicts. Diverse groups inhabiting Anatolia throughout the centuries brought an array of ethnic, religious and cultural differences to a land that benefited from this enrichment. Instantaneously regarded as outsiders by the republic, they could either submit to the rules of the new regime or instead rebel. Those who stood up against suppression of the regime found themselves facing severe clampdown at the hands of the state. Harshly quashed were certain groups that the regime considered dangerous or capable of intimidating others into action.

Turkish Political Liberalisation

Cries against these authoritative implementations by the state led to the introduction of multiparty politics in 1945. The success of the Democrat Party of Adnan Menderes came at the behest of those who had suffered under the authority of the Kemalist elite. It resulted in the breakdown of the imagination of Turkey in becoming a Westernised state, as most of the leaders in Turkey wanted integration with the Western European modernisation project. In response, the Kemalist elite maintained a discourse that legitimised their positions. It was a discourse based on a series of constructed enemies, rather than taking steps to accommodate the needs of the people. As an alternative to empowering individuals and groups who sought to integrate successfully into an ethnically, culturally and religiously tolerant society, Kemalist leaders focused on the discourse of the security state. Multiparty politics scarcely existed for a decade without anxiety over the potential loss of power among state power holders. Kemalist elites benefited from the discourse of the 'guardians of the regime', and habitually maintained the status quo through undemocratic means, for example, the military coup of 27 May 1960.

The 1961 constitution brought relatively increased openness to Turkish society, regarded as the most democratic of the Turkish charters produced by the three military juntas. During this era, different elements of society were able to mobilise politically. For example, the Workers Party of Turkey, a socialist revolutionary party founded in 1961, was able to secure parliamentary representation. All the same, the state did not always recognise the freedoms gained during this time. In 1971 the military interfered with parliament once again. After the 12 March memorandum, ordinary members of society became targets of state elites exercising their exasperation against the masses. Many affected by the authoritative policies of the state were on the left, and tensions grew as the state took control of the population. The Islamist National Order Party, established by Necmettin Erbakan in 1970, closed down only a year after its founding. On this occasion two camps emerged, rightist and leftist activists. During the 1970s the Nationalist

Movement Party (MHP), with its close links to the Grey Wolves, fought on behalf of Turkish ethnic ultra-nationalism, while the Kurdistan Workers' Party (PKK) mobilised Kurds around ethnic nationalism lines. The state perceived such conditions as threatening. The problem remained unresolved when there was a third coup in three decades, the last carried out on 12 September 1980. Kenan Evren, the leader of the coup, claimed that the military moved in because of the serious conditions facing Turkey at the time. This junta's goals were to strengthen the secular principles of Atatürk and to rebuild state authority. This endeavour underscored how the Kemalist elite understood democracy; that is, for rule to be democratic it needed to be under the dominant hegemony of Kemalist ideology and its attempts to homogenise society.

From the newly formed Motherland Party, Turgut Özal became prime minister in 1983, following the military coup of 1980. During his rule, through political and economic liberalisation from the Kemalist state order, the republic opened up to the outside world. Throughout the Özal years there were new perspectives on Islam. In tandem, the petit bourgeoisie from the provinces overcome the opposition it faced from the nationalist oligarchic bourgeoisie, for example through organisations such as Turkish Industry and Business Association (TÜSİAD) (Alam 2009). Constituent social groups, who had formed a new conservative middle class, began to search for a political establishment that best responded to their needs and demands (Çarkoğlu 2008). The economic success of a new Muslim bourgeoisie paved the way for Muslim identity in the public sphere. From the 1990s onwards the opening up of the economy and the end of the Cold War helped Özal to pursue further liberalisation policies. These developments were responsible for the electoral achievement of the Welfare Party of Erbakan in 1995. The post-Cold War period saw the rise of new varieties of postnational citizenship, which undermined traditional models of national citizenship (Koopmans and Statham 1999). These events, together with the growing importance of international law and human rights, destabilised the power of the military to interfere with everyday politics. The liberal ideology also soon became the dominant global paradigm towards the end of the twentieth century.

Capitalist globalisation affected the four corners of the world. Growing awareness of differences in Turkey accelerated the process, causing not only Kurds but also veiled women to demand their rights (see Chapter 7) (Toprak et al. 2009). Others suffering under the arbitrary rule of the state questioned the actions of state institutions but the process of EU integration helped to somewhat improve the human rights conditions of the country (Müftüler-Baç 2000). Through developments in communication technologies and their spread to the outer areas of the country, groups developed greater opportunities to connect with others. They were able to formalise group relations based on collective cultural, linguistic, religious and political struggles (Çaha et al. 2010). The opening up of society made accepting different norms and values part of the richness of society.

Turkish Differences Today

In attempting to understand religious pluralism and monoculturalism, in the move from an empire to a republic, various limitations have emerged due to the complexity of the Turkish historical experience. The idea of a clean break between premodern and modern times in Turkey is overly simplistic. There were continuities in social, cultural, political and religious developments in Turkish society during these periods, including the synthesis between Islam and modernity through the ages (Mardin 2005). A few key issues remain essential to consider when combining the historical and contemporary in an analysis of the ways in which ethnicity, culture and national political identity have come to shape interethnic relations.

The Ottoman period sanctioned different religious minorities to coalesce as subjects (and then citizens under the Tanzimat of 1839) within a huge polity and across wide geographical borders. The Kemalist period reversed the mechanisms inherent in the functioning of this model. Here, Kemalists attempted to eliminate differences and replace them with a monocultural understanding of Turkish national political identity. A narrowly defined state-maintained secularised Islam was a political and cultural tool to keep the masses restrained and to repress dissent. The state became the dominant political entity, narrowly defining national identity. It increased its grip on the citizens of the country during the middle of the twentieth century, but it also added a securitisation dimension. This further reduced the will of the many to succumb to the will of the few. After Kemalism Turkey's various different cultures went into retreat, leading to isolation and the reproduction of reciprocal mistrust. In the post-Cold War context, ethnic and religious identities have emerged as growing transnational political forces. Part of this also explains the rise of various and often-unsettled intercultural dynamics in the Turkish Republic. Domestic identity claims, the opening up of the media, the economic liberalisation of markets, international investment and the development of communication technologies led to innovative configurations of belonging and citizenship.

The military juntas played a particular part in maintaining this reality, ultimately bringing down existing governments and carrying out military coups periodically until 1980. The situation was unstable. It crushed the activities of civil society, which are crucial in establishing democratic institutions and processes. The state political machinery, coupled with the military apparatus, led to ongoing tensions that are yet to be resolved. The mobilisation of Islamic cultural and political norms and values directly conflicted with a secular republican political establishment, which sought to impart a monocultural perspective on national political identity. During the rise of the Welfare Party in the 1990s and since the establishment of the AKP in 2002, Islam politically mobilises a significant body of the conservative population of the country. Islamic values gain popular appeal through the public sphere, but also through access to television and print media. 'The growth of the modern media and the expansion of universal education, instead of weakening the influence of Islam, have led to its redefinition as a dynamic form of political and social consciousness' (Yavuz 2003: 266).

The new Turkish Islam has a pluralistic dynamic past, with influences from Sunni Hanafi traditions that shaped centuries-long social, cultural and interethnic norms and values. Immediately after the War of Independence, Turkish Islam was used as a political project to bridge ethnic and cultural differences within the Muslim populations of a territory that later became Turkey. Specific ethnic, linguistic, cultural and religious differences surfaced as Kemalism narrowly defined this brand of Turkish Islam in its own image. Its characterisation was restricted to privileged urban groups along with established middle classes that had a specific educational and cultural heritage. This new Islam left behind the vast majority of the country, which then became the lesser developed regions of Anatolia. 'The old Turkey was based on a conscious attempt to forget the Islamic-Ottoman past. The new Turkey, in contrast, is evolving on the basis of remembering and building on the deep-rooted legacy of the Ottoman-Islamic past' (ibid. 274).

A Theoretical Synopsis

There are numerous historical, political, cultural and sociological studies on Turkish society. While many analyse the transformations from Ottoman to modern and postmodern society (Ahmad 2003), few have considered the process through the sociological and political lens of religious pluralism and monoculturalism. Here, class structure, as well as ethnic and religious differences, is important in governing the relations between communities. Social conflict as analysed through the prism of religious, ethnic and political relations in Turkey remains unique. Table 2.1 presents a summary of the nature of different historical periods and their implications for society as explored in this chapter.

In the twentieth century various populations in Anatolian Turkey began to urbanise in sizable numbers. It affected employment and education patterns, as well as the dynamics of class stratification and social mobility. Minorities diminished and virtually vanished at the end of the nineteenth century, and the break-up of the Ottoman Empire led to their wide dispersion (see Chapter 3). With the establishment of the Turkish Republic all Muslims were defined as Turks, but there were also non-Muslim citizens

Table 2.1 Changing ethno-national and religio-cultural identity politics in Turkey

Historical period	Forms of truth	Differences– social structure	Analytical framework
Classical Ottoman Turkey	objective → absolute	accepted → open	assimilationist – religious plurality
Kemalist Turkey (1920s–1980s)	absolute → subjective	suppressed → closed	assimilationist – monoculturalism
Postmodern Turkey (post-1980s)	subjective → objective	increasingly recognised → opening up	assimilationist – neo-liberal

in the territory. Today, all Turks are defined as Muslims (irrespective of piousness), but non-Muslim Turkish-born minorities are considered to be lesser Turkish citizens (Lewis 1968; Çağaptay 2006; Jenkins 2008).

The Ottoman Empire reigned over a religiously plural social structure. However, the heirs of Ottoman heritage, the founders of the Turkish Republic, did not preserve this attribute. In its place, they established a new state with a monocultural society. At the end of the Ottoman Empire, a 'Turkification' nationalism project was under way, especially during the second constitutional period (1908–18), but a form of Ottomanism also existed alongside this policy approach (Ulker 2005). Strongly influenced by French liberalism and positivist philosophy, the Young Turk movement, originating in the 1880s and embracing a programme of Ottomanism, gradually came under the influence of (pan)Turkist notions (van Bruinessen 1992).

Together with the 1908 Young Turk revolution there emerged a wider liberal discourse seeking freedoms and rights, which later became another absolutism as a reaction to the counter-revolutionary movement of 1909. Rebellions led by religious leaders strengthened the modernist discourse of the Young Turks, paving the way for successive changes under the Kemalist regime in later periods. When the state was not required to temper differences within society, as it had under foreign threat during the War of Independence, it attempted to create an imagined Turkish society based on a nationalist discourse. The state introduced a series of reform packages, which frequently operated against the will of wider society. Once the state felt secure against the threat of external powers it initiated a further series of revisions that eventually eradicated the remnants of the Ottoman legacy. As part of the social engineering project of the newly founded republic, the date of 3 March 1924 is crucial. The caliphate was abolished. In its place, the state established the Directorate of Religious Affairs as a national institution, along with the introduction of changes to legal and education systems according to the principles of secularism. The state took control of religion and under this directorate assembled a body of imams working as state officials. Through this specialisation in religious matters within state institutions, religion was taken from its social and 'folk Islam' base and replaced with the political discourse of the state. The Kemalist elite were unable to suppress religion successfully.

Rather, state ideology ignored ethnic and religious differences and resorted to enforced assimilation as a solution.

In essence, the Turkish Republic created a monocultural understanding of society that proved to be limited in prompting social transformation. Because of these state initiatives and with differences overpowered, hegemony reappeared in the Turkish political scene, but under an entirely different guise. The authoritative implementations of the state maintained secularism and national political homogeneity for the purposes of the state, making religion and ethnicity subservient to it. For the religiously oriented seeking religious freedoms, including traditional Sunnis, the state became a barrier to their freedom of expression. Since the post-Cold War liberalisation of society, 'soft-Islamisation' has seen religio-cultural norms and values re-emerge in the public and political spheres. Staunch secularists and liberals regard the current social and cultural transformations of Turkey as suspicious (Koyuncu-Lorasdaği 2010). Whether Turkey is able to shake off its inward-looking dynamic and fear of all outsiders, in spite of the forces of secularism or Islamism, is another lingering question (Haynes 2010).

One group significantly affected by this experience is the Kurds. They continue to demand acceptance and rights largely because of their share in the demographic structure of the republic and their success in coming together as a local and global political unit. The debate on whether the Kurdish struggle for recognition is rooted in socio-economic disadvantage or in political dissatisfaction has still to reach conclusive outcomes (Sarigil 2010; Ekmekci 2011). The reality is arguably an amalgamation of both factors. The ambitions of postmodern Turkey have made it possible to consider an intercultural cosmopolitan social structure, not only for the maintenance of peace and stability, but also for democracy to flourish, if not to consolidate the nation. As increasing numbers of Turks accept that *being* Kurd is not incongruent with *becoming* Turk, and as ardent secularists begin to perceive minority *and* majority religions as worthy of respect on their terms, the evolution of a globally cosmopolitan Turkish society will come into existence (Efegil 2011). It potentially benefits society as a whole, resulting in robust understandings of cultural and social cohesion, and national political identity. Perceptions of cultural memory (*and* forgetting) continue as contested concerns in Turkey (Ozyürek 2007). There remains a great deal to do to ensure that Turkey can fully move on from its recent past and return to a multireligious, multicultural society that is confident and capable of looking within as well as without.

3

Insights on Intolerance towards Minorities

In Western Europe issues of ethnic discrimination in societies containing post-war immigrant and minority populations are well established in research and policy matters (Bulmer and Solomos 1999; Miles and Phizaklea 1980; Rex and Tomlinson 1979). In response, anti-discrimination legislation helps to eliminate the disadvantages that these groups suffer. This legislation, however, has had an unpredictable degree of success. Less known are the realities of ethnic and racial discrimination and intolerance in Turkey. It is a country ostensibly 99 per cent Muslim, but where, according to the European Social Survey (ESS), 7 per cent of the population define themselves as a minority (although it is difficult to discern whether this relates to classifications of ethnicity or religion, given the rules of Turkish citizenship). Whether Kurds define themselves as a minority depends on their social positions, geographical locations and political outlook. Therefore, many of those who self-identified as minorities for the survey are arguably Kurdish, but not all Kurdish groups would adhere to that definition. Conjecturally, most minorities in Turkey are a combination of ethnic and religious minority groups, many of which are found in the larger cities west of Anatolia as well as in Istanbul. The latter contains a population of twenty million people (unofficially), including as many as three million Kurds and nearly a million Syrians refugees.

A sample of 4,274 Turkish respondents to the 2004 and 2008 waves of the ESS explores how tolerance is a factor in understanding perceptions of discrimination among minorities and majorities in Turkey (further details of the study's methodology are contained in the Methods, see Appendix). The primary question is how do minorities in Turkey perceive discrimination, and to what degree? That is, if there is intolerance, are Turks intolerant towards all minorities, or only some? How does use of language or religiosity explain intolerance? These questions help to understand how minorities and majorities perceive and relate to each other. It also helps to appreciate the impact of perceptions upon discrimination, intolerance and prejudice. Analysing the results of these questions helps to comprehend the nature of interethnic and interreligious relations as a variation of the Turkish experience (Ince 2012). Analysis of ESS data finds that minorities in Turkey suffer greatest discrimination, but exhibit greater tolerance regarding majorities. Majorities are least likely to experience discrimination, but more likely to show intolerance concerning others. Respondents on the right of the political divide, and classifying themselves as more religious, are least likely to show tolerance regarding others. The analysis offers vital insights into intolerance and its relationship to discrimination.

As discussed in the previous chapter, contemporary Turkey is a nation with an authoritarian and conservative culture. Broad-based religio-cultural norms and values define the country's identity, but there are ongoing challenges of tolerance, discrimination and racism. This chapter provides a unique picture of ethnic minority life in Istanbul and in Turkey, connecting the local and the national, and the micro and macro in an investigation of diversity, equality, and ethnic and religious intolerance and discrimination across the nation. From re-examining history to determining national models in the present climate, from discussing ethnic cleansing to exploring ethnic gentrification, this chapter endeavours to determine a holistic understanding of interethnic relations and intolerance towards minorities in Turkey.

Historical Paradigms

There are around fifteen million Kurds living across Turkey, with major concentrations in the south-east of the country (Heper 2007). Other minorities in Turkey include Christians, Armenians, Alevis, Circassians, Bosnians, Arabs and Jews. The extent to which these groups would classify themselves as minorities is less clear in light of the Turkish nationalist project in assimilating minority groups (see Chapter 2). Minorities face different experiences of integration, assimilation and incorporation in Istanbul, and all over Turkey, in areas ranging from successful entrepreneurship to aspects of the informal economy (Ergin 2014). Compared with European nations, in recent years

Turkey has been the least tolerant, especially of Jewish groups (Zan et al. 2012). There remain particular issues affecting recognition and acceptance of specific minority groups in Turkey. These issues occur despite the effects of greater economic development and globalisation on society. They persist even as Turkey attempts to improve its position on democratisation, representation and participation in the social, political and economic sphere.

At the turn of the twentieth century more than a million Jews, Christians and other minorities lived in the vast Ottoman Empire, with its total population of fifteen million people. Most of these minorities were of Greek and Armenian origin, notwithstanding the numerous Alevis and Jews. Greeks, Armenians and Jews made up a diverse population profile in the past, but the combined number is said to be no more than around 100,000 across Turkey today, with over twenty million additional minorities (consisting of fifteen million Kurds, three million Circassians, one million Bosnians, half a million Roma, half a million Laz and the remainder being Arabs, ethnic Bulgarians and others) (Kaya and Baldwin 2004). Since the Syrian conflict began in 2011 there are as many as two million refugees in Turkey. The Roma population is over half a million, based on official records, but unofficially it could be as high as one million. Roma live throughout Turkey but have no official legal recognition or protection.

Over time Jewish groups in Turkey left for Israel, married out or died out. Barely 17,000 Jews remain, mostly located in a few districts of Istanbul. Under the millet system, the Ottoman rulers were open to religious differences and respected them, but ethnic differences remained pronounced, in particular with regard to the Alevis and the Kurds (Barkey 2008). There is legal protection for non-Muslim minorities in the 1923 Treaty of Lausanne. It continues in generally the same configuration today. In spite of this, crucially, the treaty only recognised three minority groups: Armenians, Greeks and Jews (Toktaş 2005). There remain issues in the current period, including the 2007 assassination of Armenian journalist Hrant Dink in broad daylight in Istanbul. In 2005 and 2006 a Christian priest and missionaries were murdered. Most regard these incidents as activities of ultra-nationalists. Others view them as the workings of the 'deep state', which at the time aimed to derail the EU integration process and to create the opportunity for the return of military rule (Ulusoy 2011). Until recently, perceived by some as a credible alternative to existing governments, military intervention at times of national crises have been considerably minimised as a result of AKP reforms.

Gentrification ostensibly refers to clearing out the old in preparation for the new. It presents numerous problems for the identities and cultural memories of variously affected communities. It also weakens notions of shared existence or the appearance of diversity. Yet, nothing quite evokes the question of ethnic cleansing or ethnic gentrification than the Armenian genocide of 1914–15. The Armenians in Turkey, the Armenian diaspora, the Turks in Turkey and across the Turkish diaspora relentlessly debate this particular period in history. There is limited agreement about its causes and its consequences. Nevertheless, some facts are established.

The Armenian Genocide

Attempts to eliminate the Armenians from Ottoman territory date back to the late nineteenth century. There is particular interest in the period 1914–15, as this is when the Armenian Genocide occurred. Killed or forced out of Turkey by 1922, the cause of the genocide seems to present a particular point of contention for different groups in Turkey. Attention at one level is on the despotic tendencies of tyrannical rulers. At another level, there is the suggestion that more nuanced understandings did exist at the centre, but that the killing took on its own momentum at the periphery (Akçam 2004).

The Young Turks believed a policy of Turkifying the nation was necessary to preserve the remnants of a declining Ottoman culture. Various elements of society, in contrast, began to resist this forced assimilation, given the multi-ethnic and multireligious position of the empire at the time. The Young Turks concluded that the vision of a new Turkey could not integrate Christians. Reputedly schemed by Sultan Abdülhamid II (1842–1918), the initial massacre took place in broad daylight so that the public could witness it. This pogrom targeted Armenian marketplaces and properties. The intention was to break the nationalist fervour emerging among the Armenians, who responded to the repression they were encountering at the hands of a fading empire. The early massacres explicitly targeted men in demographically specific locations across Turkey.

The actions of 1915 included women and young children, not just men, and involved deportation as well as extermination. Because of the far-flung geographical locations of Turkey's Armenian populations, the cover of war prevented Istanbul-based journalists from unearthing the true horrors of the deportation policy until long after the events had occurred. The policy was not merely to remove the Armenian population from Ottoman territories, but to abolish all memory of their existence. This included burning properties, confiscating land and destroying records and personal effects. It was ethnic gentrification in every sense of the concept. It comes as no surprise that Adolf Hitler famously said in a speech in 1939, 'who, after all, speaks today of the annihilation of the Armenians?' Various scholars have argued that the Armenian genocide inspired Hitler in his actions against the Jews and other minorities in Germany and Western Europe. Undoubtedly, the parallels between the Holocaust and the Armenian genocide are instantly recognisable. Both used race as a central concept in outlining a form of fascist ethnic nationalism. The dispersal of ethnic minorities to reservations was also noticeable. Moreover, both the Young Turks and Hitler used the explicit concept of ethnic cleansing (Travis 2013).

The Armenian genocide coincides with the modernisation project in Turkey at the turn of the century. The telegraph and the railroads made communications and transportation effective. Orders issued at the centre but executed at the periphery came with an efficiency and speed previously unknown in Ottoman military history. Authorities did not need or keep records specifically because of the telegraph. It masked the actual events on the ground until many years later. In effect, the railroads helped to remove populations without the gaze of others bearing witness. Not only did the Armenian genocide seek to exterminate an entire population, but it also removed the associated memories of that group from popular culture. Those Armenians who managed to flee the persecution found themselves in places far away from home. They carried the memories of devastation connected with their kith and kin. The events traumatised an entire population that now bears the heavy burden of permanent loss. The Armenians were scattered all over, their legacies torn apart. Other consequences were the lack of justice and the continuous disavowal by the inheritors of history. Caught between suffering the shame of their ancestors they tried to maintain some national loyalty to the newly imagined nation. The process of refutation and repudiation was reproduced generation upon generation (Hovannisian 2003).

Because of the murky business of war and the politics of remembering and forgetting, the numbers of deaths and aspects of the annihilation process documented in letters and memoirs of the time required independent verification. Even now, there remain many attempts to polarise the debate. The Armenian diaspora has been effective in promoting a universal truth about how Armenians were brutalised and systematically devastated by a waning empire. On the other hand, the overriding Turkish rhetoric is to focus on the view that the events were isolated examples, and local actors operating independently did much of the decision-making, ostensibly sullying the good name of the Ottomans, both then and now. Polarisations linger in the international context as part of the recognition of the Armenian genocide. There is much by way of renunciation and minimisation in Turkey (Bloxham 2005).

Alevis and Kurds in Reality

The Alevis are thought to number as much as 20 per cent of the country's population (fifteen million people), concentrated in urban centres throughout Turkey. Although the Alevis have broadly assimilated into the secular national Turkish republican model with greater success than other minorities, their existence has not been without misery. In the mid-1990s a number of high profile murders of Alevis in the Sultangazi district of Istanbul heightened tensions facing this group. In 1993, in a hotel in Sivas, many Alevi intellectuals were allegedly burnt alive by far-left ultranationalists (Kalaycioğlu 2010).

Under the Turkish secular model all religious groups have the same rights, freedoms and protections as other religious communities, but this has not materialised in reality. Alevis believe that the Turkish republican system unfairly favours adherents of Sunni Islam over the Alevis' own variation of Shia Islam. The Diyanet (Turkish Presidency of Religious Affairs) now recognises Alevi places of worship in many Turkish provinces and the government has made some apologies for past indiscretions against the Alevis, but ongoing concerns persist about the acceptance of this group. It is secular but also traditional on matters of the headscarf and gender separation, even when compared with the conservative Sunni Hanafi majority. Alevis in Turkey have traditionally supported secularism, and the EU is an ally in raising awareness of Alevi concerns, but the AKP has been unwilling to deliver on their promises. Alevis often shift their political allegiance in order to achieve their demands, that is, to the Republican People's Party (CHP), but the net result is to consign the fate of the Alevis firmly rooted in the domestic political sphere of Turkey (Çarkoğlu and Bilgili 2007).

The Kurds are Turkey's most significant and largest minority, and their situation is the most concerning (Heper 2007; Yavuz 2001), especially in the current period. Although much of the 'Kurdish issue' focuses on demands for political recognition, there are matters of socio-economic inequality that persist at a deeper level. 'Kurds live in an environment of insecurity both materially and non-materially' (Içduygu et al. 1999: 993). The assimilationist policies of the early republican period not only proved inadequate in meeting the needs of the Kurds but also entrenched racism and inequality (Saatchi 2002). The formation of the republic suppressed the articulation of Kurdish language and culture in society. Attempts made by the Turkish state to maintain its Kemalist ethno-nationalist model of Turkishness were exclusivist and self-selecting. The Kurdistan Workers' Party (PKK), established in 1978, soon became militarised in its efforts to attain recognition and status. This locked the Turkish state into a guerrilla war with militant groups in the south-east of the country. Ever-problematic skirmishes between the PKK and the Turkish army have presented considerable questions about the Turkish state and the Turkish model of nationalism (Çelik 2000). The eastern and south-eastern regions, where the concentration of ethnic Kurds is greatest, remain the least socio-economically developed and the most neglected regions in Turkey (Somer 2002).

The 'Kurdish issue' is a vital question for regional stability, but also for the formation of a national Turkish identity (Galletti 1999). It is crucial to appreciate that no single Kurdish ethnic identity captures the variety of diversity found across the four regions of Turkey, Iran, Syria and Iraq. Therefore, Kurdish nationalism is in a state of evolution as much as is Turkish majority national identity. There are also huge variations within Turkey regarding how different Kurds regard their Kurdishness as relative to their Turkishness. Hence, scope arises for a negotiated space in the interests of ethnic majorities and minorities in the Turkish context (Kasaba 1997). A persistent theme that ran throughout historical paradigms in relation to the formation of the Turkish republic is that Kurds were 'Turks still in the making', such was the power of the Turkish republic among ethnic majority Turks (Yeğen 2007). Moreover, because of ongoing socio-economic and political marginalisation, many Turkish Kurds remain disaffected as well as somewhat suspicious of the Turkish state. The status quo serves to maintain their concerns, which continues to prompt Kurdish nationalism in response to marginalisation, exclusion and disenfranchisement (Sarigil 2010; Ekmekci 2011).

A permanent solution to the 'Kurdish issue' remains uncertain, whether it is over rights and recognition, or racism and equality. Notwithstanding regional intensities and a great deal of ethnic mixing among the population of Turkey, particularly in Istanbul, where one in three Kurds in Turkey reside, anecdotal evidence suggests a large minority are in mixed marriages with Turkish partners. This demographic fact alone complicates the 'Kurdish issue'. It is unlikely that many wish to 'return' to a newly formed 'Kurdistan', even if it were to be created. The rise in Kurdish nationalism has also resurfaced in the light of globalisation. Because of the tangible character of Turkish repression, it has strengthened its resilience (van Bruinessen 1998). The mythological status given to Kurdish history goes back to the Persians, with the story of Newroz continuing to be a powerful narrative in growing support for the Kurdish cause (Gunes 2013).

Turkish Exceptionalism

Since the foundation of the Turkish secular republican model in the 1920s there has been a number of politically destabilising periods. These have involved transformations of the urban sphere into secular nationalist models of monoculturalism. It was combined with loyalty to an ethnic nationalism based on the secular designs of Turkishness. Military coups occurred every decade for three decades, and a sharp divide between 'secularists' and 'Islamists' developed. While it is necessary to appreciate these are contested terms, and interlinkages exist between the concepts, there are also weighty issues dividing these two foremost segments of Turkish society.

A popular post-Islamism prevails among majority conservative Turks in the current climate. This idea of post-Islamism refers to a position that goes beyond the notion of a purely Islamic system of governance dictating the needs of a Muslim population as a whole (Bayat 2013). Rather, post-Islamism incorporates secular and liberal notions of democracy and human rights while maintaining a respectful glance back to the classical Islamic age. Simultaneously, there is also the observation that Turks are hostile to outsiders, not just non-Muslims, but also non-Turk Muslims. This occurrence stems from memories of the break-up of the Ottoman Empire and the internal and external prevailing hegemonic forces that generally provoked the process (Haynes 2010). Therefore, it is necessary to understand how the complex nature of Turkish exceptionalism permeates wider society. This exceptionalism was first observed in anthropological writings as early as the 1920s and 1930s (Maksudyan 2005), and it persists in today's popular press, for example concerning the ongoing negative description of Kurds in leading national newspapers (Sezgin and Wall 2005). Turkish nationalism has yet to meet the needs and wants of diverse communities that comprise Turkey (Suvari 2010).

The historical and political formation of the Turkish nation is rather different from Western European conceptualisations. As such, the complex ethnic and racial tensions that exist in Turkey remain less well understood. This presents a unique opportunity to categorise the ethno-cultural problems of racism and discrimination in Turkey based on the analysis of secondary national survey data. It answers a range of imperative questions in order to develop a better understanding of the issues in play (Banton 2008). Thus, a series of findings based on the respondents from 2004 and 2008 waves of the ESS in Turkey suggest a range of noteworthy insights on the type of ethnic relations in the country, as shown below (see Methods (Appendix 1) for details on the data and the variables).

- Approximately one in nine respondents spoke Kurdish as their first language at home.
- Speaking languages other than Turkish at home was the main predictor for perceiving discrimination and tolerance.
- Ethnic minority respondents were more than fifteen times more likely to report discrimination that ethnic majorities.
- Ethnic minority respondents were more than ten times more likely to report discrimination when adding the additional control variables.
- Ethnic minority respondents were more than 2.6 times more likely to express a tolerant attitude than enthnic majorities, and approximately 1.3 times more likely to state that they were tolerant

when adding in the additional variables, although the latter is not statistically significant.

- Impact of ethnicity was significant even when adding together all the other explanatory factors, suggesting that ethnicity was a critical factor in determining the extent of discrimination perceived by groups and the level of tolerance expressed by them.
- Respondents suggesting that they held conservative political values were on the more religious side of the religiosity scale.
- The greater the predisposition of respondents to place themselves on the right of the left–right political scale, the less likely they perceived their group to be facing some kind of discrimination, and the less tolerant they were towards other ethnic and racial groups.
- There was no significant difference between men and women with regard to discrimination, but men appear to be less tolerant than women.
- Marital status (living with a partner) had no impact on perceived discrimination or level of tolerance, nor did economic status.
- Younger Turks were more likely than those aged fifty-five and over to perceive discrimination *and* to be tolerant. The impact of age in the model for tolerance was broadly insignificant.
- Impact of qualifications was insignificant in the model of discrimination, but it was highly significant for tolerance. This impact was in the expected direction, such that highly qualified Turks were more tolerant than Turks with low or no qualifications.
- Living in Istanbul, compared with other regions in Turkey, increased the chance of developing views that are more critical.
- Log-linear models revealed that perceived discrimination, religiosity and tolerance were associated with each other, but not with language; but, crucially, language was associated with discrimination and with tolerance.
- Respondents sampled in 2004 perceived more discrimination and were less tolerant than those in the 2008 wave of the survey.

In the statistical models, perceptions of discrimination are a predictor for tolerance. Ethnic minorities perceiving discrimination were broadly likely to be tolerant, compared with ethnic minorities and ethnic majorities not perceiving discrimination. Therefore, the difference between minorities and majorities in terms of their tolerance level was the difference between perceptions of discrimination. Minorities experiencing discrimination were more tolerant, and majorities encountering discrimination less intolerant. Tables 3.1–3.3 present a range of significant crosstabulations based on the data from the ESS. They highlight the issues of religiosity and tolerance among respondents.

In exploring perceived discrimination, religiosity and tolerance, the relationship between religiosity and tolerance depended on whether respondents

Table 3.1   Crosstabulation of tolerance, religiosity and perceived discrimination

Discrimination on race, national, language or ethnic grounds		Religious or not		Total (%)	Cramer's V
		Not religious (%)	Religious (%)		
No perceived discrimination	Intolerant	111 (23)	370 (77)	481 (100)	–0.054
	Tolerant	528 (29)	1294 (71)	1822 (100)	(p < 0.001)
	Total	639 (28)	1664 (72)	2303 (100)	
Perceived discrimination	Intolerant	4 (14)	24 (86)	28 (100)	–0.23
	Tolerant	64 (45)	79 (55)	143 (100)	(p < 0.001)
	Total	68 (40)	103 (60)	171 (100)	

Source: European Social Survey 2004 and 2008

Table 3.2   Crosstabulation of language and discrimination

Language most often spoken at home (first mentioned)	Discrimination on race, national, language or ethnic grounds		Total (%)	Cramer's V
	No (%)	Yes (%)		
Kurdish	338 (74)	116 (26)	454 (100)	0.26
Other	82 (96)	3 (4)	85 (100)	(p < 0.001)
Turkish	3546 (96)	164 (5)	3710 (100)	
Total	3966 (93)	283 (7)	4249 (100)	

Source: European Social Survey 2004 and 2008

Table 3.3   Crosstabulation of language and tolerance

Language most often spoken at home (first mentioned)	Tolerance index for ethnic and racial differences		Total (%)	Cramer's V
	Intolerant (%)	Tolerant (%)		
Kurdish	22 (8)	239 (92)	261 (100)	0.10
Other	10 (20)	41 (80)	51 (100)	(p < 0.001)
Turkish	478 (22)	1687 (78)	2165 (100)	
Total	510 (21)	1967 (79)	2477 (100)	

Source: European Social Survey 2004 and 2008

perceived discrimination, such that high levels of religiosity were associated with intolerance among respondents experiencing discrimination. Similarly, respondents speaking Kurdish at home reported much higher levels of perceived discrimination and a greater level of tolerance than Turks reporting that they spoke Turkish at home. People speaking languages other than Turkish or Kurdish were between these two groups concerning perceptions of discrimination and tolerance of others. The results were noteworthy because they report that Kurdish-speaking respondents suggest the highest levels of perceived discrimination but also showed higher levels of tolerance for all others. All of the results in Tables 3.1–3.3 are statistically significant (p < 0.001).

The ESS offers a useful overview of some of the essential nationwide observations on minority–majority relations, and perceptions of tolerance, prejudice and discrimination using aggregated data. It is helpful in presenting a broad picture of the patterns across the country. Many variations occur in practice and no more so than when analysing experiences inside Istanbul, the cultural capital of Turkey.

Unbroken Ethnic Cleansing

For many outsiders Turkey and Istanbul are interchangeable, although in reality they are entirely different. Istanbul formed the heart of the Ottoman Empire from 1453 onwards. Previously, as Constantinople, the city was at the centre of the Eastern Roman Empire for a thousand years. The Red

Apple, as the Aya Sophia was known, was seen as the dream of many an Ottoman in their pursuit of power, glory and eternal recognition. Under the Ottomans, Istanbul was the seat of economic, political and cultural power of the empire. After the collapse of Muslim Andalusia in 1492 the Ottoman centre invited many Jews to improve its commerce, trade and architecture, as well as expand its intellectual and cultural wealth. This process involved the incorporation of religious minorities from the periphery of the empire to its centre, and because of the organic expansion of the empire in general, it led to many advantages and gains for a huge land mass, including its urban elite. Wealthy Jews and Christians, with similar levels of class and status, stood cheek by jowl with their majority Turkish counterparts, and in all walks of social and economic life. They resided in some of the more affluent districts of Istanbul. As the Ottomans waned in power and status, Jewish and Christian minorities faced the brunt of changes that affected their livelihoods and their status in society. It also shifted their situations in the city of Istanbul.

The character of a city's urbanism shapes its identity. In Istanbul, one such place that exemplifies this experience is Tarlabaşı, in the district of Beyoğlu, an area across the Golden Horn from what was once the seat of imperial power, Topkapi Palace. No other place identifies with the changing dynamics of Istanbul and Turkey than Tarlabaşı and its reconfiguration as a site of urban wealth and status defined by a neoclassical economic model. In the past the locality was notable because of its rich cultural, ethnic and religious diversities. It was where many Jews and Christians lived and worked during the height of the Ottoman Empire. Today's Beyoğlu indicates urban obsolescence or ethnic gentrification. In particular, the area of Tarlabaşı reflects issues of remembering and forgetting. It acts as a metaphor for a range of wider structural and cultural developments afflicting contemporary Turkey. The historical legacy of cultural integration and ethnic diversity shapes a selective memory, affecting the identity of the city, which acts as a microcosm for the character of a nation.

While estimates of Turkey's Roma population are imprecise, conservative figures place it at around one million. Approximately 120,000 of this number live in Istanbul and the rest live in other major cities around Turkey. Most Turkish Roma are Sunni Muslim (Kolukirik and Toktaş 2007). Since Byzantine times Roma settled in Sulukule, in the Fatih district of Istanbul.

Yet, as recently as the early 1960s, demolition of their homes began under the auspices of the municipal authority. The destruction has continued ever since. With the ban on 'entertainment houses' in 1992, the local economy of the Roma was in ruins. After the closures the population of Sulukule reduced from 10,000 to around 3,500. Many had their homes razed. Relocated to new housing complexes over 40km away to the north-west of the city, they were far from their existing social networks and opportunities for economic and cultural exchange (Foggo 2007). In 2009 the municipality destroyed the remaining Romani homes. The Roma were subsequently scattered all over Istanbul, including in places such as Tarlabaşı. New property developments in the Fatih region appealed to the rising Muslim petite bourgeoisie, the backbone of Anatolian economic success since the 1990s. Conservative groups who had moved to the district of Fatih disapproved of the Roma 'dancing girls' culture and the wider Romani entertainment industry. Because of their rising economic and political importance, these aspirational Muslims were able to influence local policy. The transformations in Sulukule illustrate the intersection of conservatism and laissez-faire economics, which has become an identifiable feature of the Turkish economy and society more generally. Other areas of Istanbul underwent gentrification policy as early as the 1980s, such as the Bosphorus and Ortaköy districts, but the experience of Tarlabaşı provides ongoing interest.

During the nineteenth century much of the Tarlabaşı population was non-Muslim and European in origin. When Ankara became the new capital most of these populations departed to work at the embassies and consulates located there. Nevertheless, Tarlabaşı remained of significant interest due to its rich cultural heritage, including theatres, museums and art houses. There were also many fashionable restaurants and boutiques supplying rare art and *en vogue* clothing. Even after the Europeans left, Beyoğlu remained one of the most distinguished parts of Istanbul. After the end of the Second World War many of the Jews in the area departed for Israel. It was then that Beyoğlu started to lose its appeal, especially as Istanbul began to expand its perimeters on all sides. Dramatic growth of the city led to different patterns of urbanisation and suburbanisation. The population spread not just geographically, but also across the class structure. The Greeks suffered severe pogroms against them in 1955. Many of their coffee houses, patisseries and fine dining restaurants, as well residential buildings, suffered extensive damage. Moreover, artists began to ignore Beyoğlu, unearthing other places to meet and discuss the latest trends in their professions (Ergun 2004). The Tünel area, also in the Beyoğlu district, altered radically because of developments in architectural infrastructure, commercial activity among small traders and artisan activity. However, grave issues remained in Tarlabaşı. As the Tünel locale became fashionable again, rents increased significantly, forcing poorer and visibly diverse groups further to the margins, specifically to areas such as Tarlabaşı. These changes coincided with migrants from rural areas moving to the inner city in search of cheaper properties. By the early 1980s Tarlabaşı had become a slum area for the poor, dispossessed and disenfranchised. The construction of a major transport system adjacent to Istiklal Caddesi was arguably the main reason that the Tarlabaşı district was effectively cut off from the economic regeneration of wider Beyoğlu. The partition of the district could only be achieved by 'demolition of 1,100 nineteenth-century buildings (some 300 of which were listed) and the displacement of 5,000 people, through the illegal implementation of an informal, local infrastructure investment plan' (Kocabas 2006: 117). The plan to separate a part of historic Istanbul in the 1980s was due to the inability of policy-makers to imagine an integrated city with its diverse populations.

In the 1990s Kurdish groups began to arrive after experiencing suppression in the south-east of Turkey. Of late, African and transsexual groups have moved to Tarlabaşı. It has become an island, physically disjointed from the central parts of Istanbul that are popular among tourists, and where many of the historical sites remain. Growing capital investment directed at an ever-globalising tourist sector has surfaced, but it is coupled with the stigmatisation associated with marginalised groups in Turkish society, such as the Roma, African migrants, transsexuals and, since 2011, Syrian refugees. Local residents regard the area as 'dangerous' and those living in the neighbourhood have become suspicious of outsiders. Indeed, the racialisation of African migrants is notable in the ascendant imagination, viewed as transient groups who do not wish to make Istanbul their home. This is especially evident in policing matters, where a constant negative assumption about African migrants prevails in negative actions towards this group (Suter 2013). For transsexual groups, their presence in the Beyoğlu district characterises aspects of modern urban centres throughout the world, where a tension exists between the old and the new, the past and the present, the traditional and the modern. Such distinctive endeavour is not new to the area. Beyoğlu was always a site that pushed the boundaries of 'normality' during the ages. That is, '[t]hroughout its history, Beyoğlu has been an in-between place, an enclave of difference and otherness. Yet it has also been a place of containment and repression' (Sandıkcı 2013).

In the mid-2000s attempts grew to gentrify Tarlabaşı. Large development corporations received substantial contracts to deliver desirable accommodation and commercial holdings. These plans are currently on hold due to resistance from local action groups. They believe that the policy is unfair to local communities, who lack both sufficient rehousing opportunities and the means to maintain an independent economic existence, currently primarily in the recycling economy. Since the 1980s, in all examples of successful regeneration projects in Istanbul, dialogue between politicians, the entrepreneurs and the local community has been essential for success (Ercan 2011). In the case of Tarlabaşı, urban planning and governance appears to have broken down. This is not because local action groups are resisting the prevailing development paradigm. Rather, they wish to be part of the process of change, and to reap some of its rewards, reflecting the lack of alternatives (Karaman 2014).

Istanbul Transformed

There are many explanations to consider in understanding the changing dynamics of Istanbul's urban centres. One indispensable element is the cultural outlook that shapes urbanisation policy and how political elites and economic interests direct the approach. Much of this reflects aspirations regarding globalisation and tourism, but local area factors such as housing prices and rent levels also put pressures on accommodation. Globalisation has the effect of normalising the function of urban centres. What is interesting about the Tarlabaşı case study is the process of ethnic and cultural gentrification that has ensued, accelerated by a top-down process that serves the interests of dominant capital. The economic motivation cannot be underestimated, but the political context is also of great importance.

The inner city areas of Istanbul have become of major interest to investors looking for a sharp return in the current period. These zones are subject to various planning reforms, which have resulted in the total destruction of property and the removal of existing ethnic minority communities. As a result, there is a distorted historical memory of Istanbul, while the social capital of Turkish residents and foreign investors strengthens. Urban spaces that were once home to thriving minority cultures and their peoples become the subject of private investment initiatives (Dinçer 2011). Ethnic enclaves are now prime investor territory as Istanbul and the Turkish economic philosophy embraces a competitive approach directed at growth, but not unrelated to an authoritarian nationalism that seeks to reinvent a Turkish identity by appropriating an imagined past for a profitable future. The Roma, African migrants and Syrian refugees are some of the least desirable groups in present-day Turkish society. They suffer the brunt of racism and discrimination in all spheres of life. Turkish families tell their young children stories about the 'treacherous' disposition of the Roma. Turkish popular presses and television programmes continue to vilify and misrepresent minorities, projecting this sense of anti-Turkishness as a potential threat to the state. The hegemonic discourse of urbanism has excluded some of the most 'othered' and marginalised groups in Turkish society. Ironically, as Istanbul becomes global, it looks away from its history of ethnic and cultural diversity, championing neo-liberal principles in the pursuit of economic and political hegemony (Aksoy 2012).

This experience also reflects the lack of democratisation, fanning polarisation and divisions in the process; such is the ironic logic of the transformative cultural and economic profile of one of the world's most recognised global cities. Urban regeneration is a vehicle to introduce (religiously) conservative-friendly economic policy in parts of historical cities in order to meet the interests of cultural, political and economic capital. Affected by these developments are some of the oldest and newest minority groups in Turkey. It is indicative of a centralised discourse on nation-building and the ensuing attitudes towards particular ethnicities. The problems remain despite resistance from intellectuals, activists and liberals, some of which has been successful in delaying various redevelopment initiatives. Protests notwithstanding, the prevailing interests of the professional middle classes and the bourgeoisie outweigh the needs of the working classes and groups regarded as the underclass in policy and planning matters in Istanbul. Minorities are priced out in a free market model that rewards the rich at the expense of the poor (Can 2013). The political, cultural and economic geography of Tarlabaşı represents the further marginalisation of already relegated groups in society. Marked by economic interests and political shortsightedness, it coalesces with a historical legacy of the characterisation of 'the Turks' and their enemies. Not only is this class gentrification, as recognised in other historical cities throughout the world affected by globalisation and neo-liberalism, the experiences in Istanbul also suggest ethnic gentrification (Karaman and Islam 2012).

In the final analysis, there is negligible opposition to the bulldozing effects of dominant interests in the inner urban areas of Istanbul. Both in Sulukule and Tarlabaşı, Romani groups are the last to benefit from such developments (Gunay 2012). Rather than deliver adequate housing, health, education and wider social welfare opportunities for an otherwise ostracised community that frequently requires support, the prevailing concern is to eradicate and replace the homes of these groups with high-rent, high-value

Figure 3.1   Tarlabaşı – young children forced to play in polluted streets due to a lack of space for outdoor leisure activities. The air was thick with the stench of sewers. Photograph taken by the author, May 2014.

Figure 3.2   Tarlabaşı – dispossessed local residents have limited opportunities for social life in confined, obsolescent and dilapidated spaces.
Photograph taken by the author, May 2014.

property aimed at prosperous Turkish majority communities (Eren 2014). The presence of Romani groups in Istanbul is noticeable, but Turkish Istanbullus disregard them and they are almost undetected by outsiders visiting the city; Romani groups are the underclass of Istanbul. In this case, beautifying a city means disremembering its past and reinventing it in the image of an international cosmopolitan city that meets the desires of global capital in pursuit of optimum leisure and services (Tok and Oğuz 2013). A well-conceived methodology, suitably balanced around community interests and wants, needs articulation in practice. The ability to regenerate for the greater good of a particular city's profile and economic and cultural status, combined with the interests of economic investors, albeit with particular agendas, remains underdeveloped (Akkar Ercan 2010).

Glocal Turkey Past and Present

Over the last decade Turkey has successfully improved its position after the financial crisis of 2000 left the country in a dire situation. Turkey now has a much stronger geopolitical profile. The Muslim world views it as a successful model that bridges Islam, capitalism and democracy. Western Europe, after enduring the financial crisis of 2008, maintains robust economic ties with Turkey. The question of EU entry has lost momentum in recent years, combined with a rising level of hostility among leading EU countries and Turkey's general ambivalence at present compounded by the AKP's stronghold internally and externally in the region. Nevertheless, the questions of discrimination and intolerance are crucial in Turkey. Is it possible to establish a liberal democracy when a degree of intolerance remains unchecked? Can Turkey acknowledge that it evolved from a multireligious Ottoman Empire to a monocultural secular republic?

To some extent, not least since the 1923 Treaty of Lausanne, ethnic and religious minorities have always faced suppression and their identities denied in Turkey (Pettifer 1998). In the 1920s, through official ideology, Turkishness became synonymous with Muslimness. In the 1930s both ethnicity and race combined with religion and language as signs of Turkishness. Here, ethnicity-through-language defined 'race' rather than phenotypical or genotypical characteristics. Learning the Turkish language is the basis for recognition as a Turk. It was linguistic assimilation (or 're-acculturation') into a shared national identity, in spite of religious and even ethnic differences. Forcibly assimilated into Turkish society through maintenance of the Turkish language, some Kurdish groups resisted. It has led to ongoing battles for status and recognition among this minority group ever since (Çağaptay 2006; see Chapter 2). 'Whiteness' within Turkishness is also crucial to bear in mind, given the powerful racialist associations that white skin and light eyes have with purity and superiority. Over a 300-year period, the latter was central to the European colonial project. The term 'white Turk' (first used by the journalist Ufuk Güldemir in the 1992 book, *Teksas Malatay*) applies to urban groups with considerable social, cultural and human capital. These groups are predominantly concentrated in Istanbul. Over time this distinction tempered due to some recognition and acceptance of the 'Kurdish issue' in Turkish society (Somer 2005). Lingering effects on ethnic relations persist as a legacy of history immediately after the formation of the republic (Çağaptay 2004). The reality is that the treatment of minorities in Turkey is tangled up with legal citizenship and it further complicates the situation. This has had a negative affect on non-Muslim minorities in much more striking ways than on the Kurds and the Alevis, particularly from the fall of the Ottomans to the implementation of the 1923 Treaty of Lausanne (İçduygu and Soner 2006). The Alevis are perhaps Turkey's largest religious minority group, numbering approximately twenty million, with lower estimates placing them at between ten and twelve million, and spread across the entire country, including in concentrated urban centres. Over the centuries they have also suffered discrimination, vilification and prejudice. A recent 'Alevi Opening' orchestrated by the AKP in 2007 began a process of conferring Alevis their full rights and identity-based claims. Though granted a greater public profile and recognition (Köse 2011), the long-term outcome has yet to be determined.

It is accurate to state that Turks and Kurds do have intra-ethnic friendship relations, and a great deal of social and physical integration between these groups in society surfaces, but a sense of fear also exists among majority Turks regarding minority Kurds. In the analysis of the ESS data, the difference between those who reported that they belong to a minority group (about 7 per cent) and those who speak Kurdish (about 11 per cent) is noteworthy. It suggests that some Kurds do not see themselves as minorities. Moreover, according to a survey carried out by the influential Turkish organisation, Foundation for Political, Economic and Social Research (Aras et al. 2009), Turks fear too great a recognition of the Kurdish identity question in case it leads to a potential partition of Turkey. In reality, the Kurdish groups do not yearn for separation but decentralisation. They seek a resolution to the decades-long economic and social underinvestment in the south-east region, combined with equality of treatment and social outcomes, as well as recognition of language, culture and heritage in wider society. Because of uncertainties held by majority Turks, there is 'visible resistance, particularly among Turks. The issue of constitutional recognition of Kurdish identity, liberalization of policies on the Kurdish language and the introduction of a liberal constitution that will address the objections of the Kurds' is exposed (ibid. 12). Among Kurds, there is greater trust in international political institutions compared to domestic, and this difference is essential in understanding local and global interconnections among majorities and minorities in the Turkish context (Karako 2013).

Gazing Forward

In light of developments from the Arab Spring, the present moment is a genuine opportunity to resolve the long-standing 'Kurdish issue' that continues to afflict the country, driven by the EU-entry process (Kirişci 2011). The opportunity remains in spite of all the political machinations between and within the three main opposition parties, specifically the CHP, MHP and the BDP (now the HDP), since the recent talks that began in March 2013 and collapsed in 2015. After the 2011 election the number of Kurdish parliamentarians increased to thirty-six, a remarkable step at the time (Aydin-Düzgit 2012). In the June 2015 election, under the banner of the HDP, a distinctly pro-Kurdish party, with 13 per cent of the national vote, eighty candidates entered the parliament. In the November 2015 snap elections only fifty-nine HDP runners won seats, with just under 11 per cent of the national vote. Thus, with Turkey's political and legal recognition and acceptance of Iraqi Kurdistan, there is some hope for Turkey's beleaguered Kurdish population as Turkey maintains its EU relations and advances its foreign policy across the region (Alessandri 2010). On the other hand, while there is considerable attention on the EU question, it is more complex than bridging an East–West or Islamist–secularist divide. It also acts as a question of how a post-Kemalist state system with pro-Islamist undertones attempts to unify with a post-Cold War model of European integration (Turunç 2011). There is also the thorny matter of the rise of Islamic State and the role of Kurdish forces who fight against this pernicious force while retaining ideological links with the PKK. This situation unsettles the Turkish national political project.

Will developing a post-Kemalist, post-Islamist cultural and political framework help to cultivate the relations between Islam, secularism, capitalism and democracy in a rapidly changing Turkish society? Some of these questions are ongoing concerns for the future of Turkey (Saktanber 2007). But does the changing nature of society, where groups have been historically neglected or suppressed for the purposes of the nation state since the foundation of the Turkish Republic, make it entirely possible to discuss a diverse and interdependent society where cultural memory (and forgetting) in Turkey are urgent themes (Özyürek 2007)? With 99 per cent of Turkey nominally classified as Muslim, youth is another important factor, as eighteen to twenty-five year-olds constitute one-third of the population. According to the ESS findings reported in this chapter, young Turks are more tolerant than older Turks, but a range of ongoing developments have placed Turkish politics into sharp focus by repoliticising the youth. Turks that are more affluent and the more religious are politically to the right and are less tolerant of others. Some were behind the rise of the so-called 'Islamic bourgeois'. More educationally qualified Turks are more tolerant of others. Hence, the education system is another substantial dynamic affecting the question of ethnic relations in Turkey. Life in Istanbul encourages its residents to be more tolerant. This is arguably because of cosmopolitanism, but also because of higher education across the city, where a growing number of universities exist and where Istanbullus are wealthier than the rest of the country per se. Nevertheless, there are also a number of risks for Turkey as it continues its drive for economic, political, social and cultural influence. This is not least due to the role of religiosity in potentially shaping a conservative social and political identity, reinforcing chauvinism and exclusivity. Meanwhile, youth unemployment remains high, while only the construction industry has benefited from expansions to the manufacturing sector of the economy, with the availability of cheap credit that fuels a consumer boom sensitive to global finance.

Arguably, there is ethnic cleansing *and* ethnic gentrification in the historical *and* contemporary development of Turkey at the periphery *and* at the centre. At the turn of the twentieth century, as war raged on, over a million Armenians died at the behest of centralised policy-making aimed at preserving the nation from its enemies. Due to the technological developments of the time, that is, the telegraph and the railroad systems, extermination became both feasible and manageable. At the turn of the twenty-first century, Turkey has undergone a series of further changes in relation to modernisation and globalisation, some of which reveal further risks for already beleaguered ethnic and religious minorities. Neo-liberal economic policy was under way from the early 1980s, when the processes of gentrifying aspects of Istanbul's historical ethnic minority communities began. Since the 2000 financial crisis in Turkey a new wave of aggressive neo-liberalism has seen Istanbul radically altered in the face of the interest of domestic and foreign capital. The parallels between these two historical periods, one involving opening up to free market principles, the other a form of accelerated globalisation, are both understood as an aspect of nation-building. Projected to the world is the sense of a better Turkey with a stronger core and a greater whole. Modernisation, globalisation and centralisation are consistent themes in both periods. As such, ethnic cleansing or ethnic gentrification, projected in the interest of a progressive 'modern Turkey', has attuned to the evolving global neo-liberal climate. Although the historical periods differ in many ways, the idea of a nation pure of race and religion lingers on.

The Gezi Park disturbances of the summer of 2013 presented many questions about trust in politics, political engagement and doubts about a form of authoritarian nationalism under the AKP (see Chapters 5 and 6). The protests began as a localised resistance project with environmentalist undertones, but rapidly developed into a national outcry against AKP policies. This raised issues of political participation and representation, and the role of youth, who came together in spite of their ideological and cultural differences, pooling their efforts to voice shared concerns against the state. Dubbed the 'bridge of civilisations', the future of a successful Turkey rests not simply on economic stability and purposive foreign policy, but also upon greater cultural and social tolerance concerning others, within and without, including the vital 'Kurdish issue'. It remains the most critical domestic cultural and political topic for accepting and valuing differences in contemporary society. It is crucial to envisage the future of Turkey as a multireligious society based on citizenship rights, rather than competing claims to ethnicity (Keyman 2012), with a model of nationalism based on the politics of recognition (Ozkirimli 2014).

4

Perspectives on the 'Kurdish Issue'

I am proud of having my son with them. In front of all Kurdistan, I am so proud that I have a martyr . . . We knew that one day we would have his death.

Your [then] prime minister [Erdoğan] says, 'Everyone should have three children!' I tell you what; if it was possible, I would have 100 children . . . Turks will never be able to eradicate us.

Selim, father of deceased Welat

The Middle East divides the Kurds into four countries, namely Turkey, Iran, Iraq and Syria. Forty million Kurds live in these lands (Yildiz and Fryer 2004), with at least fifteen million in Turkey, the largest community of Kurds in the Middle East (Gunter 2008; Kuzu 2016). In Turkey the Kurds make up anything between 18 and 25 per cent of the population (Mutlu 1995), and the 'Kurdish issue' is of particular significance. Through the 1923 Treaty of Lausanne, ideas of Turkishness were restricted to ethnically homogenous groups with modern Turkish linguistic heritage. This occurred in the larger urban zones of the Anatolian region and in Istanbul. The imprint of Turkishness was loosely associated with a secular identity that recognised different religious minority groups, such as Armenian Christians, but it did not accept the Kurds as ethnically distinct (Loizides 2010). These are the significant conundrums of the so-called 'Kurdish issue' in Turkey.

By the late 1940s the authoritarian system that Atatürk had founded was weakening. The opening up of multiparty politics gave opportunities for Kurds to vie for recognition and status. The grip of Turkish ethnonationalism, however, was vigorous. The Turkish state suppressed all emerging separate identities within the nation. The state dislocated Kurdish groups to the industrialised areas in central Anatolia (Kirişci and Winrow 1997), and to the south-east. The majority of Kurds still live on the mountain plateaus of south-east Turkey. Privileged Turks used the derogatory term 'mountain Turks' to describe the Kurds. It reflected their geographical conundrum, but it was also racialist. The fact that they are concentrated in the remote territories of south-east Turkey has contributed to perceptions of Kurds as problematic groups. At the same time, their group and cultural identities have developed as separate and unique. A discernible linguistic heritage is part of the distinctive identity of Kurds. Ongoing problems of misrecognition continue to impact on these Kurdish groups in Turkey. Both Turkish and Kurdish nationalisms arose simultaneously, arguably, much later than among many of the European nations, and habitually in direct competition with each other (Donmez 2007). Historically there have been many peace process attempts, all with limited or no success. The recent 2013 peace-building efforts began after many months of bloody fighting and a hunger strike by thousands of Kurdish prisoners. Both sides honoured the ceasefire, and most of the PKK fighters withdrew from the affected mountains in south-east Turkey. In 2014 the Kurds in Turkey grew agitated by the lack of Turkish intervention to support the Syrian Kurdish town of Kobanî, located three miles beyond the Turkish border. Islamic State was poised to overrun it. This incident over Kobanî was the beginning of heightened tensions that led to the peace process in Turkey breaking down once again. The seemingly permanent impasse between the Turkish state and the Kurds of the south-east has perpetuated the so-called 'Kurdish issue' (Bacik and Coskun 2011; Gunes 2012).

In January 2013 ethnographic and qualitative interview fieldwork was carried out in the town of Yüksekova, located in the Hakkâri district of south-eastern Turkey, close to the Iranian border. Detailed interviews and observations involving six families with members actively involved in the PKK formed the methodology of this research. The aim was to explore the impact of the 'Kurdish issue' among Yüksekovan Kurds directly linked to the conflict. The fieldwork was carried out a few weeks before the assassination of the three Kurdish activists in Paris (they were former PKK guerrillas; Sakine Cansiz was a founding member of the PKK), and approximately three months before the peace process, which began in 2013 and ended in 2015. This study was an attempt to explain the nature of Kurdish resistance through an understanding of the perspectives and perceptions of families with members involved in the PKK. Why Kurdish groups maintain a negative view of the Turkish state and young Kurdish people continue to be affected by the forces of exclusion was questioned. While attention is paid to Kurdish groups in the smaller towns and cities, and on the questions of integration and coexistence, some of the worst cases of marginalisation can be found in Yüksekova. This potentially confirms the notion that socio-economic inequalities, including ongoing patterns of racism, vilification and discrimination, as well as Turkish state repression, continue to motivate (especially) younger people to join the PKK. This theoretical perspective, combined with an understanding of the processes and drivers, was explored in this study. Table 4.1 profiles the sample in the study.

Table 4.1 Profile of Yüksekova respondents

Family	Respondent	Family members in the PKK (age) [time in the PKK] (status)
1	Ayşe (mother, wife) Rohat (uncle) Harun (son)	Sedat: husband (37) [eight years in the PKK] (living) Rojda: daughter (15) [four years in the PKK] (living) Gewero: nephew (14) [sixteen years in the PKK] (deceased)
2	Zeliha (mother) İsmail (father) Zeynep (sister)	Aynur: daughter (13) [four years in the PKK] (living)
3	Selim (father) Sara (mother)	Welat: son (13) [four years in the PKK] (died in 2011) Saniye: daughter (18) [joined in 1997, came back after two years]
4	Rojhat (brother) Rojin (brother in-law)	Zana: brother (20) [joined in 1997] (died in 2009) Selahattin: brother (18) [joined in 2010] (died in 2011)
5	Songül (mother)	Ali: son [joined at the age of 16] (alive)
6	Fatma (mother)	Esra: daughter [joined at the age of 17] (alive)

The study used ethnographic and observational methodologies to provide a grounded theoretical perspective on resistance identity politics among the Kurds in the town of Yüksekova. Grounded theory is the process by which data gleaned, in this case from interview respondents, is used to generate a theoretical perspective, which then helps to determine a hypothetical–deductive perspective on the research findings. Using various methods of snowball sampling and a trusted 'fixer', access was provided to six families who had various members in the PKK in the mountainous regions of south-east Turkey. Two visits were made to Yüksekova to conduct the actual field-work, the first in June 2012 and the second in January 2013. Planning and access took many months of negotiation and discussion in order to ensure confidentiality and trust. The interviews were carried out in the local dialect of Kurdish and transcribed into English. The benefit of an international research collaboration ensured that a British sociologist was able to work closely with a native Kurdish sociologist to ensure the matching of various skill sets and opportunity fields.

The Emergence of the PKK

In the 1970s an organised revivalist Kurdish nationalist movement emerged in the wake of growing Turkish ethnic nationalism and ongoing repression of the Kurds. The Turkish state staunchly suppressed any appearance of ethnic revivalism or Kurdish nationalism. On 15 August 1984 the PKK launched its first guerrilla attack against the Turkish Armed Forces operating within the Kurdish region. The attacks were against Turkish police in the area of Şemdinli, which is twenty-five miles away from Yüksekova, celebrated by some as the 'awakening of a nation'. One man, Abdullah Öcalan, established the PKK in 1978. He was a student in Ankara during the coup in 1970. His intentions were to revitalise a lost identity, in particular concerning the language associated with the Kurds. The PKK began with Marxist–Leninist leanings. It sought to establish equality and the rights of the Kurds, including fighting bourgeoisie groups, even those of Kurdish origin. Before 1984 there were no reported clashes between the PKK and Turkish forces. The PKK focused on internal conflict among privileged Kurdish groups, especially tribal chiefs. It has never been a class movement per se, as a host of different Kurdish interests drive its philosophy in practice. Certain class interests do remain intact, all the same, especially dismantling the institutions of imperialism using military force (Özcan 2006).

Since the 1980s the Turkish government has committed a series of injustices against Kurds, partly aiming to discourage support for the PKK. The suppression has only served to further marginalise Kurdish groups and encourage additional dissent. Caught between two competing interests, Kurdish villagers in eastern Turkey feared reprisals not merely from the Turkish state but also from the PKK. As the conflict raged on, the socio-economic conditions of Kurdish groups in the most eastern regions of Anatolia became increasingly severe. Some on the political left, or the religiously inclined, supported the Turkish state, but many younger Kurds were encouraged by the militant activities of the PKK. The ongoing socio-economic deprivation and political oppression facing Kurdish communities in the south-east of Turkey has become a particular recruiting ground for the PKK, where young people, disaffected with life and lacking hope, are easy targets. There was talk of a two-state solution as early as 1991 when the PKK considered that a federalist resolution to the Kurdish issue in Turkey would be an acceptable way forward. In 1992 the then president Turgut Özal argued for the need to accept the role of the PKK in the political process, but he mysteriously died in office in 1993 (ibid).

In 1993 the PKK announced a ceasefire. Nonetheless, the Turkish regime of Süleyman Demirel paid scant attention to permanently resolving the 'Kurdish issue'. The government forcibly relocated numerous Kurds, and ongoing conflict between the PKK and the Turkish Armed Forces led to skirmishes during most of the 1990s. It was a particularly troublesome period for Kurdish groups, who faced all sorts of hostilities, characterised both locally and nationally. In 1998, while Öcalan and some of his elite cadre sought refuge in Syria, the Turkish government placed more than 100,000 troops on the Syrian border, demanding that Öcalan be handed over to them. After various attempts to flee to Moscow, Rome, Athens and finally Nairobi, Öcalan was eventually captured by the Turkish Special Forces and imprisoned on İmralı Island in 1999, where he has remained ever since. The EU and other international actors were able to stay his impending execution, the outcome of his trial for crimes against the state. He was seen as critical in the future of any peace process.

Since the imprisonment of Öcalan the PKK has been in disarray. There have been many clashes with the Turkish Armed Forces throughout this period, some quite severe. There are various reasons for the demise of the PKK. Michael Gunter (2000) argues that it extended its reach among political actors, which over time became difficult to manage. Alternatively, Vera Eccarius-Kelly (2012) contends that the PKK placed too much emphasis on violent conflict as the only solution. Meanwhile, the south-east region of Turkey remains underdeveloped, with limited attempts made to incorporate the region into a greater economic and political Turkey. This neglect has led to ongoing frustrations among younger Kurds who see no future. Their only hope comes from the prospect of flight through the limited education system, or the anticipation of eventually finding themselves in the more established towns and cities of Turkey. According to recent surveys, most Kurds do not want to establish a separate state from Turkey, although roughly one-third of Turks think Kurds seek partition. Before the recent escalation in violence nearly half of the population of Turkey agreed that the Turkish state should maintain negotiations with the PKK, with approximately three out of five believing that Öcalan absolutely dictates the organisation (Çaha 2013). Ofra Bengio (2011) upholds that Turkey needs to build regional stability, and, given the political developments across wider Kurdish territories throughout the Middle East, a peaceful solution could finally end the most significant issue to linger from the formation of the Turkish Republic in 1923.

An Analytical Perspective

The idea of Kurds as groups yet to reach a state of Turkishness has been a consistent theme running throughout historical paradigms in relation to the formation of the Turkish Republic and its constituent parts (Yeğen 2007). Because of ongoing socio-economic marginalisation, the Kurds in Turkey have become disenchanted, as well as suspicious of the Turkish state (Içduygu et al. 1999). Concerns emerge in the light of the status quo, which continues to galvanise Kurdish nationalism in response to marginalisation, exclusion and disenfranchisement (Sarigil 2010). In many instances, this process of alienation affects Kurdish women more (Yüksel 2006). Thus, the search for Kurdish identity is analogous to a reawakening of consciousness. Then again, this identity is constrained for Kurds because of the distinct geographical realities facing many communities across four countries (Barkey and Fuller 1998). The Ottomans pursued a policy of acculturation, while the republican period sought assimilation. Ironically, the Turkish state acted in the interests of the republic to prevent a process of de-acculturation, thought to propel the search for a distinctively separate Kurdish ethnic identity (Heper 2007). The primary reasons for the maintenance of the Kurdish ethnic identity are the elimination of modes of multireligiosity found in the former Ottoman Empire and the policy of de-acculturation by republican secular ideologues.

The processes of educational reform in the early phases of the republic created Kurdish elites who began a period of resistance that gained wide appeal (Yavuz 2001). Later the PKK successfully invoked an articulation of arts, culture and symbolism as a reference to the 'golden age' of the Kurdish 'nation without history' (Gunes 2013). The present reality is that the PKK have all but abrogated hopes of regional autonomy, and the understanding of a federated system is likely to be the outcome. Even so, the politicisation of this issue deeply affects Kurdish communities in the most remote areas of the south-east of Turkey. Furthermore, limited confidence in the EU integration process means that Kurdish groups in Turkey view the future with negativity. It would seem that the only way to obtain a solution is from within the existing borders of Turkey. The PKK is an icon for the ambitions of Kurds in Turkey and, in spite of the limitations faced by the Kurds, both the PKK and Öcalan remain powerful symbols (Marcus 2007). The rise in Kurdish nationalism has also resurfaced because of globalisation. Because of Turkish repression, resilience among Kurds has strengthened in the Kurdish diaspora and at home (van Bruinessen 1998). This Kurdish nationalism raises a crucial problem of regional stability, but it also rouses questions about Turkish national identity (Galletti 1999). As no single concept of a Kurdish ethnic identity captures the immense variation of diversity found across the four countries, Kurdish nationalism is in a state of evolution as much as Turkish national identity itself. Therefore, there appears to be room for a negotiated space in the interests of both ethnic majorities and minorities in Turkey (Reşat 1997).

The interviews in this research involved the discussion of highly sensitive and personal information, and in many cases respondents found it moving to talk about their young children involved in the PKK. In talking to mothers, fathers, brothers and sisters, many different issues were addressed. It permitted the study of the intersection of history, politics, conflict, ideology and the relations between minorities and majorities, as in other sociological studies of violence, which have become prominent in recent years (Walby 2013). Moreover, when discussing marginalised groups, the question that is frequently asked is 'Whose side are we on?' (Becker 1967). As with much of sociological thinking on disadvantaged groups, the motivations are to convey the story of oppressed minorities to understand better the workings of wider societies, not because one has taken a side per se. This study endeavoured to analyse the following: first, how the issue of forced migration helps to appreciate the existential realities facing these Kurds in the study; second, the nature of Turkish state repression of Kurds, facilitated by the police and the security services in alienating and radicalising groups; third, perceptions of families and how they are affected by children or siblings joining the PKK; finally, to understand how respondents view the ethno-national conflict at the heart of wide-ranging problems facing Kurds in the south-east corner of Turkey, and what might lie ahead. This analysis presents a perspective almost never heard outside of the areas studied. It narrates the stories of marginalised groups associated with armed conflict against a mighty foe, which has spent most of twenty-five years and billions of Turkish lira pursuing a conflict that resembles civil war in all but name, and which shows no signs of abating.

Forced Migration and its Impacts

Various political pressures displaced many Kurdish families from their homes. Families and communities had to leave behind their possessions, their livestock and their land, receiving no compensation from the Turkish state. Forced eastwards to towns such as Yüksekova and adjoining areas, they also moved to the western areas of Anatolia. Divulged and routinely repeated, stories of this forced migrated persecution circulated within the households of the respondents. These stories invariably affected how children understood their realities and the wider political paradigms encompassing them. Importantly, the narratives seemed to create deep politicisation among young people. Compounded by limited education or employment opportunities in Yüksekova, it is apparent that the stories may well have played a role in encouraging some young people to join the PKK. Also evident from the narratives was that the PKK and related groups organised many demonstrations and political rallies in the local area, and some young people participated. Many respondents talked about their migration experience. The comment below is from Rojhat, whose two brothers joined the PKK at a young age. He alluded to exile, which characterises the memory of the Kurdish migration experience, and which sustains the feeling of ongoing state repression. Rojhat said:

> We were exiled from our village. They [the state] burned down our village, and then we came here. It was 1989. The state gave us two options: 'either you will be a part of the Village Guard[1] system or you will be exiled.' We did not accept becoming village guards . . . The state [Turkish soldiers] gave us an ultimatum, which was ten days to get ready to leave the village and relocate. But we could not sell all our livestock and it was not possible to get ready within ten days. Then they came and burned down our houses. We brought our sheep and came here, to Yüksekova. At that time, we had nothing here: no house, no job, nothing. I tell you it was really hard, leaving a place, going somewhere else and becoming exiled.

Similarly, Ismail, a sixty-two-year-old retired butcher, shared his migration story. He also talked about how the Turkish military regime placed considerable pressure on him and his family to leave their homes. Ismail and his family were not given sufficient time to prepare their exit. His resentment towards the state was palpable. He said:

> We were living in our village at the time, a place called Zere, in the Oramar region. We migrated from the village to Yüksekova in 1995 because we were forced by the state . . . The military accused us of helping the PKK.

---

1. The Village Guard system was established by the Turkish state as a way in which to employ local Kurds to monitor and police their own communities. Villagers had specific ultimatums that required individuals to act as guards of their own villages, working alongside the Turkish military establishment. Paid salaries, they adhered to the demands of their employers, which often created another layer of tension within the communities (Criss 1995).

'You are giving bread to the PKK,' they said. 'Either you will evacuate your village or we will burn down your houses with you inside them.' Of course, if there is any killing, or burning our village, we had no choice but to go. We had young children and families that we had to take care of.

Zeliha, who had eight other children at the time, talked about the experience of being forced out of her village. Her story was remarkably similar to the others. She described how the Turkish military regime gave little or no notice to families. They had limited time to prepare leaving their places of birth. Families who had no choice but to leave had immense suspicion directed towards them. The experience left a particular stain on Zeliha and her family. They had to face the reality of starting over with nothing at their disposal, losing all their property, capital and livelihood in the process. She said:

> The fields were planted and the corn had matured. It was the time of harvest. All the gardens were ready for the following year. We left all the produce that we worked on in the fields . . . They did not let us prepare anything. We evacuated the village in one day. We went to another village, which was in Oramar too. We were desperate on the way there, with our kids, until my husband brought a car from Yüksekova . . . We sold every- thing for half the price. We could not sell any of the livestock. We really had no choice at that time. Some of us became porters or runners. What can I say? It was a nightmare for us . . . We did not get any help or support from the state at that time, not even one lira.

Ayşe also explained her situation. She recalled a conversation with her hus- band, 'I heard from my husband that the state burned his village and then left them there in 1993. We had not married yet. I came here [Yüksekova] from another village'. All the six families in this study reported that they were forced to move by the state, mainly during the early to mid-1990s. Stories of being compelled from their places of birth were told and retold among the families, directing the narrative of Turkish state oppression. Young people in the families listening to these stories were affected, not merely by the experi- ence, but also by the memories associated with it. Forced migration was a topic much mythologised and lionised by families, and among the wider community of Yüksekova Kurds in which they eventually found themselves.

Turkish State Repression

Forced to their new homes, the Turkish state maintained a particular degree of authority over the Kurds. In many cases, it turned into repression mediated through institutionalised policing and security activities. There were many accounts of raids on homes and of various methods of police brutality. These became routine practices in some instances. Individuals targeted on a systematic basis believed they had no option but to join the PKK to escape these localised experiences of state terrorism. Selim explained how the security services had captured and tortured his son, Welat. He said:

> Let me tell you. I am a member of the party [PKK]. I am active in its politics as well. I have been tortured many times because of this issue. But I did not want him [his son] to go there [to the PKK]. He was my heart. My son saw the tortured scars on my body with his own eyes. During 1997 the police forces were holding me captive and torturing me a great deal. For instance, once they seized me, and we went to the Terror Point of the city. There was a person, Huseyin Commander; he tortured me for thirteen days. All my family knew that. I was involved with the party politics of the PKK, and that is why the police forces captured me many times.

During a lengthy monologue about his brother, Rojhat talked about the reasons why Selahattin went to the mountains. Affected by Turkish state repression in many different ways, it was also apparent how one family member changed the history of others. This particular narration offers an interpretation of events. Selahattin seemingly had no choice but to join the PKK as a way to escape his localised experiences. Facing the possibility of arrest and torture at the hands of security services, Selahattin took the only option he felt he had left. Rojhat recalled the events:

> My nephew, Şehit Gever, his friends, Şehit Zerdest and Şehit Heyder, came to Yüksekova. They came and stayed for a year . . . there was a ceasefire at that time. The police forces made a complaint about Şehit Zerdest and Şehit Heyder. The wealthy people of Yüksekova, from the Doski tribe, gave information to police forces and now both are dead because of them . . . There were twenty-eight people at the funeral procession of Şehit Zerdest. The police got all the names of those attending that funeral procession.

Selahattin [Rojhat's brother] was at that funeral too. I can say that after that funeral the police forces got their hooks into him . . . [Later] the police forces swooped on our house. Special experts came all the way from Hakkâri and Ankara. If they had caught him [Selahattin] that morning, they would have executed him. They brought some computers to the house. They were looking for ammunitions hidden underground, including bombs and C4. They could not find anything . . . Of course, after that event, my brother, Selahattin, came back to us. He said to us, 'Either the state will execute me, or they will want me to be a betrayer, or they will torture me. Soon, they will kill me or let me live only under their control.' He thought there was no other option for him. He asked us, 'What should I do? The only way is to go to the mountains.' We said, if you wish, then go. He then went to the mountains.

Zeliha, mother of Aynur, talked about her perceptions of the Turkish state. Aynur, who had disappeared to the mountains as a young teenager, knew of all the stories told in the home. Not only was there a migration history, but there was also ongoing persecution by the Turkish security services that had directly affected Zeliha's brother, Seyfettin. She explained:

She [Aynur] knew all the stories. We were talking about those days, not only with her but also with all our children. We were telling them that the state made this and that oppression against us. For instance, at that time Turkish soldiers came to our village and took four people with them to stand guard. My big brother was taken with them. Sometimes he was with those soldiers standing guard for a week. In those days, someone hung a photograph of Abdullah Öcalan on the Aslan Hotel's wall. Someone from Yüksekova came to the village and told us 'someone did that in Yüksekova, and that's why nobody dared come to the city centre.' My brother was with those soldiers at that time. Now, listen to what I am about to tell you. The police forces arrested someone and tortured him. He was afraid and they took advantage of him. This person told those police officers that he had hung the photograph of Abdullah Öcalan, with Seyfettin, my big brother. Seyfettin was there with soldiers standing guard. They found my brother and gave him electric shocks for twenty-five days. After twenty-five days he came back to the village. When he came back you could not say that he was the same person. He had totally changed in twenty-five days. He lost his balance. When he lost his balance we could not do anything, so we took him to Elazığ [for hospital treatment] for three months but it did not help. I took him to Van, Erzurum. Nothing changed.

Further exploring some of the experiential dynamics affecting young people, Selim, father of Welat and Saniye, talked about his son, Welat. Welat felt that the security services would eventually create problems for him, irrespective of whether he was directly or indirectly associated with any criminal activities. Welat feared for his future, but felt greater security, extraordinarily, in going to the mountains and joining the PKK. Selim said:

> The head of his school hit him once, and then he [Welat] went to the Party [PKK] and told them that he had been hit because of his politics at the school. He was always so aware of his rights. He was asking for Kurdish language in the school. He was saying that, 'We don't want Turkish rules here. They catch us, kill us and torture us. We don't accept this in our country.' He told us, 'I will go [and join the PKK], as there is no other way!'

These narratives show how various patterns of subjugation by the local police forces and security services as representatives of the Turkish state had alienated a body of people already feeling the pressures of isolation and disenfranchisement. Family members tortured by the Turkish security services combined with episodes of persecution and repression. It negatively affected the Kurds in Yüksekova. It encouraged some to enthusiastically join the PKK, or join simply because they lacked any alternatives.

To the Mountains

It is vital to explain all the background factors motivating individuals to join the PKK, including how the process worked in practice. The experiences of surveillance, securitisation and police brutality ostensibly created the conditions for some to join the PKK. For others, hopelessness led to romanticism or heroism as superficial ways out of local problems. For others still a distinctly political ideology developed. There were many different reasons given for why young people went to the mountains. Zeliha, mother of Aynur, emphasised that her daughter was merely a young teenager when she decided to go to the mountains. Aynur had romanticised her life in the PKK to such an extent that she had taken a bag containing make-up and jewellery, which was later returned by a visitor who knew the family. Zeliha said:

> When he [Ersin, a cousin] went to the mountains to join the PKK, he gave a picture of himself to my daughter. She was young and he was on her mind. One day we saw him on the Kurdish TV channel, that he was guarding Murat Karayılan [after Abdullah Öcalan, head of the PKK]. It was kind of a live broadcast. We all screamed, 'Here is Ersin, on the television.' We all saw him there. At that time, my daughter's mind turned and she started to think about him . . . When she was thinking to go to the mountains she told her sister. She went later that year. Do you know how she went there? She had that big accessory bag with her. She took so many accessories with her to the mountains . . . She thought she would wear those accessories there, even put on make-up. She thought that she would have fun there. She had no idea about life there. She was so young. When she took that bag with her to the mountains, one of her cousins visited her. She said to us, 'I was so sorry for her when I saw that bag with her there. My heart was really broken for Aynur.'

Some young people romanticised the conflict. For others it was about adventure and pride associated with a legitimate cause. Some mothers felt a degree of comfort in their daughters being in a place that did not necessarily put them in danger. There was an explicit acceptance on the part of Ayşe that her daughter had indeed joined the PKK. Ayşe rationalised that her daughter was in a better place among the PKK rather than at home. She explained:

> I do not want my daughter to come back here. It is better for her to be there. When I compare her here with me and her in the PKK I can say that she is better in the PKK. She has more knowledge [there] than here. In all cases, she is better off there than here.

Harun, whose father and sister had joined the PKK, stated that he did not have any educational ambitions, 'No, I don't have any. I will not study anymore. I don't want to study anymore.' Would Harun join the PKK? He replied, 'If my father allows me I will join the PKK as well.' As the only son in the household, his mother placed considerable restrictions on Harun's movements, including limiting his visits to the mountains. The idea that neither the PKK nor existing family members compelled children to join their siblings or parents was also prevalent among other mothers. Ayşe regularly visited her husband and her daughter, seeing them on a frequent basis, but she was keen to emphasise that the PKK were not actively encouraging her or her other children to join. Rather, in the extract below, Ayşe emphasised that her daughter was discouraged from joining, and encouraged to concentrate on her education. She said:

> We were once visiting my husband there, with my son and daughter. The guerrillas told my daughter, 'Do not come here to join us, you should study.' My daughter was coming to the mountains with us of course. We all went to visit my husband there.

The PKK respected women and their status was equal to that of men, continued Ayşe. The shackles of materialism or individualism did not bind women in the PKK, nor did the forces of patriarchy inhibit them, she argued. Ayşe added, 'The *hewals* [guerrillas] give respect to me and also to anyone else there, especially women. They have more value for women than men. There is no value for us in the cities, but in the PKK we are valued by them'. Harun, Ayşe's teenage son, added that the PKK provided empowerment and emancipation, rather than curtailment of freedoms or values of various kinds. It appears that not only were there push factors creating the conditions that encouraged young people to join the PKK, but the PKK was also perceived as liberation from everyday discontent. Harun said:

> They act so differently. They open your heart and mind. They are taking your soul out. It is not like here, in the cities. Here, you are just ordered to do something. But there is freedom for anyone there. You become a free person. I feel like my father is freer than here. [It is the] same for my sister too.

Entry into the PKK was a venerable move for some, which did not necessarily lead to engagement with unquestionable violence among young people. The PKK commanded respect and status among many Kurds and for families with their closest members actively involved in the campaign. For them, joining the PKK was not terrorism per se, but as a way to engage with a community of those faithful to a meaningful political and cultural cause regarded as urgent in the milieu of dislocation and disempowerment.

Facing Conflict

In speaking with families about the essence of the conflict, and what helped them to appreciate its nuances they regularly mentioned the media and the physical manifestations of political protests that occurred on a regular basis. The nature of these rallies, combined with the oppressive responses of the state, not only created tension and alarm but also galvanised further support for the PKK. Demonstrations were also vital for 'spotting' people, young or older, who were vulnerable or otherwise at the margins of society and therefore perhaps amenable to joining the PKK. Zeliha, mother of Aynur, said:

> We spoke about politics at home more than perhaps we should have, even though at times we did not speak about it at all. Our home, at one time, was in the centre of town. Whenever there was a clash, or gunfire, we witnessed all of these things in front of our home. There was always something going on in front of our home. There was always a panzer [armoured plated police vehicle] parked there. Police forces beat up kids and people, and so on. She [Aynur] saw all these things. I was attending demonstrations or funeral processions, but she never did that . . . She was only interested in her studies. It was summer time. . . In that summer, some people talked to her. We think that someone talked to her.

Participants in the study elaborated on the use of Kurdish media within the home. This included television, satellite, DVDs and the Internet (Çeliker 2009). Selim said their family had Kurdish broadcast TV on at home all the time. He also talked about the issue of demonstrations and political protest as another pattern affecting the views of many young people in Yüksekova. Selim added further detail about his son's activities in the town. He said:

> For sure! From the first day that Kurdish broadcast was established I had it on all the time at home. It is always on in my house and it will remain so . . . Absolutely, he [Welat] was at all of the demonstrations. We could never keep him at home. He felt he had to be there.

Selim explained that Welat's involvement was not restricted to attending demonstrations. It appeared that Welat was also involved in other activities. Selim stated:

Yes, he was reading some documents about the PKK. And he was singing the national song of the PKK. He was always going to the Party. In the last two years, he was coming from school and then he was going to join his friends in the Party. He was covering his face, and with his friends, he would then throw stones at police vehicles. Once he came and told me, and sorry for saying this, 'We fucked the Turkish police car. We turned it over.' But his face was 'burned' [was recognised by the Turkish police forces] because of the demonstrations. He was always at the heart of the demonstrations, especially in the summertime, and after the closing of the schools. He was going to the village and then going to the mountains. He was always talking with guerrillas. I hit him two or three times because he was hanging around with guerrillas. He did not listen to me, and went to the mountains and talked to them whenever he found a chance.

Families were hopeful this conflict would end one day, despite the historical political discord between the various political actors in the Turkish and Kurdish political context (Satana 2012). A solution seemed a distant concept, with conflict as the normal state of reality. The position of the Kurds in south-east Turkey was seen as difficult, without any real sense of hope in the near future. For parents who had endured the impact of the conflict, their pain and suffering was amplified when their own children felt that they faced increasingly limited horizons, and that joining the conflict was the only way forward. Ayşe talked about her daughter Rojda. She said:

I am praying to Great Allah all the time . . . My daughters and I sat in the kitchen and cried every night after she went. For seven days we could not go to the room where she slept. We were sitting on carpets in the kitchen, crying and crying until morning. My eyes were always checking the door. I was telling myself that she would come back. Anyway, she is gone. God willing, and with the help of Allah, she will be fine . . . To be honest, it is hurting a lot, it is so painful. I haven't seen any pain like this. If you have a child on the mountain, I am not only saying this for myself but for all mothers, this is just such an unthinkable thing. I have lost three children before, when they were [still]born, but I cannot compare those losses with the loss of Rojda! It is hurting. People can be sick, become blind, or any other bad thing. But this is something else, believe me, this is something else.

Though parents believed that their children joining the PKK would not engage in actual combat, profound concern about their welfare was indeed apparent. The emotional cost of losing their child weighed heavily on the minds of incessantly worried parents. In such cases, a post hoc rationalisation may have given them additional pride that their children were prepared to sacrifice their lives for a greater cause. But this was also conflated by a lack of choice in the matter, largely because of local conditions and the ongoing political persecution and vilification they faced at the hands of the Turkish state. Selim explained:

> I said to my son, 'My son, maybe you will regret the step that you are taking when you go to the mountains' . . . I can tell you that no one wants their children joining the PKK. This is suicide. It is obvious. But, we have to accept that, we are under the control of [the Turkish government]. We are not free, but we want to be free. Even now, if I get an order [from Abdullah Öcalan], I will kill myself.

In the eyes of some, Abdullah Öcalan is the key to resolving the ongoing conflict. The international community, in particular the EU, sees Öcalan as important in any process involving negotiations with the PKK. The stay of his execution, originally ordered by the Turkish courts after his capture in 1999, demonstrated this. But any efforts made by the Turkish state towards peace met with ambivalence and mistrust among local Kurdish communities. The comment by Selim below suitably captures the essence of the sentiment held by participants. He said:

> There is no other way. There should be a process because even our infants wake up with the name of Abdullah Öcalan in their eyes. Absolutely, we will win this war. Either we will be killed or we will take our rights from them. We will all burn or kill ourselves. We have to. We do not want any land of the Turks, we don't want their idol [referring to Atatürk], we don't want their rules and regulations, and we want our rights. We want our land. This is our land. This Kurdistan is ours. We want to stay in our land, and have no other government rules and oppression. This process cannot be contemplated without him [Öcalan]. There is no way it is happening without him. Without him, there will be no resolution. Whatever he says it will be [the outcome].

Loyalty to Öcalan was consistent among those active in local community politics, including some who had to live with the terror resulting from the misrecognition of their ethnic, cultural and linguistic heritage. Much of this was a male domain, with heroism a noticeable pattern. For women, and in trying to understand their perspectives in a traditionally patriarchal society, a feeling of deep loss permeated the conversations. Young women joining the PKK did so out of some romantic impulse, rather than one borne out of ideology or politics. Venerated were the young women who had joined the PKK in the mountains. Ultimately, parents rationalised their sons and their daughters going to the mountains and joining the PKK as a just cause. Some parents were proud that their children had died fighting, which only further hardened their political resolve. Beyond romanticism or heroism, they believed in the greater good of the political project. Ultimately, respondents considered a range of issues in formulating the narratives in relation to the processes of joining the PKK, and the importance of political memory and social context in understanding the wider experience. The significance of forced migration and the ongoing role of the Turkish state in patterns of repression of Kurdish groups influenced how individuals joined the PKK, the family members in their visitations, and in ultimately how Kurds comprehended the conflict and its ramifications. Most of the respondents consistently presented views on repression, marginalisation and alienation. It has a devastating impact on families when young people join the PKK. Placed on a pedestal and idolised as heroes or martyrs in a wider political and ideological struggle for recognition it becomes a cyclical process for the young caught up in the fight. Writing in early 2016, the political outcomes presently appear bleak for the 'Kurdish issue'. In the meantime, the conditions of families worsen in instances of growing isolation and disenfranchisement.

Kurds associated with the PKK and the conflict, rather than their socio-economic conditions, the challenges faced in attaining social mobility, or recognition as a whole, is the general focus of attention in this analysis. Foremost when thinking of a post-resolution situation in south-east Turkey, concerns exist over the well-being of communities in otherwise banished areas of the country. This is especially among Kurdish women, often more excluded and ostracised than Kurdish men. Undoubtedly, Kurdish civilians have borne most of the consequences of the conflict (Smith 2005). Some of the stories and the narratives outlined above have demonstrated exactly how this has happened.

Competing Ethnic Nationalisms

The widening use of communication technologies and the importance of globalisation create the conditions for heightening Kurdish ethnic nationalism in the Turkish context. Moreover, due to the recent establishment of Iraqi Kurdistan as an autonomous region, and the role of the Syrian Kurds in fighting Islamic State, these precedents may focus the minds of Kurds in Turkey in relation to their own separatist nationalist ethno-cultural movement. Overall, existing literature on the Kurdish issue generates inconsistent assertions about the forces of ethnic mobilisation, drawing on social movement theories (Romano 2006), nationalism literature (Loizides 2010) or the formations of social capital (Ayfle 2005). This research on families with members in the PKK has demonstrated that specific local area grievances combined with historical patterns of persecution and contemporary policing, intelligence and surveillance draw attention to the behaviour of the Turkish state in fanning the flames of Kurdish opposition. Simultaneously, the radicalisation of Kurds in the south-east of Turkey is a result of both grievances and opportunities driven by the political and military arms of the PKK. An interdependent multifaceted cyclical dynamic continues to polarise groups in the search for a peaceful solution to competing ethnic nationalisms.

Since the end of the Cold War contemporary nationalisms have produced the conditions for conflict because they have placed ethnicity as the dominant paradigm in the creation of national identity. Such conditions are important for understanding the 'Kurdish issue' within the Turkish context, although race-based class conflict analysis also applies in this case. Faruk Ekmekci (2011) argues that this particular configuration of nationalism is ideological rather than a question of socio-economic inequalities, while Murat Ergin (2014) contends that racialisation of the ethnic category has created the specific problem. This racialisation is an outcome of Turkish national political dogma that resists Kurdish claims of ethnicity. Today some Kurdish elites no longer consider ethnicity as an obstacle to realising a peaceful solution to the existing conflict (Gurses 2010). Perhaps an alternative to boundary changes or policies of assimilation to resolve ethnic conflict between groups within states (Aktürk 2011) could rest on identity assertions based on an inclusive and cohesive mode of national citizenship (Keyman 2012). The essential question is whether Turkey is ready to move on from its past (Bakiner 2013), where the popular vernacular is to equate Kurdish identity politics with 'terrorism' (Barrinha 2011). Still, the suggestion that marginalisation and disadvantage explain all the reasons for joining the PKK is overly simplistic, as these issues affect practically all Kurds in Yüksekova. Although Kurds are Muslims, and they are engaged in armed conflict with fellow Muslim Turkish majority groups, there was no mention of religion as an identifiable motivator. This wider situation is a specific function of the Turkish republican context, where secular authoritarian nationalism subsumes religion. In other studies on the motivations of those joining deviant groups, such as the Revolutionary Armed Forces of Colombia (FARC), religion is not as vital a factor (Florez-Morris 2007), although Islamic symbolism and the idea of becoming a *şehit* (martyr) was evoked in the Yüksekova study.

There is extensive discussion over whether a leftist–Kurdish struggle is directly in competition with an Islamist–rightist single party rule over a national conservative political project in Turkey. In reality there is an urban elite–rural poor division, where the periphery has moved to the centre in relation to political power (Demiralp 2012). On the question of a permanent solution to the conflict, the main reason for general improvement in the political climate was that the Turkish state regarded the threat of violence as a deterrent (Aydinli and Özcan 2011). This was the case until the recent events following the emergence of Islamic State. Since the conflict between the Turkish state and the PKK has now erupted again, an even greater range of multifaceted programmes of action are required to ensure an effective long-term solution, including economic development and the importance of outside political intervention to ensure domestic success (Uslu 2007). In specific major urban areas, including in parts of Istanbul and other large cities such as Izmir, Kurds are an observable minority community. There needs to be a move away from considering such groups as the 'permanent Turkish other'. Instead there is a requirement to mobilise a greater appreciation of attempts at integration and coexistence by all. The urban spaces of towns and cities to the west of Anatolia are vital sites for the discussion of what it means to be Kurdish in Turkey today (Saraçoğlu 2009). There are ongoing transformations in both Kurdish and Turkish ethnic nationalism. Therefore, convergence and divergence needs greater understanding within these wider frames of reference.

The issue of spatiality and geography is imperative in Yüksekova, which is potentially an important recruitment region for the PKK. Yüksekova is a tremendously political space, well known for its struggles and demonstrations. From his prison cell on Imralı Island Öcalan has sent his greetings to the people of Yüksekova on a number of occasions. Approximately three–four million Kurds were forcibly migrated from their villages over the period of Turkey's repression of the group. Many ended up in Yüksekova. Moreover, the motivations of young people joining the PKK needs detailed scrutiny. In the case of young women, there may be questions of romanticism and for young boys, heroism. Finally, a serious concern is the understanding of cross-cultural comparative perspectives on indigenous resistance within nation states with historically wider cultural, ethnic and racialised borders. Specific cases include Palestine, Latin America and Mali, where anxieties exist around the formation of internal capital in order to achieve domestic representation. Groups want fundamental rights and the recognition of culture and heritage, including language and education. This is a common concern among many resistance organisations across the world.

The Kurds of Yüksekova do not exist in isolation, as the ethnic category of 'Kurd' has wide-reaching resonance across a huge geography and at an international level. As such it is important to consider the development of Iraqi Kurdistan and the Kurdish awakening in Syria and their impact on Kurdish nationalism in Turkey, along with Turkey's responses to it. A wider Kurdish milieu ensues in the countries where there are sizeable Kurdish populations, that is Iraq, Syria and Iran. All have Kurdish nationalist movements of various sorts. Yezidi Kurds in Armenia, numbering no more than 150,000, are also of interest in understanding localised Kurdish resistance. Thus, though there may be some 'imagined community' of a nation of Kurds in parts of Turkey today, 'a nation without history', undeniably a wider factionalism affects all groups in all locations. It is also essential to consider how the position of the Kurdish diaspora might motivate processes locally (Eccarius-Kelly 2002; Ayata 2011). The Kurdish diaspora has helped attract increased global

Figure 4.1   Yüksekova – parents pose proudly in front of a large photograph of their 'martyred' son, killed by the effects of sarin gas used by Turkish Armed Forces. Photograph taken by the author, January 2012.

Figure 4.2   Yüksekova – family members in the PKK eulogised and memorialised. Photograph taken by the author, January 2013.

awareness of the conflict, and with the ongoing developments to Turkey's foreign policy, this new landscape has provided the PKK with opportunity (Sezgin 2013), and exposure. Enormous toil is required in order to build trust in the domestic political process (Karakoç 2013), ensuring the outcomes are sustainable and equitable, with a focus on the politics of toleration rather than those of competing ethnic identities (Ozkirimli 2013; 2014).

5

The Gezi Park Awakening

During the long hot summer of 2013 the eyes of the world were set on Istanbul as dramatic protests unfolded in Gezi Park, in the city's central Taksim Square. Numerous articles, commentaries and op-eds in the international media suggested that the Gezi Park protests were a 'Turkish uprising'. They likened the events to various 'Occupy' resistance movements that had already engulfed most of the Middle East, along with the cosmopolitan capitals of Western Europe and the US in 2010 and 2011 (May 2013; Rodrik 2013; Örs 2014). Many explanations were put forward, emphasising 'combination[s] of structural and conjectural [openings] . . . which may or may not be the beginning of a larger protest cycle in Turkey' (Gürcan and Peker 2014: 86). While the anthropological, sociological and political context of the episode was important, the Gezi Park events also suggested a significant breakdown in social and political trust in Turkey. Never before in the recent history of Turkish politics have the far left, the conservative right, Kurds, the LGBT community and headscarf-wearing Muslim women united in a show of solidarity around a single cause.

The Gezi Park movement began with localised resistance against government plans to raze a historical public park in central Istanbul. The movement quickly escalated into a national outcry that manifested in wider criticism of AKP policy. How did various protestors in Gezi Park comprehend and respond to the concerns raised by the movement? How did a local event trigger such a degree of national political activism among a host of different community participants in Turkey, and among those otherwise habitually, ideologically and culturally opposed to each other? Qualitative research carried out in Gezi Park during the protests found that various patterns of political disenfranchisement developed alongside the wants and needs expressed by disenfranchised Turks. Caught between conservatism and secularism, and between nationalism and majoritarianism, a host of groups came together in an unprecedented moment. A range of responses given by protesters in the park generated a holistic perspective on the Gezi Park movement, uncovering its overarching themes. These highlighted how historical ethno-political and ethno-cultural distinctions unfolded during the protests to produce both interactive and transformative urban social and political opportunities.

The Gezi Park movement sparked considerable discussion about matters of citizenship, political participation and Islam in Turkish society. Moreover, this political episode was a fundamental incident during the rule of the AKP. Rather than reflecting a decisive turning point in national politics, the Gezi Park events revealed the dwindling profile of the secular–Kemalist opposition and the prodigious command of the AKP. In December 2013 various allegations of corruption were directed squarely at the then prime minister Recep Tayyip Erdoğan emerged, along with his family and other members of the AKP cabinet. The accusations, which purportedly came from Hizmet, exposed a deep fissure between the two principal conservative Islamic forces in Turkish society. The Gezi Park movement could well have hastened the realisation of an effective Turkish civil society, one benefiting from local and global aspirations, which in the end suggests a determined and democratic polity in Turkey. Ultimately, the events merely played a temporary role in weakening the political base of the AKP. They severely affected the June 2015 elections outcome, which resulted in a hung parliament. Snap elections held in November 2015 returned the AKP to majority representation and the ability to form a government on their own. The solidarity once realised between different political groups in Turkey during the Gezi Park events now appears as a distant and forgotten past.

This research is based on first-hand interviews carried out in Gezi Park on 15 June 2013, the day when Turkish police evicted protesters camped inside the park. Perspectives on social and political issues affecting the groups of protestors were diverse and disparate. Questions asked in English and translated simultaneously into Turkish or Kurdish, with responses translated back into English, and then coded and analysed in English, revealed detailed insights. Table 5.1 highlights the characteristics of respondents and their pseudonyms. These respondents reflect a theoretical sample of the many different types of protesters camped in the park, some affiliated with various political organisations, others there purely out of curiosity. A grounded theory approach was adopted to help conceptualise and theorise various observational, qualitative and life history data.

The analysis to emerge from the data, as expressed by respondents replying to open-ended questions about their motivations and aspirations in relation to the Gezi Park movement, uncovered thought-provoking perspectives. This issue was very much on the national and international agenda at the time, and those taking part in generating the momentum, camping at the park or making repeated visits to it, reflected on their concerns and wants. While there were only fourteen respondents interviewed in depth on the day, there were a host of observations incorporated into the contextualisation, analysis and discussion. These sampled individuals fittingly echoed the diversity of opinion, as well as the ethnicity, social class, age profile, ideology and political background of the protesters in the park in general. They all helped in probing the dynamics of the Gezi Park movement and the consequences it raised for politics, social cohesion and ethnic relations in Turkey. First, based on an analysis of the political and sociological context there is a chronological

Table 5.1 Profile of Gezi Park respondents

Pseudonym	Age	Profession	Place of residence	Gender	Ethnicity
Ali	52	medical doctor	Istanbul	male	Circassian
Azad	25	unemployed graduate	Istanbul	male	Kurdish
Welat	26	student	Istanbul	male	Kurdish
Merve	22	nurse	Istanbul	female	Turkish
Nagihan	32	school teacher	Istanbul	female	Turkish
Seda	25	student	Istanbul	female	Turkish
Okan	27	banker	Istanbul	male	Turkish
Sabiha	58	retired	Sydney, Australia	female	Turkish
Samet	30	shipmaster	Istanbul	male	Turkish
Emre	25	customs officer	Istanbul	male	Turkish
Can	26	student	Istanbul	male	Turkish
Jale	53	retired	Bursa	female	Turkish
Sinan	57	retired	Bursa	male	Turkish
Ali	35	press adviser	Istanbul	male	Kurdish

overview of the Gezi Park events. Second, the data analysis is divided into four distinct analytical spheres: anti-authoritarianism – that is, how different political interest groups coalesced to oppose the then prime minister; the lack of confidence in the opposition; issues of social conflict; and how the so-called 'Kurdish issue' was subsumed into the wider movement. The events highlighted a decisive moment in recent Turkish history. Below the surface, however, there were wide chasms between the people of Turkey and the reformist but authoritarian AKP government, which is, at the same time, pro-Islamic, laissez-faire, conservative and globalist (Moudouros 2014).

Voices from the Margins

The Gezi Park movement began as a peaceful environmentalist campaign to protect a public park that dated back to the 1940s. Protestors hoped to prevent the park from its planned erasure and replacement with a brand-new leisure complex catering for the richer classes and their consumer lifestyle choices. In recent periods an economic (and political) paradigm has transformed a historic city into a global megacity, with vast tracts of open space now used for the purposes of real-estate development (Aksoy 2012). Gezi Park is one of the last remaining green spaces in central Istanbul. The threat to the park inspired a number of activists who wanted to preserve the trees and the space from imminent levelling. Space became central to discussions of political protest (Karasulu 2014), and notions of political and social conflict because of the search for place (Lelandais 2014). The AKP has upheld certain neo-liberal economic and social policies, invariably gentrification and corporatism (Çavuşoğlu and Strutz 2014), including the reinvention of an Islamic traditionalism that has narrowly defined space and place (Gül et al. 2014). It was these concerns that mobilised protestors and then the rest of the country when the policing eventually turned violent and ugly.

From all accounts, the first four-day sit-in at the park was peaceful. In spite of this, on the morning of Friday 31 May, the police conducted a forceful dawn raid to evict protesters. Activists, environmentalists and people living and working in the local area, and those who had peacefully occupied the park over the preceding days, found the police moving in aggressively. Police used pepper spray, tear gas and a considerable measure of heavy-handedness to remove protestors. The response encouraged others to get involved in various organised and unorganised actions to resist the police. Over the following weeks the scenes turned nastier as forceful protesters replaced peaceful activists. Some engaged police in face-to-face combat, destroying public and private property in the process. What began as a local area environmentalist project amid a backdrop of general concerns around neo-liberalism and urbanisation became a national outcry against the policies of the AKP, and police brutality as representatives of the state. As local events developed into a national uproar, the state clamped down on the Gezi Park protesters with maximum power. On 15 June police dispelled campaigners camped in the park with an enormous show of force. From leftists to rightists, Islamists to secularists, young urbane sophisticates to older 'mothers of the protesters', all encountered the full wrath of state authority. Other related mass protests occurred: the 'earth tables' during the month of Ramadan 2013, where fasting and non-fasting Turks sat together at sunset to break the fast in public spaces, and the case of Erdem Gündüz, the 'Standing Man', were all illustrations of ongoing anti-government protests that characterised the summer of 2013 in Istanbul and across Turkey. Aspects of Turkey's LGBT community also co-organised against the policies of the AKP. Others resorted to painting rainbow colours on prominent flights of steps in the centre of Istanbul and in other parts of Turkey. For some observers a radical national movement was under way that had gained an extensive momentum (Sözalan 2013).

The majoritarian conservatism of the AKP has reconfigured the memory of the Turkish nationalist project through the projection of a future that is neo-Ottoman, neo-Kemalist (neo-nationalist) and pro-Islamic, although, primarily, through the lens of a past once considered glorious. In light of the Gezi Park demonstrations, challenges emerged in recovering from the muscular authoritarian secularism of Turkey's Kemalist past (Bakiner 2013). For many in the secular establishment, the demonstrations possessed a spirit that channelled local, national and international forms of resistance against an apparent authoritarian regime, with Recep Tayyip Erdoğan, who has since become accustomed to even greater power, at the helm. Erdoğan was seen as micromanaging every aspect of people's lives. He made pronouncements on the number of children that families should conceive to their practices as observant Muslims, from regulating private alcohol consumption patterns to discouraging Caesarean sections and abortions. In addition to these invasions into their personal lives, pious Muslims joining in the protests were also concerned about authoritarianism, neo-liberalism and police brutality. All these anxieties brought together a body of different interest groups, including environmentalists, educated youth, LGBT, anti-capitalist Muslims, the hyper-secular nationalists, Kurds and Alevis. The overall aim was to show collective resistance against related concerns (Kuymulu 2013).

At the time of the disturbances, a great deal of disapproval was simmering within Turkish society. Apprehension about state violence, police brutality (Amnesty International 2013), infringement of civil liberties, routine arrests of lawyers, doctors and activists, the silencing of political dissent in the media, and the co-opting of individual media pundits and analysts, led many to believe that the state was abusing its power. Cited too were human rights abuses, particularly given the widespread police deployment of tear gas and pepper spray (Adams 2013). Comparisons with Occupy movements in the West and other resistance movements in the Middle East and North Africa, on the other hand, were somewhat underdeveloped. The events that occurred in Istanbul and across many of the cities of Turkey were responses to specific forms of economic inequality and repressive leadership. There was also a national consensus among a broad spectrum of political actors that signalled disaffection with AKP policies on matters of privatisation, urbanisation and authoritarianism (Eraydin and Taşan-Kok 2014).

In some respects, the Gezi Park movement was the venting of frustration through a bottom-up process that included many different layers of society traditionally opposed along ideological and cultural grounds. The protesters were not merely a few 'chapullers' (Anglicised term referring to 'plunderers' or 'looters', as used by Erdoğan). The initial police response ignited much trepidation across Turkey, fuelled by social media, in particular, by Twitter (Varnali and Gorgulu 2014), which remains a foremost site for social and political activism in Turkey (Genç 2014). For many, the AKP's pursuance of the free market economic agenda, which reconfigured the urban sphere in many of the larger cities across Turkey, was unacceptably unrestrained. The resulting outward democratic deficit reached boiling point, with Erdoğan deemed as the essential reason for the severe stance; '[a]n authoritarian and undemocratic way of policy making accompanies these policies . . . there is no tolerance for resistance and no time for discussion, a blatant use of coercion and of public relations . . .' (Elicin 2014: 155). Given the precise role played by Erdoğan, some argued that the AKP confirm an 'institutional and ideological framework through which neoliberalization is accompanied by authoritarianism' (ibid. 155).

There is little doubt that the AKP government managed matters hastily. The initial police action was problematic, but, then, as issues got out of hand, the environmentalist numbers swelled as left-leaning and marginalised groups (including Kemalists, fascists, Marxists, Leninists and anarchists) joined the fray. Protests turned into insurrections. Cars burnt throughout central Istanbul, and angry groups damaged public property. Police attacked innocent protesters. The mishandling of the initial resistance to the prospective levelling of Gezi Park escalated the dissent. Minorities and majorities, men and women, mostly young but also older groups, leftists and rightists, atheists and religionists, all fused together into a national outcry against the police responses to the protesters and the heavy-handedness of the state that surfaced over several days and weeks. Volunteers distributed food left for the campaigners in the park. Yoga classes were set up in Gezi Park at noon every day. Bands played music, and kebab venders sold their wares. There was an almost carnival-like atmosphere in the park, bringing together a wide cross-section of society never before witnessed in Turkey (Yel and Nas 2013). The events created a national swell of sympathy and ownership. Throughout the suburbs of Istanbul and in as many as eighty out of the eighty-one provinces in Turkey, small but vocal groups paraded through the streets, armed with their pots and pans, all chanting anti-government slogans.

With these images in mind, this chapter attempts to delineate the events and their repercussions. Though these occurrences seem unprecedented in modern Turkish political history, the need persists for greater sociological appreciation of questions relating to urbanism, citizenship, political representation, nationalism and majoritarianism in a secular Muslim-majority country. This chapter is an effort to generate a conceptualisation and contextualisation of the events using a sociological grounded theoretical and analytical framework based on fieldwork carried out in Gezi Park during the height of the protests.

Coalescing Anti-authoritarianism

Many different groups had set up tents in the park. The Kurds were at the left corner, adjacent to Taksim Square. The Kurdish section consisted of tents that displayed PKK flags and pictures of Abdullah Öcalan. Using the Kurdish language facilitated locating interviewees who otherwise seemed reluctant to talk. It also reassured respondents. Azad was a Kurdish protester. He had a bachelor's degree in sociology. Azad explained his reasons for joining the protesters. He said:

> We know that the first demonstration was based in Gezi Park itself; however, I believe here [in the park] are all these different groups, which for ten years, twenty years or 100 years have been suffering from despotic regimes, now representing themselves in this park. After a couple days, it became a mass movement; it was not like a typical party action. As you know, when it became a mass movement it included many different components; the purpose is to show opposition. It doesn't matter whom you are fighting against.

Azad elaborated further about who or what he and his associates were battling. Azad chortled, and offered the following comment:

> We all know that the current government is bad. Some came here just to be against Recep Tayyip Erdoğan. Some came here because they think that the state system is unfair. As a Kurdish group, we are here because of the state. We are not here just to be against Tayyip Erdoğan, but we are here to be against all government policies. Not only against the current rule or power, but all.

Okan was twenty-five years old. He worked in a bank and identified himself as a Turkish leftist. He was enthusiastic about taking part in the research, saying that it was the third interview he had given to researchers and journalists visiting the park in recent days. He was assertive with his answers. When speaking with him in English, he became expansive with his replies. It was an opportunity to ask detailed questions about why he was at the park. Okan stated that:

> What brought me here is that in Turkey there is a regime that I am not happy about. There were many demonstrations against this regime, but

this is the biggest one in the history of Turkey. It is the biggest one because many people give their support to this issue . . . For instance, when you go to work, you take the bus or metrobus and you can see that everybody talks about Gezi Park. Everybody has an idea about the Gezi Park protests. Not only organised people, but also unorganised people came here . . . These protests show us that there is a chance to overthrow Recep Tayyip Erdoğan and the AK Party. This is what brought us here. What if this is *the* opportunity. Maybe we will not be able to do it but the achievements of these protests will be great . . . Now, the government is Tayyip Erdoğan, which is why we are against him specifically. And I believe that it is a normal situation that we have a reaction against AKP or Tayyip. In all the discussions of neo-liberalism, capitalism or the system, the problem of the system is Tayyip Erdoğan.

Emre was the lead spokesperson of the 'Didier Drogba Party', an ultra-Atatürkist group (Didier Drogba was an Ivory Coast international footballer of some repute. He played in the Turkish Süper Lig for the Istanbul club Galatasaray during the 2012–14 seasons). Emre was twenty-five years old. He said he had been there from the beginning. He worked as a customs officer by day, returning to the park at night: 'we are workers during the daytime and insurgents at night'. He presented his main reasons for being in the park:

We are here because we want to protect our nation and republic from all injustices; and also, to protect our future from the one [the Erdoğan] who tries to bring sharia to our country, the one who calls himself prime minister [at the time], the one who slowly separates our country, the one who tries to be *padişah* (Ottoman sultan) in the republic, Recep Tayyip Erdoğan . . . We, as the Turkish nation, celebrate our important national days and religious days too. We used to celebrate these kinds of important festivals. However, in the last couple of years, he interfered with these [secular] days. They [the AKP] are banning all the things that comprise the republic and Atatürk . . . Before Recep Tayyip Erdoğan and President Abdullah Gül came to their positions they made some speeches. The president made a speech ten–fifteen years ago, 'We are coming to destroy the republic regime and bring the sharia regime to Turkey.' They are clear! They are serving the Gülen movement and to make money.

Figure 5.1   Gezi Park – a burnt-out police car sprayed with political graffiti and dragged on to the steps of the entrance to Gezi Park.
Photograph taken by the author, 15 June 2013.

A profound anti-authoritarian, almost uncompromising stance was found among many of the interviewees, and among groups who would otherwise be ideologically and politically opposed to each other on many fronts. These individuals were contesting the government because they felt that there was no credible alternative. They were making a particular stand against the neo-liberalism of the AKP.

Villain of the Piece

Sabiha was a retired Turkish woman with Australian citizenship. She was part of a group known as 'the mothers of the protesters'. They held hands and formed circles that circumnavigated the central areas of the park. As we approached their tent, these mothers held hands and formed a chain inside the park. Sabiha chose to stay behind and speak to us about her motivations for joining the Gezi Park movement. She stated that:

We want this government to quit. Quit and go! We don't want them to govern [anymore]. We want a decent government, which gives us more human rights, and doesn't see us as dirt. We are human beings. We should respect each other. The government should respect us, and we selected them . . . The issue is the government, and the governor who is governing the country now. He is trying to establish a dictatorship. We see things like that. Also, recently, they [the AKP] have been passing legislation which is against the rights of the nation. I am a member of the Turkish Labour Party. I used to follow the CHP [Republican People's Party], but that changed after Kiliçdaroğlu, who is the current head of CHP. He is not doing well in opposition, not doing well at all.

Sabiha continued her responses in English. She was asked what she thought were the main issues that united the different groups. She responded:

The last thing that happened was the remark from the prime minister [Erdoğan at the time], who said that Atatürk and his best friend, Inonu, were *ayyaş* (drunkards). This was so offensive to us. The second thing he said was that we are *çapulcular* (plunderers or looters). He also said in the past that all women should have three kids. Why? Why? Why? Then there is the abortion issue. They are trying to introduce fundamentalist Islamic sharia inside Turkey.

Jale and Sinan, a couple in their fifties, were originally from the city of Bursa. They had travelled to the park that Saturday morning, and found themselves sitting among the group of Atatürkists who called themselves the 'Didier Drogba Party'. A handful of young men, grouped among them, drank, smoked and discussed politics. A conversation about football started with one of the young men in the group, and this offered an opportunity to address the group at large. In discussing the Gezi Park movement with the couple, Jale answered:

Our aim in being here is because of these younger generations. I had little hope about these youngsters. I am from the 1977 generation. I am one of the 1 May 1977 protesters. I almost lost hope because we are suppressed and suppressed. I was really unhappy about it. When I see these protests, I see myself born again. I came here to feel the old days of 1977. I see a much better situation here. These youngsters are active and excited. They give me hope again. This is very important for me. We came here just today, and we will go back at night . . . I am a CHP supporter, have always voted for CHP. Each time I say, 'God damn this party', but there is no other alternative for me. I think all leftist parties should be incorporated into one. We cannot even breathe anymore. We want the AKP to go.

Interview and observational data suggested that many in Gezi Park possessed similar anxieties about existing government policy. Azad and Welat commented on why there were so many Kurds and Kemalist groups with shared political goals in relation to their positions within the park. Welat, a postgraduate student in Istanbul, seemed eager to respond. He informed us that the police had singled him out a few days earlier. Imprisoned for three days, he told us he was tortured. He showed us the cigarette burns on his arms and legs before adding:

> For instance, about twenty years ago, Islamists were supporting us against the government; however, now that Islamists are in power it is the Kemalists who are the ones fighting [government] policies. It seems that these Kemalists are combatting state policies and supporting us. The purpose of the Kemalists is to overthrow Tayyip Erdoğan. This is a mass movement, do you understand? This is why you see flags of Kurdistan and Turkey on the same picture.

Okan, focusing on the economic and political standpoints that united groups in the park, added that a collective outrage positioned itself against the machinery of elitist self-serving government, irrespective of the ideological position of the different groups involved. He said:

> As a party, we are against a system that puts pressure on workers because of neo-liberal policies. Specifically, there is someone with a lot of arrogance; Tayyip Erdoğan is the one to be against. To be honest, we are against all mass parties or older parties, it doesn't matter for us whether it is AKP or MHP or any other party. They are all the parties of the system.

There was a palpable suggestion among the leftist-socialist groups that a growing bourgeoisie oppressed the people of Turkey because of their proletariat status. Samet was thirty years old, a university graduate and a shipmaster. He identified himself as a Leninist. Samet spoke of what the Gezi Park protests meant to him. He stated at length:

> I would like to give some information here before starting. Now, the AKP sees itself as *the* party and that it has *no* opposition. TUSIAD [the Turkish Industry and Business Association] and some other organisations tried to make the CHP an alternative party, but it did not work. It is because the CHP has no desire to solve the main problems of Turkey, such as the Kurdish issue, the sub-contractor problem, and so on. Even the CHP created all these problems. That is why the CHP cannot be an alternative to the AKP . . . I believe the AKP is losing its power. The AKP is now talking with Abdullah Öcalan. The AKP gives some compensation to the Kurds, on the one hand. On the other hand, the AKP puts more pressure on workers, and tries to make everyone the same. It banned worker days in Taksim. It has tried to impose its ideology on the people. Therefore, people have some anger against the AKP. When these environmentalists were attacked by the police forces, the anger of the people blew up . . . And now, it is not about the trees of Gezi Park, and nobody talks about it. Now everybody talks about democracy, freedom and human rights issues . . . We are against this system. It doesn't matter whether it is the CHP or AKP or MHP. They are all the same. Now, we have the AKP. That is why we are against the AKP. Our main goal is to construct a proletarian dictatorship. If we don't construct that proletarian dictatorship, all ethnic groups, all workers and all citizens will be under the control [of the state]. They will not be free.

In commenting on the lack of an alternative to the authoritarianism of the ruling party at the time and, in particular, Erdoğan, many respondents also mentioned fears about class inequalities and the oppression of workers at the hands of the state. They felt that the state promoted bourgeoisie interests at the expense of everyday folk. Part of the frustration of groups was that the political parties they supported could not offer a viable political alternative to the electoral advantage that the AKP had gained.

Figure 5.2   A depiction of Recep Tayyip Erdoğan in Gezi Park – founded in 2006, the Youth Union of Turkey, Türkiye Gençlik Birliği, is a far-left, anti-imperialist, doggedly nationalist, often racist, and vehemently anti-AKP Kemalist revolutionary youth organisation.
Photograph taken by the author, 15 June 2013.

'Enemy of my Enemy'

Many in the park were anarchists; that is, they sought to destabilise the government based on some specific ideological struggle. Although various groups displayed identifiable political differences, the overarching concern was that the AKP had become too dictatorial, and that Erdoğan's behaviour was akin to that of a 'sultan'. The range of comments, from ideologically opposed sections of society, indicated that in spite of apparent political differences, all believed in the existence of further marginalisation for many and an increasingly unequal society for most. A collective conviction brought them together in a unified struggle against the alleged authoritarianism of Erdoğan and the AKP. Although leftists, secularists and Kurds united under the rubric of anti-authoritarianism, social revolution and class-consciousness, the 'Kurdish issue' was still not far from people's minds. As illustrated in the following section, granting Kurds little autonomy or civic freedoms, but somehow inhibiting their apparent centralising project, occupied the minds of many Turks. While a number of issues brought groups together in shared protests against government policy, beneath the surface there lay deeper struggles between groups that remained unresolved. In discussing this problem with Emre, it became evident that particular political and ideological emotions dominated. He said:

> We are really uncomfortable about Kurdish flags and pictures of Abdullah Öcalan. This event is strange. Sometimes you see someone hold a picture of Apo [a derogatory term for Abdullah Öcalan] and someone else holds one of Atatürk, and they are hand-in-hand . . . Nothing is happening now, but in the first discussion between us this will be an issue. I can say that the enemy of my enemy is with me now. However, the next enemy will be those Kurds. We have police friends here too. They have been doing their job for many days now. We talk to them too. We ask them, 'You are attacking us, but when will you attack these PKK groups? When will you take out those flags?' And they said that it is their first mission to do that. We are uncomfortable with this situation . . . Listen, they [Kurds] took advantage of these protests. They were around ten to twenty people at first; however, they now have a large nomad tent. As a nation, we don't have any problems, but Abdullah Öcalan is our biggest enemy and terrorist.

Given his statements, Emre discussed how he had developed a ranking for those he viewed as 'his enemies'. After Abdullah Öcalan, who is number two, three and so on? He replied, 'Tayyip is two. Three is Bülent Arınç. Four is Abdullah Gül. Five is Melih Gökçek. Six is others.' Sabiha divulged that she believed the Kurds were manipulating the issue, and wished to take advantage of the present discord. She felt she could not trust Kurdish groups. She added:

> To us, the Kurds are doing wrong because they are trying to divide our country. We want to be one country – together. It is stronger that way. You know what imperialists do is to divide and then rule, separate and control. He [Erdoğan] is listening to the CIA, listening to America, and to what Obama says. We don't want that, we are looking towards the

East. We want to be good neighbours with Syria, Russia, Iraq, with all our neighbours, because Atatürk said 'peace at home, peace in the world'. They [the Kurds] can speak their language but you know that in Australia your language is English. I am Turkish-Australian. When I go to the government or to some other institutions, I have to speak English. They can provide me with a translator if I cannot. In one country you cannot have two or more official languages. We have one language, one nation and one flag. They [the Kurds] are trying to manipulate and divide this country.

Issues raised among the Gezi Park protesters ranged from general concerns about authoritarianism, to deep disaffection with the opposition. There were agitated Marxist–Leninist groups, but also profound divisions between Kemalist and Kurdish groups. Many respondents pointed out that the Gezi Park movement was a reflection on the so-called problem of Islam in the public sphere and how the AKP projected the faith. In reality most protesters were there because of what they regarded as unhindered power on the part of the state. The brutal nature of police operations created deep disaffection in society, reflecting the seemingly excessive powers of the state. Yet, underneath the façade of a collective consciousness, there remained intense currents of ideological, cultural, political and ethnic difference bubbling close to the surface. Many leftist and secular Turks felt concerned by the fear of Kurdish nationalism, while feminist, 'anti-capitalist Muslims' and LGBT activists were open to the Kurdish struggle.

Questions of spatiality and political orientation are also important to consider. During the protests, when urged to do so, the police reined in protesters from the Taksim Square-facing side of the park. That precise boundary was where the tents of the most marginalised and extreme political organisations (that is, Anarchists, Marxists–Leninists) were found, while on the other side of the park, the 'liberal and peaceful' environmentalist and green movements were situated facing the affluent neighbourhood of Osmanbey. On another side were vociferous supporters of the three Istanbul football teams – Beşiktaş, Fenerbahçe and Galatasaray – who had been active in the protests from the beginning. Largely, the geography of the Gezi Park resistance project became a snapshot of the rifts and markers of identity conflict within the current political order of Turkish society. In spite of deep-seated differences, different groups such as leftists, rightists, Kurdish, ultra-national, green, conservatives and liberals, coalesced around the issues of anti-authoritarianism that temporarily unified a nation (Sarfati 2015).

Mourning the Loss of Culture

From the mid-1800s onwards most of the Muslim world fell under the spell of European political and economic colonialism. Turkey avoided it but the emergence of Turkish secularism is a rather atypical phenomenon (Çağaptay 2006). Post-Islamist Turkey is often seen a model for other nations, but many secular Turkish political and cultural actors disparage the presentation of Turkey as a progressive Muslim country. Presently, pious Muslims are organising themselves and engaging in the political process more than ever, but wide-ranging backlash often results. Many Gezi Park protestors felt that the AKP was somehow Islamising the state, given the discernable Islamophobia inside Turkey (Yel and Nas 2014), in the EU and further afield (Canan-Sokullu 2012). Invariably, groups inspired by Islamist ideals do operate close to the Turkish state, but these *cemaats* (Islamic communities) are not the same as those frequently considered problematic due to their absolutism and theological indifference to non-Muslims in parts of the Middle East, North Africa and across Asia (Esposito 1993). In Turkey there is also growing concern over the rise of Salafism over the last three decades (Ahmad 1988).

In many ways Turkey has witnessed a reconfiguration of a post-secular and a post-Islamist identity politics. The idea of the post-secular is the prospect of a neo-secular movement; that is, Turkey is on the way to becoming the new, without having fully overcome hyper-nationalism, and only slowly embracing pluralism because of globalisation. A specific Turkish post-Islamist dynamic suggests similar compelling forms of hyper-nationalism and the embracing of a variation of Muslim pluralism. Secular young people emerge from the same ethno-cultural fabric as their pious Muslim counterparts, but their ideological and religious outlooks diverge. The secularist old guard has been forced to retreat in the face of the expanding new Muslim presence in Turkish society. These ideological, philosophical and political forces, as well as Turkish concerns regarding the 'Kurdish issue', came into sharp focus during the Gezi Park events (Demir 2014). 'Who we are' has become a function of 'who we are not'. In the context of these wider transformations, the fault lines between Islamists and Kemalists has blurred. In the past it was theoretically imaginable to be liberal but not secular, Islamist but not liberal, secular but also Islamist. Now it is possible to be conservative and liberal, but neither Islamist nor secularist. The Gezi Park events exposed a toxic tribalism bubbling to the surface. People were afraid of the future and their positions in it. With the apparent rise of Islamism, for some a loss of Turkishness pervaded, which added to that fear. It created polarisation over what it meant to be Islamist and Kemalist. The traditional model of laicism that characterised the Turkish state since the foundation of the Republic referred to a secular lifestyle within a state-sponsored Islam. However, being Turkish was to possess particular blood or racial heritage. In this context, Islam was not a feature, but instead an extra-national entity cut from history. A cultural purity defined a Turkishness that the Turkish state perpetuated. In effect, the dismantling of the Kemalist state has made Turkey insecure about its new Turkishness. It remains 'under construction' in the light of ongoing developments. Globalisation has affected the identity of Turks and Turkey as a nation. What it means to be Turkish has shifted to reflect local and global apprehensions.

The Muslim rebranding of Turkishness began in the 1980s, and expanded into the new Muslim bourgeoisie. This group has now become politically powerful. They have high degrees of social and cultural capital, and economic wealth (see Chapter 6). The AKP has also instrumentalised a combination of piety and profit to achieve its ends (White 2012). The perception is that the AKP not only uses the lens of Islamism to advance new policies, there is also alleged egoism of Erdoğan to outwardly project the view that only he can save the nation from demise. Having developed a successful 'theology of secularism', that is, a secular democracy run by pious Muslims, the AKP and younger Turks on the streets were both operating within a post-Kemalist and a post-Ottomanist frame of reference. The AKP has successfully projected the new Muslim Turkey across the globe, but because of intergenerational disconnect and widening social divisions, many young Turks feel left behind. Religion and consumerism have gone hand-in-hand, and the modern Muslim is remodelled in the light of this outlook. A form of social progress remained robust over a decade-long period, but at the time of a national crisis, namely the Gezi Park events and breakdown in the recent peace process, the AKP response is to return to authoritarianism, in a similar vein to the unforgiving Kemalism of days gone by.

Until late 2013 the Turkish economic and political success story attracted global praise. It acquired individual and collective configurations that benefited much of society. In particular, it empowered the Muslim middle classes and gave them a stake in society that would have been unprecedented a few decades ago. It also reflected a change to the social order of Turkey that metamorphosed neo-liberalism, Islamism and Kemalism without the specific understanding of what will be, or might be, the end. Ongoing ideological and cultural worries notwithstanding, class-consciousness converges within these disquiets. A telling account of the Gezi Park movement reflects on class divisions and class conflict. Islamism, secularism and Kemalist understandings of nationalism blur to such an extent that they no longer demarcate separate or competing blocs. Social divisions in the classical Western European economic discourse were foremost worries among the protestors. As such, the Gezi Park movement in Turkey mirrored recent Occupy movements in other parts of the world, particularly in European and Western economies, and in parts of the Middle East after the so-called Arab Spring. In most of these instances, the protests were led by the middle classes and educated urbanites. The situation in Turkey was no less different, although a wide variety of classes were involved in the protests inside the park and across Turkey over time (Tuğal 2014). For the most part the disturbances were also leaderless. They reflected cross-class societal frustrations with the ruling elite's neo-liberal policies (Farro and Demirhisar 2014). The Gezi Park movement exhibited both a neo-liberal and a Kemalist self-critique of Turkey, operating simultaneously but in opposite directions.

Those in the park represented the collective cries of Kemalist, Kurdish, secular, Islamist, LGBT, feminist, Marxist (including Leninist and Trotskyite) and other marginalised groups. Outside of the park, including mothers banging pots on their balconies at nine o'clock every evening, the combined perception was that the future of Turkey was out of their hands and placed into those of groups from the so-called backward provinces of days past. At the heart of the events was the question of whether too much power and a degree of popularity gave unwarranted confidence to the AKP, and whether age-old 'deep state' penchants that beleaguered Turkey in the past had resurfaced in an alternative guise. Because of these wider fears, demonstrations increased dramatically over a few days and spread all over Turkey. Many came in response to the excessive powers of the police at the behest of the government, which escalated the police action further. In many ways, through empowering the middle classes, and by further opening up opportunities for civil society to expand, the AKP became a victim of its own success.

After Gezi Park

The Gezi Park disturbances involved the amalgamation of various political interest groups, but some argue that the dominant and overarching theme was that of culture, especially the presumed fragmentation of secular political culture at the behest of a pro-Islamic authoritarian nationalist conservative party. As the AKP made crucial inroads into the secular elite by promoting liberal democracy, these same secular elites began to resist what they observed as the Islamisation of society. To that end, the actions of the AKP were understood as a betrayal of the Kemalist historical paradigm that had defined the identity of the nation throughout the twentieth century. Secular groups organised themselves in response to what they saw as a threat to their cultural norms (Atay 2013). Pious Muslim and pro-Islamic protesters, who also engaged in the resistance activities, including mothers of traditional Muslim backgrounds, even in the much smaller towns and cities in Anatolia, were somewhat separated from the machinations of the urban elites. Fittingly, aspects of the secular media capitalist classes invariably attempted to benefit from the unsteady few months that the AKP endured during the summer of 2013. For some, the defeat of secular popular culture was the net result. For others, authoritarianism plagued their relations with the government, combined with concerns about wide-ranging economic policy.

It is undeniably true that 'governments have a profound effect on social cohesion' (Capshaw 2005: 75). They possess a distinctive purpose to create social glue by establishing and resourcing the institutions of social life. The relationship between social capital and social cohesion in society is complex, but unmistakably, significant features of social cohesion broke down during the Gezi Park events. The events also created opportunities for new forms of social capital, helping to bridge communities against the seemingly authoritarian conservatism and unrestrained neo-liberalism of the AKP. Arguably, the Gezi Park events were a key factor behind the AKP losing votes in the June 2015 election, unable to form a parliamentary majority government at the time.

Rather than leading to deterioration, the Gezi Park events should have sparked renewal. The greater good of a wider Turkey should have become prominent in the eyes of those who held power and those who aspired to it. Before the Gezi Park events Turkey managed to develop a positive image internationally. It helped lessen the Orientalism long characterising Western perceptions. Until the Gezi Park events Turks grew confident both looking within and looking out to the wider world (Clark 2012). The reconfiguration supported the possibility of widening citizenship and participation, and expanding Turkish social cohesion that was both nationally and ethnically grounded (Gellman 2013). Further still, for some, the Gezi Park events mollified the intense conflict between the so-called Islamists and the so-called secularist–Kemalists (Öncü 2013). Thus, the Gezi Park movement was successful in creating the outcome it originally sought, which was to reconfigure the public rhetoric of the AKP. For a brief moment, the movement demonstrated that no Turkish government is immune to the will of its people, despite intractable power and boundless political authority. Turkish society faced the greatest resistance to its ruling elite since the foundation of the republic in 1923. The centre-periphery dualism played out asymmetrically, but the balancing out of these domains of power politics, culture and authority could have determined a very different Turkey going forward.

Unfortunately, it is unlikely that much will change in the near future, nor will much materialise to break the direction in which the AKP is taking Turkey. In 2014 Recep Tayyip Erdoğan achieved his aim of becoming the first elected president of Turkey, although his plan to bring in a new constitution remains under development. A healthy democracy requires an effective opposition. The Gezi Park demonstrators highlighted ongoing concerns around liberty and freedom of expression, and aspects of the reconfiguration of a state around specific ideological and political motivations, some of which were both implicitly and explicitly anti-Kemalist and pro-Islamist. Still, the voices of those frustrated by increasing urbanisation and gentrification need listening and understanding. The initial matter of the environmentalist initiative behind the early stages of the Gezi Park protests did not prevail. Direct attacks against Erdoğan remain ongoing, because of his 'sultanate' style of government, where there are wider ideological uncertainties culminating in a leftist-liberal [secular] vs rightist-conservative [Islamist] battle over the identity of Turkey as a nation.

6

Exploring Trust in Society and Politics

Since 2002, when the fortunes of Turkey began to shift, the changing character of Turkish society has led to all sorts of questions about social and political cohesion. Driven by exports, an expanding retail sector, increasing urbanisation and rampant consumerism (Öniş 2012), the economy was stable throughout the 2000s. Given the recent issue of decreased trust in the AKP and questions of authoritarianism as the Gezi Park events revealed (see Chapter 5), it is vital to explore the implications of Turkish social and cultural relations in a political context. Rapid economic and cultural developments to traditional modes of life can sometimes create social isolation and political disenfranchisement. It is essential to understand how these issues affect Turkish society as part of its postmodernisation and neo-liberalisation experience.

Turkey is both a post-traditional and post-secular nation, where both history and memory distinguish individual and collective values (Bakiner 2013). Moreover, it is important to consider the positions that Turks adopt between Islam and nationalism, especially when some identify these through religious values, others through secular liberal norms (Azak 2010). Thus, the primary question in this chapter is to what extent social capital intersects with political trust in Turkey, and, in addition, how the independent variables of employment status, education, ethnicity, religion and gender explain these patterns. The analysis presents a range of ethno-religious, political and sociological distinctions. A number of implicit sub-questions arise in this analysis. What are the types and levels of social capital and political trust in Turkey, that is, trust in politicians, political systems and democratisation? To what extent do Turks maintain social relations with others, and through which social formations (family, community or neighbourhood)? How do these levels of social capital affect attitudes towards political participation and engagement in society?

The theory of social capital centres on three different types: bonding, bridging and linking. Bonding social capital refers to associations, ties and networks 'with people who are like us'. Bridging social capital refers to social relations, connections and affiliations 'with people who are not like us'. Linking social capital refers to access to people and institutions who have 'influence and authority' in affecting wider social outcomes. It is also essential to concentrate on the civic dimensions of social capital, viewing it as separate from its economic definition, as well as to understand social capital as trust, or social capital as reciprocity, as both are different concepts in practice (Smith and Kulynych 2002). Furthermore, it is vital to think of social capital as composed of formal and informal networks and associations of trust and reciprocity, which vary for different nations. For example, Scandinavian countries and the Netherlands have high degrees of formal social capital, whereas social capital is informal in the south-east and southern regions of Europe. Family and social networks define the informal, whereas the formal is associational life and civic engagement (Pichler and Wallace 2007).

The present investigation offers a unique opportunity to understand social capital and political trust in Turkey. The research generates a more nuanced understanding of individual action and collective outcomes, shaped by Islamic cultural values at one level and centralised secularist democratic norms on the other. There is also an attempt to disentangle social capital from political trust. In the general literature the former deals with aspects of trust, reciprocity and civil society. The latter refers to governmentality, governance and performance. The two may not necessarily reinforce each other, and there may well be other factors shaping their associations (Newton 2001). Moreover, those of lower socio-economic status gain advantage from weak ties (Granovetter 1983), but those with higher socio-economic positions benefit from civic engagement (Li et al. 2005). People from different backgrounds from the same societies can utilise different features of social capital to determine various aspects of social trust. On the other hand, the trust 'radius' of friendship circles varies considerably from Confucian countries to Western economies, which may also affect the experience in Turkey (Delhey et al. 2011). Undoubtedly, political trust is an open-ended term because of its attention on performance, but what really defines the experience is how individuals maintain confidence in their political systems (Catterberg and Moreno 2005).

This chapter uses the combined sample of 4,272 Turkish respondents from the 2004 and 2008 waves of the European Social Survey. It explores patterns of social capital and political trust in Turkey, where social capital is defined as 'social trust' (extent of people's helpfulness towards each other and 'social participation' (derived from questions asking how often people meet socially with friends and relatives, and how frequently the respondent takes part in social events). 'Political trust' is trust in political institutions and political systems. The hypothesis states that the intersection of social capital and political trust hinges on religion and cultural identity. Data analysis and findings indicate that pious bourgeois Muslims are least likely to trust the EU, although a nationalist sense of 'Turkishness' was more critical than religious identity, even for Kurds in this sample. Ethnic minorities have lower levels of social participation and lower trust in parliament, the police and the legal system. Older and younger respondents are likely to be socially disengaged, but have higher interpersonal trust than others. Age, religiosity and ethnicity are weighty considerations in the formation of social capital and political trust in Turkey. These are potentially valuable findings for social scientists attempting to understand social, cultural, religious and political relations in contemporary Turkey.

Citizenship and Identity

Classical definitions of citizenship evoke concepts of trust and engagement, but they also allude to the development and realisation of various forms of identity politics. As a nation Turkey generally has low trust, low tolerance and low general levels of social capital (Norris 2002). Nevertheless, theory suggests that social capital brings stability and economic development, as well as a range of local area neighbourhood effects. To understand social capital in Turkey, it is vital to consider cultural identity. Strong individual and group identities build social trust based on efficacy and high-esteem, findings that social psychologists working in this area have regularly established (Smith and Tyler, 1997). Without fully contextualising the formation and shaping of identities, the realisation that strong identities can lead to strong social capital cannot exist beyond specific localised contexts.

Various political actors have contested the question of Turkey's entry into the EU. They argue that the country's stance on human rights and personal liberties, combined with its lack of political openness, are barriers to its eventual admission. Although much of this debate focuses on political culture, the issue of Islam is also under suspicion. There is also tremendous debate taking place inside Turkey about how open or closed Turkey should be to the West in general. As such, the relationship between Islam and democracy comes to the fore (Göl 2009). Rhetoric inside Europe fixates on the apparent ambivalence Turkey has towards democracy, but the view inside the nation is changeable. Contrary to widespread ongoing European discussion, based on a study of the World Values Survey (2000–8), Turks were regularly less authoritarian than others are across the world. Nationalism is potentially the political divide on the EU entry question, rather than 'Islamism' or 'secularism'. This was also the concern in terms of the adaptation of liberal democratic values in society (Dixon et al. 2013). Undoubtedly, religion in personal life is pronounced, but Islam played a strong role in the political process, especially between the 2011 and 2015 elections. It was a function of religiosity at some level, but also reflects Turkey's unique brand of secularism in practice. Until recently, it permitted the AKP an ability to exercise geopolitical influence, in the process evoking national pride and Islamic associations with the *ummah*. Today, 'Turkey is moving neither "East" nor "West"; rather, it is very much moving in its own direction' (ibid. 772).

A break from the nationalist–Kemalist past emerged in the 2000s. It was in pursuit of the European ideal and affirming the balance between Islam, democracy and capitalism (Michael 2008). Other studies on Turkey, on the other hand, confirm that Islam exerts no influence whatsoever on the national desire to join the EU. Rather, Turks believe their individual livelihoods and their satisfaction with democracy would improve through EU membership. National identity is negatively associated. By the end of the 2000s, however, Turks were less willing to enter the EU based on the view that their living standards would improve. This was likely to be a function of the declining fortunes of the Eurozone since the 2008 recession. Moreover, limitations placed on Turkey's EU entry inevitably had a negative effect on European perceptions of Turkey (Çarkoğlu and Kentmen 2011). Among elites in Europe, unmistakeable evidence of 'Turcoscepticism' and fears of immigration affect wider media and political discourses on this debate (Canan-Sokullu 2011).

Another crucial issue in Turkey is its youthful population. Approximately half of the country is under the age of twenty-five. This has particular implications for social cohesion, civil society and politics, as well as for policy and planning. Although there is general political disaffection among Turks as a whole, it transpires that younger Turks tend to under-participate in the political process. Younger Turks often feel demotivated and immobilised, particularly among present-day generations. As such, there is a predisposition to leverage personal and family associations to find solutions to social conflicts. This results in disengagement with the political process, though this happens in the context of a centralised and hierarchical government (Ontas et al. 2011). When analysing perspectives on legal status, identity and civic virtue, a left–right divide is noticeable among young Turks (Senay 2008). Liberal respondents hint at their discontent with the 'state-centric conception of Turkish citizenship, preferring a rights-based and individual-centric model of citizenship' (ibid. 972). As for the question of Islam, young Turkish–nationalists regard their ethnicity and religion as fundamental aspects of their identity. Young Kurdish–Islamists are likely to assert specific ethnic identities, compared with young Turkish–Islamists who affirm their rights on the specific basis of religion. For Kurdish groups, the importance of socio-economic opportunity is imperative in any appreciation of motivations on matters of integration and adaptation (Sarigil 2010).

A present concern among young Turks is how to approach EU entry as a distinct opportunity. There are different aspirations because of identity, ethnicity and religiosity fused with the nature of the relationship of the individual with the state. Here, a certain degree of Turkish–Kurdish rapport did exist in the context of the democratisation process taking place in Turkey in the early periods of the twenty-first century (Somer 2002). In spite of this, over time some Turks fear that too much recognition of Kurdish identity politics may destabilise democratisation. Others argue that this could be a positive element in the process of Europeanisation itself (Johansson-Nogués and Jonasson 2011). Overall, support for democracy is high in Turkey, as in a number of other Middle East countries, and 'it appears to be independent of "sectarian" or theological traditions across the Muslim world' (Ciftci

2010: 1460). In the light of the Arab Spring of 2011 it has become clear that these countries, including Turkey, are undergoing dramatic transformations. Until recently, developments to the democratic process and human rights, as well as the opening up of the economy, created harmony in approaches to improving Turkey's position in the region. During the 2000s the wider EU-integration question was foremost in the psyche of the nation (Mousseau 2006), even if it has dropped from the political agenda in the current period.

Intersecting Class, Ethnicity and Islam

Based on original empirical testing of ESS data, this chapter explores the relationship between social capital and political trust in Turkey. 'Social capital' is the combination of social trust and social participation, and 'political trust' is trust in political institutions and systems (see further details in Methods (Appendix)). Modelling of the ESS data demonstrated a significant relationship between trust in political parties and politicians, and trust in international institutions ($r = 0.48$, $p < 0.01$). There is also a strong relationship between trust in parliament, the police and the legal system, and trust in international institutions ($p < 0.01$). All these observations are in the expected direction, where social trust is significantly associated with all forms of political trust ($p < 0.01$). However, social engagement appeared to have no significant association with any form of political trust, and only a weak relationship between social trust and social engagement emerged, although it was significant nevertheless ($p < 0.01$).

The analysis suggested that Turks who trust each other also trust the political process and engage socially. Then again, Turks did not trust in politics, even if they are specifically trusting of one another or are socially active. It proffers the view that these groups are likely to work within their own communities to achieve social outcomes that are based on strong localised bonding and bridging social capital (see Table 6.1). Arguably, the importance of group identity and community-collective cultural norms and values are more prominent than the needs or wants of the individual (Çağaptay 2006).

According to the ESS, 99.8 per cent of the population of Turkey classified themselves as Muslims. Moreover, 75 per cent of the population stated that they are religious as opposed to less religious. Indeed, 72 per cent stated that they prayed every day. Analysis showed that religiosity had a positive and

Table 6.1 Pearson correlation between dependent variables

	Social trust	Social engagement	Trust in parliament, police, legal system	Trust in political parties and politicians
Social engagement	.08**			
Trust in parliament, police, legal system	.15**	.00		
Trust in political parties and politicians	.21**	−.03	.42**	
Trust in international institutions	.13**	−.03	.28**	.48**

Notes: ** $p < 0.01$ * $p < 0.05$

Source: European Social Survey 2004 and 2008

significant effect on trust in national institutions and national politics, but a negative influence on social engagement. It seems that religiosity did not have any significant influence on trust in international institutions, nor on social trust. Practising religion, measured by praying, was only associated with two of the models. Compared with Turks who pray every day, those who never pray or prayed less often had less trust in national institutions, but those who prayed only on special holidays had greater social trust.

Turks who defined themselves as being on the right of the political spectrum are likely to trust national institutions and national politics, but are less likely to trust international institutions (these results are significant at $p < 0.05$). It included Turks who are religious in practice and therefore more critical of Western European and US-led foreign policy than their secular counterparts. Younger Turks are likely to show trust in others but less likely to engage socially. There is a sense that young Muslims are discovering an Islamic outlook, simultaneously distancing themselves from mainstream politics (Saktanber 2007), not necessarily because of depoliticisation, but conceivably because of cynicism or even apathy. In terms of gender, men are slightly less trusting of international institutions ($p < 0.05$) and are more socially engaged than women. Marital status had no significant impact on any of these results. Ethnic minorities are significantly less likely to trust national institutions (such as parliament, the judiciary or the police), but are likely to trust domestic politics. Compared to majority Turks, there was significantly less social engagement among ethnic minorities, too. It plausibly explains the perspectives of Kurds (the single largest ethnic minority group), for example, who experience various forms of social vilification and institutional bias on a routine basis (Ergin 2014). At one level, much of the 'Kurdish issue' is about the need to gain political recognition. At another level, the Kurds have deep reservations around socio-economic inequality. Historically, assimilationist policies have proved inadequate in meeting the needs of the Kurds (Karakoç 2013; Saatchi 2002).

Economic status had no significant influence on any of the outcomes (models), but occupational positions had a significant impact on most of the outcome variables, particularly the category of managerial and professional occupations and that of service, shop and market workers. Compared with unskilled workers, managers and professionals are less likely to trust in national institutions ($p < 0.05$), but are likely to trust in politicians and political parties (national politics), and are more likely to be socially engaged. The professional classes are likely to have strong forms of bridging and linking social capital. More socially engaged service, shop and market workers are less likely to trust in international institutions than unskilled workers. The petty bourgeoisie, whose profile has grown in the last two decades, are likely to be pious Muslims whose Islamic perspectives on the state of the *ummah* have shaped their opinion of the world. Socially engaged respondents had trust in the political process, arguably because of the economic success it had personally brought them. Turks in intermediate positions followed the same pattern as the managerial and professional classes, but the influence was only significant for trust in national institutions (compare with Çarkoğlu and Kalaycioğlu 2009).

Turks in Istanbul are more likely to trust national institutions, trust other Turks and emphasise greater social engagement compared with Turks living elsewhere in Turkey. Yet, they exhibited less trust in international institutions. Urban, educated and professional, both Islamic and secular Turks in Istanbul, had higher levels of bridging and linking social capital, and they arguably shared a distrust of European and US-led foreign policy, believing it to directly or indirectly affect Turkey. Most of these observations here are significant (p < 0.01). Moreover, Turks showed more trust in international institutions in 2004 than in 2008 (p < 0.01). This could have reflected the deterioration of the Europeanisation process after 2006. It also mirrors geopolitical tensions shaping perspectives on the Muslim world since then, including inside Turkey. Both 'Islamists' and 'secularists' are loyal nationalists in spite of their localised cultural differences. Trust in national institutions was positively associated with trust in domestic politics and international institutions. It was not at all associated with social trust or with social engagement.

It seemed that Turks who are trustful of political institutions, domestic or international, exhibited loyal authoritarian nationalistic tendencies, which prevented them from trusting one another. That is, Turks trusted politics and institutions based on group interests. Divisions persisted between secularists and Islamists in terms of how they related to as well as perceived each other. Trust in national politics was associated with political trust. Social engagement was only associated with social trust. It indicated that social trust might have played a connecting function between political trust and social participation (engagement), since it was associated with both. Social participation and political trust are not associated in any remarkable way. Highly educated Turks show less trust in politics compared with those who had low secondary education. This lack of trust is significant in relation to parliament, the police and the legal system (p < 0.05). Simultaneously, highly educated Turks exhibit more social engagement than Turks with lower levels of education. Middle class and elite groups are critical of government policy and various media and political discourses that surround them. They are independently active, with forms of bonding and linking capital that set them apart from their less well-educated counterparts.

Religion and National Political Culture

Social capital is a powerful agent in the formation of political trust. The general impression here suggests that where associational ties transpire within communities, leading to forms of bonding, bridging and linking, a greater sense of well-being, trust and reciprocity follows. It potentially improves political participation and engagement, and therefore strengthens the democratic process. One argument is that because of the breakdown of associational life and a dwindling trust of others in society and in institutions, disengagement with the political process has emerged (Jacobs 1961). Nevertheless, Robert Putnam (2000) uses social capital as a collective resource operationalised at the societal level, but both Pierre Bourdieu (1986) and James Coleman (1988) use the concept to underscore how social ties support individuals involved in existing networks. In effect, the direction of change is contradictory between these positions.

Yet, civil society activists and policy practitioners have urged the need to build social capital in order to improve political trust, and thereby the functioning of democracies, where solidarity and empathy are essential concepts. Trust is at the heart of recent conceptualisations of social capital. Trust in each other and trust in the political process become equally vital. The types of social capital generated by communities refer to social actions at the individual level, and their transformation into social actions within the collective. It includes actions by the family in the home, and their adaptation at a national level. For societies invariably divided along the lines of class, ethnicity and gender, social capital influences the degree to which members feel that they are able to take part in or even shape their social outcomes. It is also worth stating that social capital is potentially a moving field, and therefore what might exist as social capital at any one point may alter over time (Keele 2005). Invariably, it would also affect formations of political trust.

In spite of these differences, there is a propensity for robust forms of social capital among middle-aged Turks with a high level of education and high incomes, who are, arguably, reasonably satisfied with their lives and the opportunity structures in which they operate. Higher incomes are associated with higher levels of social trust, though Turks with middle incomes are less trusting of Turks with much higher incomes (You 2012). Those performing well in society have strong urges of collective agency. Similarly, political trust is likely to be associated with political views in particular, and trust in wider political processes in general, with much emphasis on associational life. Thus, those with high levels of political trust demonstrated high levels of confidence in politics. It is a top-down process, where strong and stable governments encourage a sense of participation among citizens. Simultaneously, it is bottom-up process where individual and collectivised political organisations were built up from local area experiences of high social trust (Newton 2006).

It is difficult to understand the generation of social capital at a general level, although specific localised understandings revealed the most about its formation and instrumentalisation. Moreover, patent methodological concerns apply in different country contexts (Secor and O'Loughlin 2005), but the characteristics of religion, culture and identity are foremost sub-categories in the determinants of social capital. The political regimes under question are also vital considerations (Catterberg and Moreno 2005). Disaggregation on the components of social capital and the character of the political rule under observation need careful consideration to determine theoretically and methodologically rigorous understandings of outcomes and experiences (Radnitz et al. 2009). Existing research has pointed out that there is lower political participation in cases where individuals and families rely on each other for cultural and emotional support, where there is interdependency and protection from the ills of society, such as financial difficulties, ill health or even crime (Alesina and Giuliano 2011). The findings in this chapter highlight noteworthy observations in Turkey, but the local area dynamics of social capital and political trust still demand further contextualisation.

Over the last few decades, Turkey has experienced population movements from the eastern parts of the country to the larger cities, especially Istanbul. Migration status affects levels of trust in government because of the recent status of immigrants, along with indigenous minorities who are also likely to be critical of various patterns of discrimination. Emerging from the ruins of the Ottoman Empire, the secular democratic Republic of Turkey largely maintains the traditionalism of its lesser-developed urban and rural areas steeped in dominant Sunni Hanafi Islamic orthodoxy, and, thus, a conservative Muslim culture. Istanbul, on the other hand, is a global metropolis, rich in human, social, cultural and economic capital. Once the centre of the Eastern Roman Empire, it is now the cultural capital of Turkey, home to approximately 20 per cent of the entire Turkish population. This includes about three million Kurds. The political capital, Ankara, is Turkey's second city and home to major foreign and domestic political centres. In many of the larger cities a growing middle class has emerged, which has also become Islamist and conservative. Described as the 'Islamic bourgeoisie', this group has benefited from globalisation, the internationalisation of finance and commerce, and rising aspirations associated with the consumption of luxury goods and services.

Until recently two rival but highly mobile groups competed for political and economic authority – the secular middle classes vs the conservative middle classes. In the past secularists held greater influence, but have since witnessed a major decline in status. For some it is a risk to their existence and to the future of Turkey, encouraging further defence of their secular values. In order to integrate into the political and democratic process, which has exhibited increasingly Islamist traits in recent times, some secularists have even been motivated to moderate their staunch secularism (Başkan 2010). In the current period, religiosity emerges as a crucial element in the formation of national political and economic values, as well as localised social capital. These details are thought-provoking considerations for policy-makers and researchers.

Fragmented Interests

Although political trust and social capital have associations in their own right, the relationship between the two remains inconclusive. Nevertheless, a number of social outcomes are largely predictable, for example, the effects of education, gender and social class on particular social and political attitudes. Other observations show that ethnic minorities are significantly less likely to trust in national institutions, but they are likely to trust in domestic politics, measured by trust in political parties and parliament. Compared with majority Turks, social engagement is significantly less likely among Kurds, although they feel relatively protected by the state. The police often negatively target them, and they do not wholly trust the system. It is likely that their status as a minority, combined with ethnic penalties in the labour market and the wider discrimination they face in society, contributes to their lower levels of trust. They are nevertheless prepared to maintain an effort to integrate into society. These groups continue to pursue attempts towards political integration. Resolution of the 'Kurdish issue' is critical for Europeanisation. It is part of a process where improving human rights and civil liberties are worthy considerations. The results of the ESS analysis infer that Kurds in Turkey trust the Turkish political process less than majorities, despite all the modifications made since the Copenhagen criteria for entry into the EU was established in 1993 (Kirişci 2011).

For all groups, religiosity is associated with greater trust in domestic politics and institutions (parliament, the police, the legal system, political parties and politicians). Those on the right of the left–right political divide also had greater trust in domestic politics and institutions. Still, Islam did not enter politics in the way regularly perceived by Turkosceptics in the EU, although it is true that the 'Islamic bourgeoisie' have greater social, economic and political capital than ever before. This is because of the mobilisation of certain forms of civil society activism and political openings, originally shaped in the 1990s (White 2002). Both nationalist secular Turks and Islamist Turks are less enthusiastic to enter the EU, arguably because of their primary economic motivations. When it comes to the EU entry question, concepts of national identity supersede any internal conflict in terms of Islamism or secularism. This attitude also reflects complex pay-offs both groups engage with that are functions of economic performance and the parts played by pro-democracy movements and political influences that reflect their combined interests. It also indicates that Islamists and secularists have formulated strategic alliances around the maintenance of a nationalist political project at one level and an economic interdependence at another. This approach strengthens the influence of both groups, although, ironically, collating around minimising the negatives of Europeanisation (Somer 2011), particularly since the 2008 Eurozone economic recession. The AKP backed off on questions of formal entry into Europe well before the 2015 elections, given the ongoing resistance Turkey faces from the populations of the EU (Gerhards and Hans 2011). Arguably, this is due to the relatively strong economic base of Turkey, compared to a flailing Eurozone, and a much troubled Middle East since the Arab Spring of 2011 (Avcı 2011).

Much of this analysis reflects broader democratisation processes in Turkey. At some basic level democracy involves the notion of free and fair elections, but the rule of law and the judiciary are also essential considerations. Although it is possible to interpret patriarchal authority in relation to how Turks organise themselves, from the family, to the local community and to nationalism itself, exactly how these factors shape trust in political processes and politics remains unclear. Notions of the 'father figure' have historically democratised Turkey, but it also needs an organic development process separated from the past. Liberal democracy in Turkey is still under development, as arrests of journalists, students and activists have created tensions among the elites. The challenges of democratic consolidation are still in play. An embedded class structure and the interests of dominant groups that impose and sustain democracy have not yet fully advanced. Thus, the least organised, least powerful and least classed groups have immense aspirations for change (see Chapter 5). Major interest groups support economic stability and business interests, but apart from those who are arguably most marginalised, few are speaking the language of freedom in Turkey. Indeed, women are especially prone to exclusion from the opportunities for entrepreneurialism. Their empowerment is a vital ingredient in the development of human and financial capital (Çetindamara et al. 2012).

In-groups and out-groups prevail in all societies, as well as hierarchical inclinations and structures contained within these social relations. Then again, it is likely that Turkey has not moved on from the authority of the group to which most Turks belong. Urban and rural divisions are distinct, although urbanisation has been rapid in recent decades. Furthermore, it is impossible to ignore Islam among Turks, as there is the still-evolving issue of nation-building. Individual liberties are limited in Turkey, especially for women, who are some of the least influential in society. Social capital, regarded as the engine of civil society activism, with its resultant impact on local area experiences of bridging and linking, is largely an urban phenomenon. Rural and provincial Turkey is traditional, conservative and emphatically patriarchal in the main. But rural Turkey has its own forms of bonding social capital that help to galvanise various cultural, religious and ethnic norms, values and controls (Çarkoğlu and Cenker 2011). Acute divisions exist between civil society activists of a secularist hue, compared with those of a more Islamist outlook. They may well have similar and shared aspirations, but they ultimately work independently of each other (Özler and Sarkissian 2011). The distinct issues facing civil society organisations in Turkey set them apart from their counterparts in established democracies of the West (Heper and Yıldırım 2011).

A Clash of Cults

The AKP gained political success in the 2002 elections partly because it played down its pro-Islamic roots. It also appealed directly to the aspirations of the secularists to pull Turkey out of the financial crisis. The mandate concentrated on economic development, EU engagement and a forward-looking foreign policy concerning nations to the east and the west. Until the AKP's third general election victory in 2011, Turkey's position was strengthening dramatically due to sustained economic growth, rising exports and the resultant impact on the service and leisure sectors. At the same time, the AKP began to take a particular interest in Iraq, Palestine and other areas of the Muslim world, actively expressing its apprehensions on the global stage. Turkey had the status of a net investor economy, which grew in the light of the collapse of the Eurozone in 2008. It was able to sustain this status until the corruption allegations that started in late 2013. This began to affect business confidence. The opposition, consisting mainly of the CHP, but also the MHP and the HDP, was unable to counter the march of social and political concentration in the hands of the AKP. Despite attempts at derailing the local and municipal elections of March 2014, and the presidential election of August 2014, the AKP remained sturdy. However, the June 2015 elections put a significant dent into the power base of the AKP until the November 2015 snap election gave the AKP the fourth victory it so desperately wanted.

The Gezi Park events of 2013 illustrated how different aspects of society at the margins of the political process were able to galvanise around a social project in response to the neo-liberalism and authoritarianism of the AKP (see Chapter 5). The corruption allegations that began in December 2013 exposed a drastic cessation in relations between Hizmet and the AKP, a situation that continues to worsen for Hizmet. As the civil war continues in Syria, Turkish foreign policy is in question, especially given the events in Kobanî in late 2014 and the emergence of Islamic State terrorism on Turkish soil in 2015 and 2016. There is also concern over nearly three million Syrian refugees in Turkey, predominantly in the major urban centres and in camps near the Syrian border. Despite insufficient developments in the EU integration process, the issue remains on the political agenda. Underpinning all of these fears in Turkey is the issue of trust, which is at the heart of formations of social capital and political engagement, as separate realms on their own as well as at their intersections. Fundamentally, it is a breakdown in trust in Turkish politics and society in 2013 and 2014 that has led to apprehensions over the future of Turkey. Although many of these processes were under way well before these recent events, anxieties have deepened due to these developments.

At one point Hizmet and the AKP were close allies in the reconstruction of a twenty-first-century Turkey that saw its Ottoman past positively, while moving forward with a progressive neo-liberal Islamism that appealed to moderate sentiments in the West and economic and cultural aspirations in the East. Once regarded as the ideal model to connect Eastern and Western ideas of economy, civil society and democratisation, there is less confidence in Turkey's position in the current period. From the mid-1990s Hizmet developed a strong international profile, weaving education and business together into a successful formula that created opportunities at different levels of society, as well as helping to maintain a conveyor belt of loyal devotees and followers. This form of civil Islam advocated interfaith dialogue and coexistence. After 9/11 the powerful rhetoric of Hizmet appealed to many in search of an antidote to radical violent jihadism and the popular appreciation of 'the clash of civilisations'. Towards the end of the 2000s Hizmet also began to garner significant attention from a wide variety of interest groups, including governments, international faith organisations and communitarians across the world.

In 2010 relations between these two foremost actors, Hizmet and the AKP, began to evaporate, leading to the recent malaise. Historically, both benefited from each other's positions, with Hizmet helping to mobilise vast swathes of the population to actively vote for the AKP in the 2011 elections. Simultaneously, the AKP provided Hizmet with preferential treatment, in terms of public recognition, civil service appointments and prime Istanbul locations for the development of physical infrastructure. In 2010 public disagreements appeared over Turkish domestic and foreign policy. In 2013 the AKP alleged that Hizmet orchestrated a direct political attack on the then prime minister, Recep Tayyip Erdoğan, converging on his family amid aspects of alleged involvement in corruption on a massive scale. Given the particular personality of Erdoğan, now the president of Turkey, Hizmet received extensive backlash. The AKP dubbed Hizmet part of a 'parallel state', and targeted its institutions for censure or closure.

In December 2014, approximately one year after corruption allegations, the AKP government arrested twenty-six journalists and senior editors of the

Zaman newspaper group. Zaman was an extension of Hizmet, and published the bestselling English language daily in the country, *Today's Zaman*. Until 2010 Zaman and the AKP joined forces on many aspects of policy-thinking and social commentary. After the dramatic breakdown in relations at the end of 2013 Zaman adopted a strong anti-AKP line that led to a great deal of disapproval, ultimately causing the state to silence the newspaper. The government arrests and detains journalists on a regular basis in Turkey, but this was the first instance of a major newspaper becoming the target for political action in Turkey. As a final blow to Hizmet, its bank, Bank Asya, came near to collapse in 2014. The AKP took the bank into administration in 2015. With its vibrant development and civil society charity, Kimse Yok Mu, already barred, the Journalists and Writers Foundation, established by Gülen in the mid-1990s as a pro-dialogue and coexistence organisation, had its offices raided by Turkish police in late December 2014. In March 2016 the AKP placed the Zaman newspaper group under new management.

Precarious Futures

At the heart of the battle over social and political trust is the question of the future of Turkish Islam. Although it is evident that the opposition is all but mollified, Turkey's future direction is less apparent. The mainstay of any industrial society is its economy, but there are worries about a credit bubble that may burst, causing a hard landing that would be difficult to overcome. Both Hizmet and the AKP have benefited from the liberalisation of the economy. Arguably, one reading is that the conflict between these groups is a function of the competition for power, status and profit. Emphasis on the economy, however, is not restricted to the prominent civil society groups in the country. Instead, it reflects concerns affecting a wide range of the population, where social and economic divisions are widening, and where the processes of development and innovation have fixated on the few rather than the many. The collapse in relations between prominent actors centres on the motivation of industrial, entrepreneurial and business elites and organisations, which are civil and political, liberal and conservative. It is where profit supersedes piety. The lack of trust in the AKP rests upon the perception of its indefatigable pursuit of self-sustaining neo-liberal policy, and the charges of corruption and clientalism that remain unchecked.

The 'Kurdish issue' is another contentious debate in Turkish society. Hopes of resolving it have diminished to new levels in the current period, largely due to the Syrian conflict. In the international arena, local problems have bubbled up and become regional. Turkish foreign policy concerning Syria remains blurred, even though the conflict has raged on since 2011, spilling over the border on numerous occasions. In October 2014 the Salafi–Takfiri group Islamic State launched a siege on the Syrian Kurdish town of Kobanî. This move drew the international community into the war, as Kobanî is merely a few miles away from the Turkish border. There were concerns that the conflict would embroil Turkey in a quagmire, as there are many Kurdish sympathisers in Turkey. In January 2015 Kurdish *peshmerga* fighters helped Kobanî to stave off a massacre. NATO-led forces unleashed missile sorties from the air while Iraqi and Syrian ground forces, supported by the American military establishment, joined the assault. Turkey, despite having agreed in parliament to take action, kept its tanks firmly at the border, avoiding the possibility of physically entering Syrian territory and thereby creating a scenario that would engulf the nation. This action disaffected Kurdish voters in Turkey, who had previously been loyal to the AKP. They showed their displeasure by voting in eighty parliamentarians for the HDP, a pro-Kurdish party in the June 2015 elections, exceeding the 10 per cent threshold needed to enter parliament. This was, arguably, why the AKP was unable to form a majority government at the time (the other opposition parties, CHP and the MHP, did not experience any significant shifts in their votes). In June 2015 Islamic State fighters returned to Kobanî in an attempt to take the town once again.

Kurdish populations inside Turkey were outraged that the Turkish government failed to follow through on its stated actions regarding Kobanî. There were major protests in the majority Kurdish city of Diyarbakır in late 2014, where police action produced many civilian casualties. At the same time, street violence broke out between pro-Kurdish, German-born Kurds with Turkish citizenship, and pro-Islamic State German-born Turks. The latter were ultra-secularist and uber-nationalist in character, but they aligned themselves with pro-jihadist groups in direct opposition to the Kurds. Kurdish communities, across the world and in Turkey were further enraged, when, at the time of the attack on Kobanî, Turkish armed forces air-bombed sites in Hakkâri, in the south-east corner of Turkey, for alleged crimes against the Turkish military. The lack of any obvious direction on Syria and Turkey's ambivalence abroad led to unrest and then the collapse of the Kurdish peace process at home.

The issue of trust has become critical in Turkey today, and relates to an array of subjects. Anxieties surface about the economic system, namely the problems of neo-liberalism. Questions materialise over the silencing of critical voices, in politics and at all levels of society. The authoritarianism of the AKP has led to attempts to rewrite Turkish history, projecting an Islamist past in the hope of a prosperous economic future. There is also the Kurdish peace process, and the complex disquiet about the relationship Turkey has with its neighbours to the east. Social capital relies on reciprocity and trust between individuals and communities, but political trust centres largely on political performance and governance. As social divisions between communities widen because of economic, cultural, religious and political issues, the political elite have been transforming society in their own image. The AKP has been rewriting history, reshaping the economy, reordering the public sphere and revising the position of women, including the matter of the headscarf. The headscarf was prohibited for seventy-three years until the AKP ruled it permissible for Muslim women to wear it in public institutions, such as schools, universities and hospitals in late 2014 (see Chapter 7). Meanwhile, the free market has become sovereign.

As the fourth term of AKP rule begins, Turkey now epitomises a conservative approach to the role of religion in the public sphere, and religion in private life. Given how Turkey has developed over the last hundred years or so, from an empire into a secular republic, the approach used to deliver this new political project is authoritarian and inevitably patriarchal. The 'cult of the father figure' in Turkish society, cemented during various stages of Kemalism, has predominated under Erdoğan. Moreover, given the huge discrepancies between the educated elite in the major urban centres and the wider Anatolian population, challenges to the state remain limited in their degree of intensity or impact. Consequently, Turkey typifies a majoritarianism that is self-selecting and self-reproducing through the political process. This authoritarian conservative majoritarian nationalism nexus seems unbreakable in Turkey.

Although a spotlight on religion, society, politics and economy is essential for any analysis of progress in a society, trust is a concern that also involves free speech. Turkey has the unenviable reputation of being among the countries most likely to jail journalists. Allegations against reporters and writers rest on the view that they are working against the interests of the state, and matters of concern here date back many years. In early 2016 numerous Turkish academics signed the 'Academics for Peace' petition to raise awareness of the human rights abuses that have arisen in the clashes between the Turkish state and the PKK in the south-east of Turkey. Many of the academics faced arrest and jail for signing the petition. It is interesting to note that most of those incarcerated happen to be Kurdish in origin. In general, journalists, bloggers and activists in Turkey live in constant worry about the risk of imprisonment because of their writing on all aspects of Turkish society, especially the political process.

Reassessing Turkish Politics

Analysing social capital and political trust in Turkey reveals a thought-provoking set of observations relevant in the understanding of religious, cultural and economic interdependencies in everyday life. The data offers a useful overarching perspective on the situation in Turkey, but there are also further critical observations and descriptions to advance the appreciation of the situation on the ground (see Chapters 4 and 5). Yet, there is a need to move beyond a focus on the Gezi Park events and families with members in the PKK. There remains a lack of understanding of specific localised experiences. The ways in which they affect social capital, social engagement and political trust also remain less well comprehended. Given the extensive research and policy-maker attention given to Turkey, there is room for further detail on these debates.

Social and political transformations are vigorously altering Turkey. The country acts as the channel between east and west in terms of tradition, modernity, religion, secularism, cosmopolitanism and globalisation. It is also necessary to appreciate how political, intellectual and media elites, who operate within the nation state, shape, direct and comment on the democratisation process in general. The ESS analysis suggested that specific social outcomes are in the expected direction. Minorities with high forms of bonding social capital demonstrate lower levels of political trust, combined with lower levels of social participation. Majority Muslim Turkishness is associated with greater trust in domestic politics and institutions (parliament, police, legal system, political parties and politicians). Placed on the right of the left–right political divide is associated with greater overall trust in domestic politics and institutions. Anti-Europeanism among nationalists compared with Islamists implied that notions of national identity superseded internal conflicts between Islamism and secularism. With past limitations on Islamism, specifically linked to military influence on Turkish politics, the triangular relationship between Islamism, secularism and the machinations of the centre–periphery quandary clearly still affects Turkish politics (Hürsoy 2012; Kuru and Stepan 2012). Questions on the authoritarian conservatism in Turkey, and the social fissures, persist. Questions raised by adjustment to the dominant hegemonic narrative on Islam and nationalism continue.

Turkey has experienced many changes to its economy and society in the last two decades, but it generally has weak social capital compared with Nordic and Western European countries (Adam 2008). In countries with high levels of social capital and political trust, where both are features of social cohesion, such as in the US and the UK, the most imperative threat to cohesion comes not from ethnic diversity, but from the challenges of social mobility and meritocracy, which have traditionally characterised the successes of liberal societies (Green et al. 2011). Research indicates that societies regarded as fair experience greater levels of social trust (Freitag and Bühlmann 2009). A noteworthy departure is that a simple Islamism vs secularism dichotomy is no longer sufficient to understand recent Turkish politics and society. Rather, it is a move towards conservatism, underpinned by economic expansionism and globalisation, with the existing political elite arguably more politically Islamist than many of the civil–Islamist organisations popular among the urban and rural poor and the middle classes. Historically, the centre-periphery dualism carried much weight, particularly at the end of the Ottoman Empire, when an elitist and centralist authority viewed the periphery as a backward marginal entity, marginalised and repeatedly excluded so that the centre could maintain a degree of power and control. The centre held on to its authority through its ideas of 'Turkishness' in the light of a secular republic model (see Chapter 2) (Demiralp 2012).

The AKP promotes Islam among individuals and in society, taking forward nationalism to a new level of conservatism (Somer 2012). Enduring tensions over how the AKP embraces the needs of the population of Turkey still persist. Turkey's political journey has taken a path from territorial–civic, to religio-ethnic, to reach an Islamo-conservative dominant ideology. The latter has created ongoing tensions between the Kemalist–secularists and the Turkish Islamists, where the position of religion between nationalism and Islam remains the dividing line between these two camps.

7

Conclusions

Since the AKP came to power in 2002, Turkey has experienced unprecedented developments. However, it remains a nation much mired in controversy, ambiguity and unease about its identity and its place in the world.
Though Turkey is a vast country exhibiting considerable diversity in various
forms of political, religious, cultural and ethnic tribalism, it is the present-day
battle over religion and politics that defines the immediate outlook for the
nation's future. Crucially, this clash also affects the nature of the relationship between Islam, democracy and ethnic relations. The economic model
underpinning the success of Turkey has come under the microscope. There
are significant concerns over the sustainability of the economy, where easy
access to cheap credit has helped drive its success. Furthermore, while there
is considerable attention paid to protagonists such as Erdoğan and Gülen,
the place of Muslim women in Turkey is also important, both now and in
the future. Turkish society seems fixated on the headscarf issue, but gives far
less thought as to how Turkish Muslim women are profoundly changing the
fabric of society in ways unimaginable.

The boundary between 'secularism' and 'Islamism' has certain limitations in the Turkish setting, hence the need to problematise both terms. The
onus of authority is in the hands of urban elites who dominate the periphery.
Before the founding of the Turkish Republic, the Ottoman Empire was a
formidable centre of the Islamic world. Earlier still, before the Muslims,
Istanbul, as Constantinople, was at the centre of the Eastern Roman Empire.
Furthermore, the land of Turkey was a critical part of the ancient civilisations of the Hittites, Greeks, Persians, Romans and Seljuks. While all these
great histories help to form an appreciation of an immense country today,
Turkey still has its challenges. The twentieth century was full of idiosyncratic

developments that saw Turkey shift from an Islamic empire to a secular republic, from a state fraught with military coups to end up as a globalising democratic neo-liberal society riven with ideological and political discord. In the twenty-first century, many in the Muslim world in particular consider Turkey a 'success story' still unfolding. Empires undoubtedly rise and fall, but the important question is, to what extent Turkey has fully awakened from its dogmatic past? On the other hand, does the future hold greater challenges at various levels? Accordingly, in determining a conclusion to the various analyses in this book, it is crucial to look at lessons from history. In the aftermath of Turkey's twenty-first-century revolution of sorts, only two major players remained most powerful, and both were competing for absolute power, status, authority and popularity – the AKP and Hizmet. Over the last three decades, Turkey has emerged as a leading power in the region. Economically it grew strongly, achieving an average of 5 per cent year-on-year GDP growth rate over the first decade of the twenty-first century. Part of this development has seen the re-emergence of Islam in the public sphere, typified by the role of Islam in the formation and rhetoric of the AKP. Islam also emerged out of the domestic sphere and into public life. Since a legal ruling in 2014 Muslim women who wear the headscarf can now legitimately work in public institutions without fear of persecution. In addition, an Islamic bourgeoisie has gained extensive political power, cultivated out of the commercial, industrial and trading successes of small and medium-sized businesses in Anatolia and in Istanbul.

In Turkey, pious, conservative and authoritarian people view Islam as a vehicle for economic gain and political purchase. The success of Turkey is characterised by material advantage, but an Islamist reconfiguration also transpires. Moulded by a revitalisation of Sufi Hanafi Islamic values and norms, and underpinned by an emphasis on humanistic goals and aspirations that bond communities, it engages civil society groups and emphasises justice, tolerance and dialogue. As the AKP rose to power much of its early success is attributable to how Hizmet galvanised an otherwise protracted and polarised body of Muslims from below. Though there is extensive disagreement about how to explain or understand Hizmet, the organisation inspired by Fethullah Gülen is variously described as a social movement, a Sufi *tariqah*, an ideological undertaking or civil society activism. In fact, it is all four. Until 2010 there was a steady and stable relationship between these two principal power holders, one political, the other religious, but both inexorably linked. In spite of this, the relationship became troubled after a series of events triggered a wave of discontent with the senior ranks of the AKP. In December 2013 corruption allegations broadcast on YouTube and Twitter implicated Recep Tayyip Erdoğan's immediate family. Hizmet was blamed for this apparent attempt to dissuade AKP voters in the run-up to the local elections and the presidential elections in 2014. This event publically severed all relations between the AKP and Hizmet. Hizmet responded by instigating a direct condemnation of Erdoğan's inner circle, a move that many in Turkey regarded as a step too far. Hizmet allegedly tried to challenge the country's political destiny. Meanwhile, Hizmet argues that it operates outside of the political process, despite the many allegations against the organisation. Given the intense authoritarian responses to the Gezi Park protests and the particular personality of Erdoğan, it was clear who was going to get his way.

Profit in Piety

Hizmet arguably reshaped the relationship between being 'overly political' and 'passively political' in the Turkish political context. Still, there is a need for better understanding of how the Islamic values promulgated by Hizmet are 'mild, moderate, liberal or peaceful', and whether there is an effective relationship between postmodernity and Islam (Hendrick 2013: 8). Until recently Hizmet sought an opportunity to remodel the future direction of Turkish Islam. The free market, nevertheless, frames Hizmet activities, as they too are a product of globalisation rather than a fundamental reaction to it. This process is the marketisation of Muslim politics in Turkey. For the most part Islam exists outside of politics in Turkey, but has recently resurfaced, albeit from a range of different perspectives. Effective democratic participation has only emerged in the last few years, namely through the AKP, but Hizmet has also worked to achieve this end through use of its well-established community-grounded identity networks. Because of these polarised perspectives, one as political and the other as civic, it is possible to appreciate the conflict that emerges through their interactions, as both groups found themselves competing for the same territory in the pursuit of overall dominance.

For the AKP, the traditional notion of political Islam is 'rationalised' based on market forces that result in a type of 'market Islam'. Processes of rationalisation create opportunities for those in positions of power in the economy and in politics, but also for civil society organisations, namely Hizmet. Hizmet schools became highly desirable global commodities, successfully exported across sub-Saharan Africa and increasingly into Central Asia and South Asia. In these locations schools and universities are also established. The domestic media in Turkey, whether print news or television broadcasting, has also become a site for a competitive market Islam. This market economy system has successfully advanced the political opportunities for the AKP, and until recent events, Hizmet explicitly viewed its own position as being outside of the political process. The organisation argued that its aspirations were strictly at a community level. Nevertheless, many within Hizmet, which gained significant influence in Turkey and abroad, argued that the success of the AKP was precisely because of them. Furthermore, in co-opting intellectuals who supported a political view of Hizmet and emphasised its impact on the success of the AKP, a Muslim entrepreneurial class formed, benefiting both Turkey and Hizmet. 'These contradictions suggest that although non-political in name, the GM [Hizmet] had a dramatic political impact in practice' (ibid. 239).

Hizmet created its brand of Turkish Islam based on excellence, quality and specialisation, which invariably came at a price in an open, competitive and relatively free market economy. Due to its efforts, Hizmet generated political implications for the AKP because of its determination to substantiate its own Islamic product. Hizmet 'does not seek to generate a new civil society; it merely seeks to reform Turkey's current civil society' (ibid. 241, original emphasis). As Hizmet advanced its efforts to mingle different aspects of its activity through this market economic formula, promoted within Turkey, the organisation underemphasised its influence to indicate that it was firmly outside of politics. This is neither the reality nor the perception, but it creates consternation among those sectors of Turkish liberal society that see Hizmet as guarded or certainly lacking transparency. Since the events that caused the breakdown of relations between the AKP and Hizmet, some have argued that Hizmet's political ambitions were finally exposed. The AKP emphasised the surreptitious attributes of the 'parallel state', painting Hizmet as

Turkey's most sinister threat. The charisma, cultural and spiritual influences of Fethullah Gülen, who is at the pinnacle of this movement, carries this spirituality forward in earnest. As the inspirational head of Hizmet, Gülen challenged the negative consequences of secularism and individualism that are seemingly plaguing European and Western societies today (Yavuz 2013). There is a suggestion of godlessness, which has affected societies in negative ways. Turkey too is experiencing the negative consequences of westernisation as it comes to terms with modernisation, industrialisation, urbanisation and globalisation. A loss of spirituality has also affected cohesion in society, especially where the secularisation thesis has failed to produce the outcomes promised.

From within this rupture, Hizmet emerged as a central bridge between enlightenment of an Islamic nature and secularism of a political and economic character. In the last two decades or so various aspects of Turkish society have shown confidence in the importance of Islam in people's daily lives, in wider society and within the home, '[i]n this Islamically inflected milieu, the citizens of Turkey are becoming more enlightened and more religious at the same time' (ibid. 244). Hizmet legitimised an opportunity to fashion a kind of Islam that can hold its own in a new global age. The Islamic teachings of Hizmet have met the challenges of modernity, which is to be plural and open, moving ahead from traditional–literal interpretations that have clouded the experiences of other Muslim countries. 'For Gülen, Islamic revival and Turkish secularism are inherently intertwined with each other; one could not have existed without the other' (ibid. 245). Hence, Hizmet has filled a vacuum left by secular Kemalism. Nevertheless, while it is essential to explore the character of religion in modern societies, the function of religion also strays into the political arena. The teachings of Gülen have challenged the power of elites to divide society and to fragment social structure. For Gülen, these elites are self-serving and self-interested, myopic and authoritarian. For Hizmet, the solutions are through education, economic development and by fostering dialogue. This is, arguably, one reason why the AKP considers the organisation a threat to its own authority. The neo-liberalism of the AKP advocates an economic capitalism well attuned to Western principles of individualism and consumerism, partly directed at a local and global 'halal market'. The latter is presently realised in the promotion of economic transactions with Gulf state economies, including increasing tourism from the Arab world. Some of this now dominates aspects of central Istanbul and other holiday destinations as 'halal tourism', which is becoming a growing sector of the Turkish economy.

One standpoint suggests that Hizmet is a product of the marketisation of Islam in Turkey, while another argues that it is a third space between modernity and Islam. Adopting and adapting principles of modernity distinguish Hizmet, benefiting a movement steeped in spiritual and community consciousness. The movement also seeks to build a better Turkey and create a beneficial Islam for others to appreciate and reconcile, for Muslims and for non-Muslims alike. Charisma and the personality cult are uniquely Turkish cultural features, which have helped to sustain Gülen in his position. As a result, Gülen and his efforts have acquired Turkish and global appreciation. One perspective on Hizmet is the rational analysis of a rationalising entity, while the other is a deeply layered appreciation of the impact of the individual and his mission. In spite of this, there is distinct unease about the future of the organisation, given the history of religious movements in Turkey during the early republican period. The magnitude of Hizmet suggests variations in styles, approaches and ideologies, all of which exist under a single homogenised notion. For these reasons, it is overly simplistic to take a generalised perspective on Hizmet. Moreover, the success of the organisation has led to many criticisms from different parts of Turkish society, including minority groups, such as the Alevis and the Kurds, as well as wider populations of Islamists and secularists. Then again, all of these groups present their criticisms because of challenges to their practices, although there is no direct opposition from Hizmet. Hizmet attempts to develop spirituality and community instead of individuality and competition. It creates the conditions for power and status for itself. Unquestionably, there is genuine philosophical, ideological and religious thinking that Hizmet strives to maintain, while enhancing positive engagement with members of diverse religious and ethnic communities.

Headscarves Revisited

In Western Europe, the debate over Muslim women who wear headscarves is of great interest to social thinkers and policy-makers. Particularly in the post-9/11 climate, the forces of Orientalism, xenophobia, Islamophobia and exoticisation have come to the fore and have concentrated around this issue. The 'Muslim woman' question has become prominent in the dominant political discourse and the wider public imagination (Fernandez 2009). The headscarf, veil, burqa, chador, hijab, jilbab and other such references have all become part of the iconography of fear (Saktanber 2006). An analysis of the Islamic headscarf for women would not be complete without under-standing the debate in Turkey, as well as some of the implications raised for the reproduction of gender as a social discourse. Without doubt the headscarf has become one of the fundamental fault lines between secularists and Islamists. This is due to gradual opening up of the position of Islam in the public sphere, as well as the part it plays in the political and ideological project of the AKP (Demiralp 2012). Although there has been a shift away from considering the headscarf as piety in private, there is the question of freedom of religious expression implicitly tied up by its function (Saktanber and Çorbaciolu 2008). It is not only an issue over what Muslim women in Turkey should or should not wear, but also an enduring cultural question that routinely emerges on the political landscape. In many ways, the discussion reflects ongoing struggles between the old secular Kemalism and the new conservative Islamism.

In spite of the changing position of the AKP on Islam in the public sphere, it was not until 2014 that Muslim women could wear the headscarf in public institutions. There has now been a relaxing of policies in public institutions, with female civil servants, schoolteachers and university lecturers, for example, now permitted to wear the headscarf. Yet, they cannot always obtain employment in sectors held as the preserve of the secularists, such as banking, corporate management or television. Fundamental tensions endure between the spheres of dominant secular society and the localised Islamic piety of conservative Muslim communities. There are continuities to an Islamic phi-losophy and discourse, but given the historical nature of the formation of the Turkish Republic, there are also cultural barriers to change. In some ways Muslim women no longer dictate the issue. It exists on a much wider political platform concerning all sections of society (Çakır 2007). Ironically, wrestling with the emancipation of Turkish Muslim women, vis-à-vis the headscarf in public institutions, may enforce patriarchy in wider society, specifically against women who wear headscarves. There is a risk that widening participation for headscarf-wearing Muslim women in educational settings could produce a generation of unemployable young women discriminated against in the labour market, and in wider secular society. For many conservative political actors, modernisation provides religious freedoms, but for secularists the headscarf is regressive and anti-modernisation, ultimately undesirable for postmodern Turkish society. It opens up a conundrum that suggests that Europeanisation could be associated with Islamisation in Turkey (Onar and Müftüler-Baç 2011). This paradox exacerbates the situation because it is a 'challenge to the secular image of women and, thus, a question for the secular identity of the society' (Seckinelgin 2006: 765). In banning the headscarf in public institutions, Turkish Muslim women had to choose between their piety and their roles in the public sphere. Women were at the centre of this Turkish modernisation project, objectified, instrumentalised and marginalised in the process. Few were in a better position to articulate the nature of the debate than Merve Safa Kavakçı. A politician turned academic, she catapulted Turkey's headscarf debate to an international level. Newly elected to the Turkish parliament in 1999, she chose to wear the headscarf during her swearing in. She encountered jeering on an unprecedented scale, which eventually forced her to leave the parliament building. She later had her citizenship revoked, and was effectively exiled from the country of her birth (Kavakçı 2010).

At the heart of this rhetoric is a distinct type of Orientalism that subjugates Turkish Muslim women from within, despite Turkey being one of the first countries in the Middle East to recognise women in the political process. Exacerbated by postcolonialism, Turkey sought to reify westernised systems of modernity, cosmopolitanism and internationalisation. It is one of many contradictions conflating concepts of citizenship and national culture with political allegiance. All have ramifications for the centre-periphery divide, along with associated uneven regional economic and social development that lingers to this day. For Kemalists, veiled women belonged to a lesser developed past, which was contradictory to the secular republican model of the present. The challenges remain acute today, as the nation views Islam in the public sphere in ever more acceptable terms, which reflect the dominant political hegemony of the ruling party, as well as the bottom-up social mobility of pious Muslims, who have gained significantly in the last three decades. Resistance to the restrictions imposed on veiled Muslim women in Turkey began in the early 1980s, and it appears this will continue beyond the recent legal ruling. As such, Muslim women in Turkey are at the forefront of social change. Moreover, the wider international community, including the modernisation and Europeanisation dynamic, remains important when considering the freedoms of women in Turkish society. In ideas of spatiality, geography and identity politics, which affect different aspects of Turkey, for example, in the urban–cosmopolitan spaces of Istanbul, Turkish Muslim women are leading from the front. These spaces contain the secularised places of existing established elites and newly socially aspirant groups, which then become sites that intersect 'race, class, ethnicity, and sexuality' (Gkarksel 2012: 15). In the smaller cities and towns of Anatolia, there are different articulations of Islamism regarding Muslim women. Here a traditional reality persists, where patriarchal norms and cultural values intersect with custom and tradition, as much as with Islamic thinking and practice. The 2015 constitutional court ruling to relax marriage laws by removing the need for a civil registration of marriages for couples married by Islamic law will lead to exploitation and vulnerability for young Muslim women. It will reinforce patriarchy in rural areas, potentially placing Muslim women found in these areas at a further disadvantage in the battle for recognition and acceptance in wider Turkish society.

In Istanbul middle-class Islamist and secularist women share the same spaces, follow similar fashions and articulate equivalent philosophies of globalisation and consumerism that, at various levels, affect an entire nation (Turam 2015). Such a mode of being potentially liberates Turkish Muslim women from the confined categories of Islamist or secularist. As a result, it is an opportunity for radically revising understandings of the position of women in Islam in general and in Turkey in particular. It does so despite the limitations that may emerge because of patriarchy and the reinforcement of traditional cultural norms and values concerning Muslim women in society, paradoxically fortified by the agenda of the dominant political hegemon (Arat 2010). A wider political and cultural deadlock still lingers, but on the ground and in the streets of Istanbul young Muslim women are pushing ahead with new hybridised religio-cultural identities that liberate them from the existing paradigms of Islamism or secularism in the Turkish context (Genel and Karaosmanolu 2006). It is necessary to understand the experience of Muslim women in Turkey, not on their formation through national identity politics but as one grounded in the lived experience. Turkish Muslim women need to be unshackled from the constructed rationalisation of the permanent hegemony of male patriarchy, as well as the homogenisation of Islam (Gole 1996).

Erdoğan's Feats

There are many factors important in understanding potential scenarios for the future of Turkey, all of which are susceptible to wide fluctuations in intensity and impact. For one, an economic bubble risks overheating due to the credit boom, which has driven individual consumption patterns and extensive borrowing by the state. Simultaneously, an oligarchic power structure reproduces itself at the uppermost levels of the AKP hierarchy. However, in understanding the class structure of Turkey a range of issues are distinct.

Authoritarianism began with the Ottomans. It ran through Kemalism and now persists in postmodern Turkey. The AKP project is a type of revolution, where the revolutionaries eventually turned into totalitarians. Furthermore, as history shows, these innovators turn on themselves, battling it out for supremacy and vying for absolute power. Their motivations are ideological but also highly competitive, based on desire and the hunger for power. The new AKP state reflects such political and cultural histories found elsewhere, such that Erdoğan reproduces equivalent models of authoritarianism found during the twentieth century. At the same time Kurdish nationalism has grown stronger, not weaker. It is arguably a function of globalisation, where the search for identities is stronger in the light of competing interests and different opportunities for their mobilisation. In the past this model was under the rubric of modernisation. Today it is in the vein of Islamisation, but remains strictly an instrumentalist philosophy. More integrated Kurds in society are often those who are more loyal to the AKP project, but leftist Kurds continue to feel marginalised. Both 2015 elections showed how the Kurds could fare on their own.

Erdoğan and the AKP have usefully managed the idea of the intersection of Islam and capitalism, but inherent contradictions remain. Islam implies community, but capitalism infers individuality, competitiveness and self-gain. From an Islamic perspective, capitalism is unclean (*najas*). As such, Islam is merely the canvas for the reality of neo-liberalism that directly supports elite interests. It is an instrument of the hegemonic discourse of the AKP. Nationalism remains resilient in Turkey, where there is an allusion to the past and future. It is the continuation of Kemalism, which was about modernisation from the centre and the authority of those in power to rule in the interests of the people expected to believe what they are told. For Kemalism, modernisation became the religion of the progressives. Kemalism is a relic of history but the symbolisms of authority and leadership are the chain of power, directed from the centre towards the periphery. To believe in Erdoğan is to believe in Atatürk, which is to believe in the Ottoman sultans. Erdoğan is thus both neo-Ottoman and neo-Kemalist. Ultimately, the understanding of a radical new society is essentially normalisation in the use of symbols. In relation to women, their bodies represent a perspective on culture, nation and even religion. Still, while the AKP allow women to wear the headscarf in the public sphere, there are headscarf-wearing Muslim women who want more of the political domain, access to and influence in the media, and greater control in all aspects of society.

The Alevis are a noteworthy case study in identity politics because they represent a distinctiveness shaped by geographical concentration, surrounded by Sunni Muslim countries on all sides and compounded by the Turkish nationalist project. There was no sense of politicised Alevism until the end of the Ottoman period. It is a group identity defined by persecution and subjugation, which lingers to this day. In the 1960s and 1970s it was practically a case of civil war, and the burning of Alevi intellectuals in 1993 in Sivas is merely a recent example. Alevism is partly about regional autonomy, but generally about the need to escape persecution by the state and to avoid the misrecognition experienced by other groups (for example, the Armenians, who could not escape a genocide and ongoing vilification). At present the AKP still chooses not to fully recognise Alevi places of worship, and there is yet no official acceptance of the Armenian genocide. As for the Roma, both their memory and geography gradually erodes from Turkish society. The marginalising of Alevis, Roma, Kurds, Greeks and Jews reflects the normalisation of ethno-national Turkey, first through modernisation and then through Islamisation. In such instances a case of AKP ethnic majoritarianism and religious nationalism defines the current period.

In the snap general elections of November 2015 the AKP returned to majority government with nearly 50 per cent of the national vote. In the months leading to this election, campaigning concentrated on the idea of the enemies within *and* without. The conflict between the Turkish state and the Kurdish south-east has brought new lows for Turkey. Meanwhile, pressures on the economy because of a flailing Eurozone and the aftermath of Arab Spring create further tensions. In spite of these challenges, Erdoğan reached out to the population of Turkey, once again in the hope of saving it from its enemies. The AKP increased its vote by luring voters who had stayed away from the polling booths in June. It also gained disaffected voters normally found on the political right. The HDP lost one million or so votes largely because some Kurds returned to the AKP while the other Kurdish voters stayed away due to the re-emergence of the conflict. The strategy worked, and the election and the country were back in Erdoğan's hands. Nevertheless, the exercise was not without cost or implication. The East–West divide that Turkey has balanced since the turn of the twenty-first century has now moved from a broad spectrum of inclusive philosophies to a narrowly defined but precariously poised axis. The identity crisis carried over from the twentieth century lingers at an intense level, creating a passion over politics rarely witnessed elsewhere in the world. Furthermore, many have argued that the ATP victory in November 2015 was not a win for democracy. Fears and apprehensions of the authoritarianism of the president loom large. No longer is there talk of freedom or individual expression. A national political project still in a state of evolution is about to be shaken by its roots if President Erdoğan finds a way to reform the constitution. His 'ambitions to raise a religious generation' may now come true. In the pursuit of absolute power, disorder is back in Turkey, whether in relation to the 'Kurdish issue', the Syrian refugee crisis or because of terrorism at the hands of foreign or domestic actors. Rising levels of intolerance in a nation that is multi-ethnic and multireligious will not subside under an aggressive ethnic nationalism. More than mere bluster and bravado will deliver the solutions that bring order from this chaos.

One of the most testing challenges facing Erdoğan is the issue of Islamic

State. The so-called rebels are the militarised Sunni groups supported and funded by the US and Saudi Arabia through Turkey. Russia is on the side of Assad, as it has been since the beginning of the conflict. Turkey is bombing the Kurds in Syria (the PYD) because they are close to the Turkish border and have powerful alliances with the PKK. At the same time, Turkey is attacking Kurds in the PKK in the south-east of Turkey. Turkey is in a complicated position. The year 2016 will be the worst year for the displacement of Syrians into Turkey and through it into the EU. Senior figures in the EU are quite aware of this fact and this is why they are playing politics with the idea of closing borders, trying to keep the refugees in Turkey, or even working towards a political solution in Syria itself. In spite of the realisation that Islamic State is a real threat inside the borders of Turkey, the security and intelligence apparatus is weak and susceptible, as proven by attacks on civilians in Istanbul in January 2016 and on military personnel in Ankara a month later. An information management war on the part of the AKP, from detaining journalists and academics, shutting down media and broadcast outlets to regulating the Internet may appease part of the population, but it will not solve the long-term problems. The violence that has ensued since the bombings in Suruç in July 2015 has made the last few months of 2015 and the first month of 2016 some of the bloodiest in Turkish history. Erdoğan is on the brink of absolute power but Turkey is floundering.

Turkey on the Global Stage

The emergence of Islamic State has thrust Turkey onto the global stage for very different reasons. It brings Turkey's foreign policy on Syria and the wider Middle East into sharp focus. Critics argue that Turkey could have made greater inroads in restricting its borders, making it more difficult for foreign fighters to enter Syria as well as for Islamic State actors using Turkey as a route into Europe. A strategic ally of NATO, Turkey's position in the region is sensitive and critical. Questions asked about the precise nature of the relationship between Turkey and Islamic State reveals inconsistencies and ambiguities. Russia and the US are right at the heart of matters, but there are also regional players that have their own divisions going back many centuries and who are deeply politicised, that is, in the form of Saudi Arabia and Iran, the two strongholds of Sunni and Shia Islam. Russia is bombing the Free

Syrian Army. The US and its allies are bombing Islamic State, and supporting the Kurds. The Turks bombard the Kurds in Syria. Then again, the Kurds are doing most on the ground to fight against Islamic State. Meanwhile, Islamic State is exultant at the thought of civilian casualties swelling the ranks of their numbers. As the troubles continue in this sensitive area, Turkey faces resistance by the Kurds inside its own borders, while some Kurds join Islamic State as a response to Turkey's war on the south-east. More generally, in Turkey there is a sympathetic attitude towards Islamic State across the conservative and pious Muslim populations of Anatolia.

As early as 2011 Turkey's support for the Free Syrian Army was a means of actively trying to oust Syrian president Bashar Assad. Weapons from Turkey flowed freely into Syria as well as training and other logistical support. With this backing, in 2014 Islamic State established itself as an offspring of al-Nusra and al-Qaeda. In 2009 Erdoğan's status inside Turkey and across the Middle East rose dramatically when he spoke out publicly against Israel's president, Shimon Peres, in relation to the atrocities in Gaza. Lionised and eulogised, Erdoğan's popularity soared and his power base in Turkey strengthened. However, Assad's hesitance to bring in reform at Erdoğan's request met with agitation. Turkey's relations with Russia have been troubled for more than a century and a half. With Putin's Russia directly involved in supporting Assad, it creates further disquiet. When Turkey shot down a Russian jet flying over Turkish airspace in late November 2015, it infuriated Putin, dramatically affecting political and commercial relations between the two nations. Then again, Turkey's role within NATO remains crucial to the US. Historically, Turkey's defeats have come not from the West but from the East, in particular from what is now Iran and Syria. Erdoğan desires to uphold a vision of Turkey that projects a glorious Ottoman past and a brave new future, but growing challenges are outweighing his lifelong dream. Aspirations by leading members of the EU to keep Syrian refugees outside of the Eurozone, within the borders of Turkey if need be, focuses attention away from the immediate crises engulfing the nation.

The demand for Kurdish autonomy is causing Turkey to panic, similar to how it reacted to Armenian demands approximately 100 years ago. Rather than find ways to accommodate and integrate groups into a multi-ethnic society, rejection, discrimination and extermination has become the norm.

For Erdoğan, there is no 'Kurdish issue', only terrorism. Instead, the AKP prepares for a referendum on the new presidential system in mid-2016. If all goes to plan, Turkey could be heading for even greater levels of authoritarianism. It will create isolation and stigmatisation on the global stage, leading to severe implications for the country. Yet, this occurs in the context of years of solid efforts to build community relations, social trust and political participation. The considerable progress made during the 2000s, from heritage restoration projects to economic development in Anatolia and cultural awareness projects, has now become a distant memory. The war on the Kurds has descended into a form of ethnic gentrification and ethnic cleansing in all but name.

The Gezi Park events revealed deep chasms that lay just below the surface of society. The events raised widespread concerns over matters of citizenship, political participation and Islam in society. The implications for Turkey were that these events could have improved opportunities for democracy within an existing authoritarian, conservative, nationalist and majoritarian project deeply loyal to a sense of a local and global Turkishness. It has been a major event during AKP rule, but rather than reflecting a significant turning point in the politics of the country, the protests sealed the decline of the AKP, along with the dwindling profile of the secular–Kemalist opposition. Crucially, the Gezi Park events could have spurred the realisation of a civil society in Turkey that has benefited from globalisation, combined with progressive EU-driven reforms, which suggest a determined and democratic polity in Turkey. Many across the Muslim world regard Turkish Islam as an example of a synergistic model of religion, capitalism and democracy. However, in the West, Turkey is criticised as a NATO member with authoritarian, nationalist and fundamentalist tendencies, bordered by Iraq and Syria on one side, Greece and south-east Europe on the other, all experiencing their own acute challenges. The questions persist. Can Turkey balance political and civil Islam with modernisation, liberalisation and globalisation? What is the future of Turkish Islam? Turkey is undergoing a rapid social, cultural and political transformation that has yet to firmly cement itself in the popular imagination. This leads to tensions, ambiguities and ongoing contradictions and inconsistencies in the imagination of the national political project.

The weight of history remains powerful in the formation of modern Turkey, where the negotiations between neo-Kemalists and neo-Islamists are tense and fraught, as competing ideological narratives periodically rise to the surface. There is no doubt that young, savvy, digitally informed, internationalised and educated Turks will be at the forefront of inevitable transformation. Nevertheless, while efforts to resolve the Kurdish issue persist, the solutions remain uncertain. There are vast challenges to the articulation of the discourses of representation and participation in society led by an authoritarian conservatism. The doctrine is formidable due to its growing pious Muslim political base as well as the advantages for populations because of the neo-liberal economic project. Variations in the conservative temperament of Turkish Muslims will be of immense interest in Turkey going forward. These are where the next battles will transpire.

Civilisational Renewal

Theories of how civilisations rise and fall have existed for some time. One of the earliest was established in the fourteenth century. In many ways Ibn Khaldun is the bona fide founding father of sociological thinking. His work analysed the rise and fall of civilisations up to his time. Not only did Ibn Khaldun contribute to the study of tribal societies, but he also laid the foundations for development economics, population studies, social democracy and contemporary sociology. Ibn Khaldun's work is also the science of history, society and law. He produced a comprehensive study of society known as the *'Ilm al-'Imran*, or the 'science of culture and society'.

Many analysts and thinkers view Ibn Khaldun as an Islamic political historian, but this omits significant themes. Ibn Khaldun's meditations were an evolution of neo-Platonic rationalism (Dale 2006). Indeed, he devised a precise methodology for understanding the rise and fall of civilisations, applicable across all times and places in history. It is the most unique of his many significant contributions. Nevertheless, in spite of these considerations, Ibn Khaldun is somewhat misrepresented in sociology curricula, largely because they contain inherent Eurocentric perspectives (Alatas 2007), which predispose that modernity is the precursor to contemporary sociology, and that the onset of European modernity laid the foundations for contemporary sociological thought. Indigenous knowledge systems in parts of North Africa, and the Arab and wider Muslim world, have also yet to determine a collective consciousness around the contributions of Ibn Khaldun (Abdullahi and Salawu 2012).

For Ibn Khaldun, political administrations undergo cycles where they find themselves in periods of rise, growth and success, through to an eventual downfall, followed by their replacement by a new political establishment. Ibn Khaldun argued that the seeds of the downfall of societies are contained within their inherent structure, and through its various forms of 'Asabiyah (described as social cohesion built upon degrees of social capital, social trust, political trust or social engagement). In the final stage of the decline of a civilisation, regimes become authoritarian and dogmatic, where leaders surround themselves with and are increasingly out of touch with mass culture and political expectation. The 'group feeling' of 'Asabiyah eventually diminishes altogether, leading to resistance and renewal. While much of the analysis of Ibn Khaldun relates to political history of the Muslim world up until the fourteenth century (al-Azmeh 2003), his theory is still relevant today. The Gezi Park events are a case in point. The Khaldunian methodology helps to gain better understanding of whether the Gezi Park events reflect a wider concern on the breakdown of group feeling across Turkey. The issue began as local resistance to an environmentalist action project, against the backdrop of general anxiety around neo-liberalism and urbanisation, but quickly grew into a national outcry. Ultimately, vast segments of the country became involved in activities exhibiting solidarity against the policies of the AKP.

Did these events spark a distinguishable shift in the popularity of Turkey's ruling party? On the other hand, were they a localised incident blown out of proportion by opposition among domestic media and political actors, combined with wider international opinion? In many ways, the AKP behaved in a manner akin to its Kemalist predecessors. The Khaldunian perspective is interested in power and the qualities of leadership in the realisation of social cohesion, but Ibn Khaldun did not make direct reference to individual leaders. It is imperative to stress this given the emphasis on Erdoğan in the minds of the protesters, and in discussing how to use the concept of 'Asabiyah to understand the Gezi Park events (Rosen 2005). Elements of the Khaldunian theory suggest that the AKP has become complacent, self-centred and dismissive. Inebriated by the success of the Turkish model and how the rest of the world perceived it, rather than revolutionise, both Erdoğan and the AKP maintained a firm hold and continued to forge ahead, accumulating increasing power. It was a sign that the AKP had not only reached its peak but that decline had already set in.

Postscript: 'A Gift from God'

After completing this book in early 2016, I decided to leave Turkey and return to the UK, the country of my birth. Merely ten days after I left Istanbul, on the night of 15 July, an attempted coup rocked Turkey and left it in a state of trauma, which continues as I write this postscript over a month later. The events of 15 July constituted one putsch too far. In dissecting the event, commentators have focused more on Recep Tayyip Erdoğan and less on the situation of ordinary Turks caught up in the malaise. This is as exasperating for Turks as it is for researchers working on Turkey. Irrespective of how matters will unfold over time, witnessed on that night was the implosion of a state, a tumultuous event occurring after eighteen months of instability, terrorism and in-fighting across the country.

Since Erdoğan became prime minister in 2003, he has steered the country away from the dark days of the early 2000s, when there was a banking crisis and huge devaluation of the lira, a situation necessitating IMF intervention. Erdoğan has grown increasingly powerful since then, but he listens far less often to the people or to those in his party who show any sign of independence. Ultimately, in the light of the events of the coup, there is no containing the fury of Erdoğan. With half of the population firmly behind him, he can do no wrong. Tensions between groups continue to grow under intense domestic pressure and international scrutiny. During the last eighteen months, Istanbul, Ankara and a number of smaller towns and cities have suffered waves of terrorist attacks. Most Turks, whether secular, liberal, Kemalist, Islamist or neutral, are worried about their futures. In a region aflame, various proxy wars at the hands of international actors continue unabated but with unclear aspirations. What will happen next remains unclear.

The failed coup left a trail of destruction in its wake. As many as 300 people died and more than 2,000 people were injured. Even the Turkish parliament building was bombed for the first time in its history. After the coup attempt was over, the AKP arrested or apprehended over 85,000 teachers, civil servants, judges and military personnel. Over 3,000 military personnel were sacked and approximately 130 media outlets were taken over. There were also allegations of torture and rape. A state of emergency in Turkey has given the government more power than ever before to arrest with impunity, but while only 3,000 have thus far been charged, these wide-ranging detentions have served to dismantle the bureaucratic structures of the state, leading to accusations of a 'witch-hunt'. The rhetoric of 'national unity' is constructed by CHP, MHP and AKP based around the demonisation of Gulenists and the PKK. The aim is to legitimise authoritarian practices as well as the exclusion of HDP and other non-mainstream opposition parties. The AKP government remains dedicated to silencing all forms of opposition. These trends confirm patterns established since 2013, all of which reflect a further shift towards the introduction an executive presidency.

Erdoğan often reacts to national crises or uproar by asserting his control over the media. Paradoxically, on the night of the coup attempt, Erdoğan used FaceTime to reach a CNN Turk television presenter in order to broadcast an appeal to the nation. The impassioned call to the people of Turkey to face down the putschists on the streets gave Erdoğan the victory he craved. The people overcame the coup and saved the country. Erdoğan used the media to hold onto power when it had all but slipped through his fingers. Later on, he described the coup as 'a gift from God'. Arguably, Erdoğan is even more the fêted protagonist. In the eyes of his admirers, he is the only man capable of saving Turkey from its enemies, both inside and outside of the country. Overturning the coup, however, could well be a pyrrhic victory as the issue of trust is more critical than ever, even inside the AKP. It will take some time to re-establish it.

Predictably, Erdoğan's popularity has skyrocketed in the wake of the failed coup. Moreover, despite all the allegations of corruption and cronyism, particularly after the graft probes of December 2013, the AKP has managed to come together under the banner of unity. As the AKP becomes increasingly bold and aggressive, however, its leaders still do not know who was responsible for the attempted coup. Initial observations suggest that the coup was well organised but failed due to its inability to shut down the media, as well as due to a lack of coordination among the putschists after a junior officer dispatched an alleged leader of the coup, General Semih Terzi. Nevertheless, the AKP was quick to blame Fethullah Gülen, portrayed as the shadowy reclusive cleric at the head of a mysterious civil society organisation, Hizmet, with sinister ambitions to take over the state from the inside. Although emphasis is placed on the Gülenists, this attempted coup could not have been carried out without the support of various actors, including diverse military personnel.

In December 2013, as corruption allegations were levelled against Erdoğan, his family and senior ministers, the finger of blame was pointed firmly at Hizmet. The significant purge of Gülenists just hours after the failed coup highlights the existing AKP agenda in relation to Hizmet. The AKP has continued its focus on effectively eliminating every element of Hizmet representation in Turkish society, including newspapers, hospitals, charities, banks and even schools and universities. Dubbed part of the 'parallel state', a fifth column undermining the workings of government, Hizmet now faces systematic demonisation. This is a battle for the future of Turkish Islam. The two sides, both Turkish and Islamist, were once competing for the same spaces but are now unable to trust each other or work together as they once did for the better part of a decade. Historically, it was an arrangement from which both entities benefited substantially. After 2013, the stage was set for this poetic but incredibly messy divorce. The purge began then, and once the failed coup came to a dramatic halt, Erdoğan unleashed his most lethal rhetoric, and the Gülenists faced comprehensive elimination from Turkish society.

The coup represents a significant opportunity for change in Turkey; however, the future is unlikely to be too different from the recent past. A particular Turkish Islamist synthesis model involving the integration of Islamism and nationalism has led to insecurity, hopelessness and paranoia as the leadership does not know where to steer the country. At the same time, the oligarchic tendencies within the leadership structure of the AKP will be difficult to disrupt. Moreover, the failed coup should not be an opportunity to reintroduce draconian policies, such as the death penalty, nor should it lead to religious extremism. While democracy has won the day in Turkey, there remain profound questions about its nature and the implications for liberty and equality in contemporary Turkish society. The challenges that Turkey faces today are crucial for its own stability and for the future of its relations with the West.

Turkey is located on the most unstable strategic fault line in the world. It is, despite everything, of great significance to NATO. As relations between Turkey, the EU and the USA begin to splinter, 'Turkoscepticism' has reached an all-time high in the West, solidifying negative views on both sides. The Syrian humanitarian crisis has given the EU a reason to engage with Turkey, not for Turkey's interests but for the EU's. The EU is unlikely to permit Turkish accession, although cautiously professing that it is considering the matter. The 'Kurdish issue' is still the main concern domestically. There remain discernible uncertainties over the PKK, the economy and the need to minimise domestic conflict. These are indeed challenging and testing times. There is a dark and menacing underbelly in Turkish society, deeply layered with ethnic, cultural, ideological and religious tensions. While the focus is firmly on purging the Gülenists, the threat from Islamic State and its targeting of tourist sites in Turkey remains considerable. The PKK continues to attack Turkish police and various other state institutions. The purge of Gülen-linked institutions was going on before the coup but this event has given new legitimacy to the AKP to continue its aggressive approach, flustering the opposition parties so that they kowtow to dominant perspectives. The founding fathers of the AKP, Abdullah Gül and Bülent Arınç have all been moved aside. There are no longer any new ideas coming out of the party.

My defining memories of Turkey are of its people and its tremendous history and culture. Istanbul, where I spent nearly six years, is a city like no other. Those who marvel at its splendour and its rich, deep and multi-layered history, and bask in its sun and seas, know this very well. When I first moved to the city in 2010, it was the European Capital of Culture. The Turkish economy was thriving in all areas, delivering on the model that it had promised, one that firmly intersected capitalism, religion and democracy. It was a stable country in every respect, and still on the up. But all good things end, as they say. If this failed coup is the beginning of a regressive phase of social and political life in Turkey, it would be an unfitting blight on its people, for they are the heart and soul of the nation.

My instinct is to remind myself that the Turkish people are deeply resilient, passionate and loyal. They may be incredibly polarised politically, they may not talk to their neighbours if they disagree with them on diverse topics, but the one thing that unites every single Turk is loyalty to the flag. As cracks in the EU project deepen, as intolerance and bigotry rise in the West, and as the destruction of Syria plays out before our very eyes, Turkey will bounce back, perhaps even stronger and greater than before the current crises. The people of Turkey seek a brighter future. Whether they get it or not will depend more on internal political structure than on sheer determination alone. Perhaps it is wise to remember that it is the people who make history, not politicians.

TA
London
August 2016

Appendix
Notes on Methods

Analysis for Chapter 3

The European Social Survey (ESS) is an excellent source of data to address the questions relating to attitudes and perceptions regarding ethnic identity and tolerance towards others. The survey explores a wide range of attitudes, beliefs, and social, political and cultural behaviours of the diverse populations of Europe. The survey was first conducted in 2001 and completed in 2002. It has been conducted biennially ever since.

This analysis is based on rounds two and four (2004 and 2008). The sample in this study consists of 1,856 respondents in 2004 and 2,416 in 2008, providing a total sample of 4,272 Turkish respondents aged 15+. There is an interesting research perspective where this study reflects on the first two terms of the AKP, which came into power in 2002.

The data analysis in Chapter 3 attempts to explain tolerance towards different ethnic and racial groups, and the perception of discrimination based on language, racial, national and religious grounds among citizens of Turkey. In what follows, the dependent and independent variables included in the analysis are presented and described.

Dependent variables

Tolerance towards different ethnic and racial groups: this variable was derived using two questions on immigration. Both questions attempt to measure the willingness of Turkish citizens to accept new immigrants of either similar or different ethnic and racial backgrounds. Respondents who agreed to permit immigration of people of the same ethnic and racial origin as majority Turks and refused to allow immigrants from different ethnic or racial backgrounds were referred to as intolerant towards different ethnic and racial groups (21 per cent). Those who agreed to allowing both groups of immigrants to enter the country were referred to as tolerant (79 per cent).

Perceived discrimination: four different questions were used to construct this variable. Each examined whether respondents belonged to a group that is discriminated against on one of the following grounds: language, race, nationality or religion. Seven per cent of respondents answered yes to one of these four questions. Ninety-three per cent answered no to all of these questions. This variable was also used as an independent factor in modelling the first dependent variable (tolerance towards different ethnic and racial groups).

Independent variables

Age: recoded as follows: 15–19 (9 per cent), 20–24 (11 per cent), 25–29 (14 per cent), 30–39 (22 per cent), 40–54 (24 per cent) and 55+ (reference group, 20 per cent).

Economic activity: measured the employment status of respondents. This variable was coded into three categories: in employment (26 per cent); unemployed (8 per cent); and economically inactive (66 per cent).

Ethnic group: ethnic minority group (7 per cent) and majority group (93 per cent).

Gender: men (46 per cent) and women (54 per cent).

Language spoken at home: recoded into three categories: Turkish (87 per cent); Kurdish (11 per cent); and other (2 per cent).

Left–right placement: whether a respondent would be placed politically on the left or the right using a scale of zero (left) to ten (right), with a mean of 6.04.

Marital status: lives with a partner (67 per cent) and lives alone (33 per cent).

Qualifications: measured as the highest qualification obtained by the respondent and recoded into four categories: 'less than low secondary' (reference group, 58 per cent); 'low secondary' (16 per cent); 'high secondary' (19 per cent); and 'tertiary education' (7 per cent).

Region: respondents in Istanbul (19 per cent); and the other regions of Turkey (81 per cent).

Religiosity: this variable measured the level of religiosity reported by respondents on a scale of zero to ten, with zero indicating no religiosity at all and ten indicating the highest level of religiosity (the scale mean was 7.07).

Sufficiency of household income: four categories were used here: 'live very comfortably on present income' (8 per cent); 'coping on present income' (46 per cent); 'having some difficulties' (29 per cent); and 'very difficult to manage on present income' (reference group, 17 per cent).

Year of survey: 2004 (43 per cent) and 2008 (57 per cent).

A range of descriptive data is highlighted in Table A.1.

Table A.2 presents two logistic regression models. The first model predicts being part of a minority that faces at least one form of discrimination (that is, as a result of language, race, nationality or religious origin), and the second model predicts being tolerant towards people of different ethnic and racial backgrounds. Each model is presented in two phases: in the first phase, the gross impact of ethnicity is examined, and in the second other controls (explanatory factors) are added.

The coefficients presented in the table are odds ratios and can be read as follows: a coefficient greater than one indicates a positive influence of the specific factor, and a coefficient that is lower than one indicates a negative impact. For example, the first important factor is ethnicity, which appears to have a significant impact upon both dependent variables.

In order to examine the relationship between language, discrimination, religiosity and tolerance further, a series of log-linear models were developed in which these four variables were included. Log-linear models permit the analysis of three or more categorical (ordinal as well) variables without determining which one is the dependent or the independent variable. It allows the possibility of understanding how these variables relate to each other; that

Table A.1 *Descriptive statistics for a range of dependent and independent variables*

Variables		(%)
Tolerance	yes	79
	no	21
Perceived discrimination	yes	7
	no	93
Gender	men	46
	women	54
Ethnicity	minority	7
	majority	93
Language	Turkish	87
	Kurdish	11
	other	2
Lives with a partner	yes	67
	no	33
Sufficiency of household income	live very comfortably	8
	coping on present income	46
	having some difficulties	29
	very difficult to manage on present income	17
Age	15–19	9
	20–24	11
	25–29	14
	30–39	22
	40–54	24
	55+	20
Economic activity	in employment	26
	unemployed	8
	economically inactive	66
Qualifications	less than low secondary	58
	low secondary	16
	high secondary	19
	tertiary	7
Religiosity		7.07[a]
Left–right scale		6.04[a]
Region	Istanbul	19
	other	81
Year of survey	2004	43
	2008	57

Notes: [a] Scale mean

Source: European Social Survey 2004 and 2008

Table A.2 Logistic regression (odds ratios) for discrimination and tolerance in Turkish society

Variables	Model 1: perceived discrimination	Model 1: perceived discrimination	Model 2: level of tolerance	Model 2: level of tolerance
Men				
Left–right scale		.84		.72*
Ethnic minority	15.67**	.82**		.89**
Lives with a partner		10.05**	2.60**	1.29
		1.29		1.05
Feeling towards household income: base = very difficult				
Live very comfortably		.96		.67
Live comfortably		.858		.99
Having some difficulties		.61*		1.07
Economic status: base = economically inactive				
In employment		1.21		1.36
Unemployed		1.03		1.24
Age: base = 55+				
15–19		2.91*		1.59
20–24		5.17**		1.03
25–29		2.57*		1.22
30–39		3.51**		.97
40–54		2.15		1.02

Table A.2 (continued)

Variables	Model 1: perceived discrimination	Model 1: perceived discrimination	Model 2: level of tolerance	Model 2: level of tolerance
Qualifications: base = less than low secondary				
Low secondary		1.25		1.40
High secondary		.96		1.93**
Tertiary		1.10		2.12**
Religiosity		1.02		.96
Language at home: base = Turkish				
Other		4.91**		3.57**
Kurdish		1.53		1.03
Istanbul		2.48**		1.44*
Perceived discrimination		2.23**		.57*
Perceived discrimination*Ethnic minority				6.57**
Survey round: base = 2008				.36**
Chi-square (df)	318.40 (2)	495.71 (22)	107.18 (2)	230.19 (24)
	p < 0.00	p < 0.00	p < 0.00	p < 0.00
Nagelkerke	0.20	0.35	0.07	0.17

Notes: * p < 0.05 ** p < 0.01

Source: European Social Survey 2004 and 2008

Table A.3   *Log-linear relationship between language, discrimination, religiosity and tolerance*

Model	Model description	Value	df	Sig.
1	[language] + [discrimination] + [religiosity] + [tolerance]	191.82	18	0.00
2	[discrimination*religiosity *tolerance] + [language *discrimi-nation] + [language*tolerance]	10.96	10	0.36

Source: European Social Survey 2004 and 2008

is, how in reality (the actual world – or the data in this case) these variables interact. How are the variables related, or do only some interact with others, and in what ways? The results of these models are in Table A.3.

Table A.3 presents two different log-linear models: the independence model (no interactions) and the first best-fit model (with interactions). In the first model the independence hypothesis that there is no relationship between the four variables is examined. With a chi-square value of 230.19, the model is statistically significant, indicating that it does not fit the data. This means that there is a relationship between these variables. The second model represents how these four variables are associated with each other. It is the first simplest model that fits the data, or captures how the variables are involved with or relate to each other.

Analysis for Chapter 6

An attempt is made to analyse the relationship between three sets of attitudes: political trust, social trust and social participation using a range of explanatory factors. In what follows, the dependent and independent variables included in the analysis are presented and described. The final sample size was reduced to 1,265 in the regression models, largely due to focusing on the 'occupational class' category. Many young people who were still in full-time education or were economically inactive (mainly women) do not work. As such they were not included in the regression analysis.

Thus, there might be a slight gender bias towards men, but since gender is included in the analysis as a control factor this bias does not impact on the results. Therefore, it is critical to remain careful in generalising the results of this study to all women, as those who do work tend to have a different social, economic and political profile compared with women not in any formal occupation.

Dependent variables

Four aggregated dependent variables were formulated from a range of questions from the ESS.

Political trust: formed from various questions which ask respondents to indicate their trust in the following institution, using a zero–ten scale; the country's parliament, the legal system, the police, politicians, political parties, the European Parliament and the United Nations. The original question was as follows, '[u]sing this card, please tell me on a score of zero–ten how much you personally trust each of the institutions I read out. [Zero] means you do not trust an institution at all, and ten means you have complete trust.'

Explanatory Factor Analysis (using SPSS software) revealed that these institutions (items) were loaded onto three different factors. In the first instance, trust in the country's parliament, police and legal system (trust in national institutions – Alpha Cronbach 0.83); second, trust in political parties and politicians (trust in national politics – Alpha Cronbach 0.88); and finally trust in the European Parliament and the United Nations (trust in international institutions – Alpha Cronbach 0.85). After constructing the factors again using the Confirmatory Factor Analysis technique (CFA, with the command Confa in Stata), it was found that the model did not converge as expected because there were only two indicators for two out of the three latent variables (factors) constructed that did not meet the minimum recommended number of indicators per latent variable. However, using Alpha Cronbach to measure the reliability of each factor (as carried out in this chapter) is common practice. Each of the three variables (factors) has a mean of zero and a standard deviation of one.

Social engagement: created out of three questions asking how often people meet socially with friends and relatives [scales range from never (one) to everyday (seven)]; whether there is anyone to discuss intimate and personal matters with [scales range from no (zero) to yes (one)]; and how frequently the respondent takes part in social events compared with others in their age group [scales range from much less than most (one) to much more than most (five)]. The answers to these three questions were added to create the scale for social engagement, which ranges from low (score of two) to high (score of thirteen).

Social trust: derived from questions A8–A10, which measure the extent of interpersonal trust (A8), the fairness of people (A9) and the extent of people's helpfulness towards each other (A10). This scale of social trust has an alpha reliability of 0.78, and ranges from low to high trust.

Independent variables

For each independent variable used in the analysis, some statistical description (in percentages for categorical or ordinal factors and the mean for interval or ratio factors) is included in this section.

Age: was measured as a continuous variable (mean = 39.42).

Economic status: was recoded into three categories: in employment (26 per cent); unemployed (8 per cent); and economically inactive (reference group, 62 per cent).

Ethnic group: was recoded as one for ethnic minority groups (7%) and zero for ethnic majority groups (93 per cent). Minority ethnicity refers to the dominant ethnic minority group. In this case, minority groups described themselves as Kurdish, but not exclusively. Moreover, not all Kurdish groups described themselves as a minority, given their legal citizenship status and their religion. Therefore, groups who explicitly identified themselves as minorities were more likely to be staunch ethno-nationalist Kurds, as well as other minority groups who live or work in Turkey as distinct and separate ethnic and religious categories.

Gender: was coded one for men (46 per cent) and zero for women (54 per cent).

Left–right placement: measured whether a respondent was politically placed on the left or the right, using a left–right scale, zero–ten (mean, 6.04).

Marital status: was recoded as one for living with a partner (67 per cent) and zero if not (33 per cent).

Occupational class: variable is a five-category version of the International Standard Classification of Occupations (ISCO-88). The categories were managerial and professional occupations (25 per cent); low non-manual occupations (8 per cent); service, shop and market workers (11 per cent); skilled manual jobs (28 per cent); and the category of semi- and non-skilled jobs (reference group, 28 per cent).

Praying: measured how often a respondent tended to pray, apart from attending religious services. Responses were recoded into four categories: never (7 per cent); on special holidays (6 per cent); once a week or more (15 per cent); and every day (reference group, 72 per cent).

Qualifications: were a measure of the highest qualification obtained by respondents. These qualifications were recoded into four categories: less than low secondary (reference group, 58 per cent); low secondary (16 per cent); high secondary (19 per cent); and tertiary education (7 per cent).

Region: was recoded into two categories: respondent in Istanbul (19 per cent); and the rest of Turkey (reference group, 81 per cent).

Religiosity: measured the level of religiosity reported by respondents on a scale of zero to ten, with zero indicating no religiosity at all and ten indicating the highest level of religiosity (mean, 7.07).

Year of survey: (round) variable was used to control for the year of survey (2004, 43 per cent; 2008, 57 per cent).

Table A.4 presents five Ordinary Least Squares (OLS) models for Turks on matters of political trust, social trust and social engagement.

Table A.4 OLS parameter estimates for political trust in Turkey

Parameter	Model 1[a]	Model 2[a]	Model 3[a]	Model 4[a]	Model 5[a]
Religiosity	0.03*	0.03**	-0.01	-0.02	-0.07*
Praying: base = every day					
Never or less than often	-0.28**	0.07	-0.06	0.08	-0.23
Only on special holidays or at least once a week	-0.07	0.05	0.10	0.24*	-0.42
Once a week to more than once a week	-0.06	-0.05	0.00	0.09	-0.20
Gender: base = women					
Men	-0.06	0.10	-0.14*	-0.11	0.74**
Left–right scale	0.06**	0.03**	-0.02*	0.02	-0.02
Age	-0.00	0.00	-0.00	0.01*	-0.02**
Marital status: base = does not live with partner					
Lives with a partner	-0.02	-0.09	0.03	-0.02	-0.18
Ethnicity: base = majority					
Ethnic minority	-0.56**	0.18*	-0.00	-0.14	-0.77**
Qualifications: base = less than low secondary					
Low secondary	0.02	-0.11	-0.10	-0.01	0.27
High secondary	-0.13*	-0.05	-0.07	0.06	0.19
Tertiary	-0.18*	-0.07	-0.08	0.19	0.51*
Economic status: base = inactive					
In employment	-0.06	0.02	-0.05	-0.04	-0.31
Unemployed	-0.06	0.03	-0.00	-0.00	-0.31

Table A.4 (continued)

Parameter	Model 1[a]	Model 2[a]	Model 3[a]	Model 4[a]	Model 5[a]
Occupations: base = semi-skilled and unskilled manual occupations					
Managerial, professional and semi-professional occupations	-0.15*	0.15*	-0.05	0.05	0.93**
Non-manual occupations	-0.26*	0.14	-0.03	0.16	0.48
Service, shop and market workers	-0.03	-0.07	-0.19*	0.17	0.49*
Skilled manual occupations	0.06	-0.03	-0.10	0.13	0.29
Region: base = other regions					
Istanbul	0.15**	-0.07	-0.12*	0.18**	0.60**
Survey round: base = 2008					
Round 2004	-0.08	-0.07	0.36**	0.17**	0.17
Trust in national institutions	–	0.26**	0.16**	0.05	0.08
Trust in national politics	0.28**	–	0.32**	0.19**	-0.02
Trust in international institutions	0.14**	0.26**	–	0.02	-0.06
Social trust	0.03	0.13**	0.02	–	0.23**
Social engagement	0.01	-0.00	-0.01	0.04**	–
Constant	-0.43*	-0.40*	0.46*	-0.70**	8.12**
Adjusted R square	0.31	0.27	0.20	0.08	0.08

Notes: ** $p < 0.01$ * $p < 0.05$

[a] Model 1 – trust in national institutions; Model 2 – trust in national politics; Model 3 – trust in international institutions; Model 4 – social trust; Model 5 – social participation, ESS 2004 and 2008 (N = 1,265)

Source: European Social Survey 2004 and 2008

References

Abdullahi, Ali Arazeem and Bashir Salawu (2012), 'Ibn Khaldun: a forgotten sociologist?', *South African Review of Sociology* 43: 3, 24–40.

Adam, Frane (2008), 'Methodological shortcomings of cross-national surveys: mapping social capital across Europe: findings, trends and methodological shortcomings of cross-national surveys', *Social Science Information* 47: 2, 159–86.

Adams, Patrick (2013), 'Amid the tumult in Turkey, human rights abuses abound', *The Lancet* 382, 13–14.

Ahmad, Feroz (1988) 'Islamic Reassertion in Turkey', *Third World Quarterly* 10: 2, 750–69.

Ahmad, Feroz (2003), *Turkey: the Quest for Identity*, Oxford: Oneworld.

Akçam, Taner (2004), *From Empire to Republic: Turkish Nationalism and the Armenian Genocide*, London and New York: Zed.

Akkar Ercan, Müge (2010), 'Searching for a balance between community needs and conservation policies in historic neighbourhoods of Istanbul', *European Planning Studies* 18: 5, 833–59.

Akman, Ayhan (2004), 'Ambiguities of modernist nationalism: architectural culture and nation-building in early Republican Turkey', *Turkish Studies* 5: 3, 103–11.

Aksoy, Asu (2012), 'Riding the storm: "new Istanbul"', *City: Analysis of Urban Trends, Culture, Theory, Policy, Action* 16: 1–2, 93–111.

Aktürk, Şener (2011), 'Regimes of ethnicity: comparative analysis of Germany, the Soviet Union/post-Soviet Russia, and Turkey', *World Politics* 63: 1, 115–64.

Alam, Anwar (2009), 'Islam and post-modernism: locating the rise of Islamism in Turkey', *Journal of Islamic Studies* 20: 3, 1–24.

Alatas Syed, Farid (2007), 'The historical sociology of Muslim societies: Khaldunian applications', *International Sociology* 22: 3, 267–88.

Alesina, Alberto and Paola Giuliano (2011), 'Family ties and political participation', *Journal of the European Economic Association* 9: 5, 817–39.

Alessandri, Emiliano (2010), 'Turkey's new foreign policy and the future of Turkey–EU Relations', *The International Spectator: Italian Journal of International Affairs* 45: 3, 85–100.

Amnesty International (2013), *Gezi Park Protests: Brutal Denial of the Right to Peaceful Assembly in Turkey*, London: Amnesty International.

Aral, Berdal (1997), 'Turkey's insecure identity from the perspective of nationalism', *Mediterranean Quarterly* 8: 1, 84–5.

Aral, Berdal (2004), 'The idea of human rights as perceived in the Ottoman Empire', *Human Rights Quarterly* 26: 2, 454–82.

Aras, Bülent, Ertan Aydın, Selin M. Bölme, İhsan Daği, İbrahim Dalmiş, Yılmaz Ensaroğlu, Hatem Ete, Talip Küçükcan, Taha Özhan, Hüseyin Yahman (2009), *Public perception of the Kurdish question in Turkey*, Ankara: SETA Foundation for Political Economic and Social Research.

Arat, Yeim (2010), 'Religion, politics and gender equality in Turkey: implications of a democratic paradox?' *Third World Quarterly* 31: 6, 869–84.

Atay, Tayfun (2013), 'The clash of "nations" in Turkey: reflections on the Gezi Park incident', *Insight Turkey* 15: 3, 39–44.

Avcı, Gamze (2011), 'The Justice and Development Party and the EU: political pragmatism in a changing environment', *South European Society and Politics* 16: 3, 409–21.

Ayata, Bilgin (2011), 'Kurdish transnational politics and Turkey's changing Kurdish policy: the journey of Kurdish broadcasting from Europe to Turkey', *Journal of Contemporary European Studies* 19: 4, 523–33.

Aydin-Düzgit, Senem (2012), 'No crisis, no change: the third AKP victory in the June 2011 parliamentary elections in Turkey', *South European Society and Politics* 17: 1, 329–46.

Aydinli, Ersel and Nihat Ali Özcan (2011), 'The conflict resolution and counterterrorism dilemma: Turkey faces its Kurdish question', *Terrorism and Political Violence* 23: 3, 438–57.

Ayfle Betül Çelik (2005) '"I miss my village!": forced Kurdish migrants in Istanbul and their representation in associations', *New Perspectives on Turkey* 32, 137–63.

Azak, Umat (2010), *Islam and Secularism in Turkey: Kemalism, Religion and the Nation State*, London and New York: I. B. Tauris.

al-Azmeh, Aziz (2003), *Ibn Khaldun: an Essay in Reinterpretation*, Budapest: Central European University Press.

Bacik, Gokhan and Bezen Balamir Coskun (2011), 'The PKK problem: explaining

Turkey's failure to develop a political solution', *Studies in Conflict and Terrorism* 34: 3, 248–65.

Bakiner, Onur (2013), 'Is Turkey coming to terms with its past? Politics of memory and majoritarian conservatism', *Nationalities Papers: the Journal of Nationalism and Ethnicity* 41: 5, 691–708.

Banton, Michael (2008), 'The sociology of ethnic relations', *Ethnic and Racial Studies* 31: 7, 1267–85.

Barkey, Henri J. and Graham E. Fuller (1998), *Turkey's Kurdish Question*, Lanham, MD: Rowman and Littlefield.

Barkey, Karen (2008), *Empire of Difference: the Ottomans in Comparative Perspective*, Cambridge: Cambridge University Press.

Barrinha, André (2011), 'The political importance of labelling: terrorism and Turkey's discourse on the PKK', *Critical Studies on Terrorism* 4: 2, 163–80.

Başkan, Filiz (2005), 'The Fethullah Gülen community: contribution or barrier to the consolidation of democracy in Turkey?', *Middle Eastern Studies* 41: 6, 849–61.

Başkan, Filiz (2010), 'Religious versus secular groups in the age of globalisation in Turkey', *Totalitarian Movements and Political Religions* 11: 2, 167–83.

Bayar, Yeşim (2011), 'The trajectory of nation-building through language policies: the case of Turkey during the early Republic (1920–38)', *Nations and Nationalism* 17: 1, 108–28.

Bayat, Asef (2013), *Post-Islamism: the Many Faces of Political Islam*, Oxford and New York: Oxford University Press.

Becker, Howard S. (1967), '"Whose Side Are We On?"', *Social Problems* 14: 3, 239–47.

Bengio, Ofra (2011), 'The "Kurdish Spring" in Turkey and its impact on Turkish foreign relations in the Middle East', *Turkish Studies* 12: 4, 619–32.

Bilici, Mucahit (2005), 'The Fethullah Gülen movement and its politics of representation in Turkey', *The Muslim World* 96: 1, 1–20.

Bloxham, Donald (2005), *The Great Game of Genocide: Imperialism, Nationalism, and the Destruction of the Ottoman Armenians*, Oxford: Oxford University Press.

Bourdieu, Pierre (1986), 'The forms of capital', in *Handbook of Theory and Research for the Sociology of Education*, ed. J. G. Richardson, Westport, CT: Greenwood Press, pp. 241–58.

Bruinessen, Martin van (1992), *Agha, Shaikh and State: the Social and Political Structures of Kurdistan*, London and New York: Zed.

Bruinessen, Martin van (1998), 'Shifting national and ethnic identities: the Kurds in Turkey and the European diaspora, *Journal of Muslim Minority Affairs* 18: 1, 39–52.

Bulmer, Martin and John Solomos (eds) (1999), *Racism*, Oxford: Oxford University Press.

Çağaptay, Soner (2004), 'Race, assimilation and Kemalism: Turkish nationalism and the minorities in the 1930s', *Middle Eastern Studies* 40: 3, 86–101.

Çağaptay, Soner (2006), *Islam, Secularism and Nationalism in Modern Turkey: Who is a Turk?* London and New York: Routledge.

Çaha, Ömer (2013), 'Public perceptions of negotiations with Öcalan', *Turkish Review* 3, 202–7.

Çaha, Ömer, Metin Toprak and Nasuh Uslu (2010), 'Religion and ethnicity in the construction of official ideology in Republican Turkey', *The Muslim World* 100: 1, 33–44.

Çakır, Ruşen (2007), 'Interview with Şerif Mardin', *Vatan Kitap Eki* [Vatan Book Review], May 15.

Calhoun, Craig (1993), 'Nationalism and ethnicity', *Annual Review of Sociology* 19, 211–39.

Can, Ayşegül (2013), 'Neo-liberal urban politics in the historical environment of Istanbul – the issue of gentrification', *Planlama* 23: 2, 95–104.

Canan-Sokullu, Ebru. Ş. (2011), 'Turcoscepticism and threat perception: European public and elite opinion on Turkey's protracted EU membership', *South European Society and Politics* 16: 3, 483–97.

Canan-Sokullu, Ebru Ş. (2012), 'Islamophobia and Turkoscepticism in Europe? A four-nation study', in *Political and Cultural Representations of Muslims: Islam in the Plural*, eds Christopher Flood, Stephen Hutchings, Galina Miazhevich and Henri Nickels, Leiden: Brill, pp. 97–112.

Capshaw, N. Clark (2005), 'The social cohesion role of the public sector', *Peabody Journal of Education* 80: 4, 53–77.

Çarkoğlu, Ali (2008), 'Ideology or economic pragmatism? Profiling Turkish voters in 2007', *Turkish Studies* 9: 2, 317–44.

Çarkoğlu, Ali and Nazli Çağin Bilgili (2007), 'A precarious relationship: the Alevi minority, the Turkish state and the EU', *South European Society and Politics* 16: 2, 351–64.

Çarkoğlu, Ali and Cerem I. Cenker (2011), 'On the relationship between democratic institutionalization and civil society involvement: new evidence from Turkey', *Democratization* 18: 3, 751–73.

Çarkoğlu, Ali and Ersin Kalaycioğlu (2009), *The Rising Tide of Conservatism in Turkey*, Basingstoke: Palgrave Macmillan.

Çarkoğlu, Ali and Çiğdem Kentmen (2011), 'Diagnosing trends and determinants in public support for Turkey's EU membership', *South European Society and Politics* 16: 3, 365–79.

Catterberg, Gabriela and Alejandro Moreno (2005), 'The individual bases of political trust: trends in new and established democracies', *International Journal of Public Opinion Research* 18: 1, 31–48.

Çavuşoğlu, Erbatur and Julia Strutz (2014), 'Producing force and consent: urban transformation and corporatism in Turkey', *City: Analysis of Urban Trends, Culture, Theory, Policy, Action* 18: 2, 134–48.

Çelik, Selahattin (2000), *Dagini Tasimak* [Carrying Mountain Ararat], Frankfurt: Zambon Verlag.

Çeliker, Anna Grabolle (2009), 'Construction of the Kurdish self in Turkey through humorous popular culture', *Journal of Intercultural Studies* 30: 1, 89–105.

Çetindamara, Dilek, Vishal K. Guptab, Esra E. Karadenizc and Nilufer Egricanc (2012), 'What the numbers tell: the impact of human, family and financial capital on women and men's entry into entrepreneurship in Turkey', *Entrepreneurship and Regional Development: nn International Journal* 24: 1–2, 29–51.

Ciftci, Sabri (2010), 'Toward democracy in the Muslim world? Modernization, Islam, or social capital: what explains attitudes', *Comparative Political Studies* 43: 11, 1442–70.

Clark, Bruce (2012), 'Shifting Western views on Turkey', *Asian Affairs* 43: 2, 193–203.

Coleman, James S. (1988), 'Social capital in the creation of human capital', *American Journal of Sociology* 94: S95–S120.

Criss, Nur Bilge (1995), 'The nature of PKK terrorism in Turkey', *Studies in Conflict and Terrorism* 18: 1, 17–37.

Dale, Stephen Frederic (2006), 'Ibn Khaldun: the last Greek and the first annaliste historian', *International Journal of Middle East Studies* 38: 3, 431–51.

Delhey, Jan, Ken Newton and Christian Welzel (2011), 'How general is trust in "most people"? Solving the radius of trust problem', *American Sociological Review* 76: 5, 786–807.

Demir, Ipek (2014), 'Humbling Turkishness: undoing the strategies of exclusion and inclusion of Turkish modernity', *Journal of Historical Sociology* 27: 3, 381–401.

Demiralp, Seda (2012), 'White Turks, black Turks? Faultlines beyond Islamism versus secularism', *Third World Quarterly* 33: 3, 511–24.

Dinçer, İclal (2011), 'The impact of neoliberal policies on historic urban space: areas of urban renewal in Istanbul', *International Planning Studies* 16: 1, 43–60.

Dixon, Jeffrey C., Yetkin Borlu and Duygu Kasdoğan (2013), 'Moving "East" or "West"?: examining liberal-democratic values in Turkey, 2000–2008', *European Societies* 15: 5, 753–79.

Donmez, Rasim Ozgur (2007), 'Nationalism in Turkey: political violence and identity', *Ethnopolitics* 6: 1, 43–65.

Ebaugh, Helen Rose (2009), *The Gülen Movement: a Sociological Analysis of a Civic Movement Rooted in Moderate Islam*, Leiden: Springer.

Eccarius-Kelly, Vera (2002), 'Political movements and leverage points: Kurdish activism in the European diaspora', *Journal of Muslim Minority Affairs* 22: 1, 91–118.

Eccarius-Kelly, Vera (2012), 'Surreptitious lifelines: a structural analysis of the FARC and the PKK', *Terrorism and Political Violence* 24: 2, 235–58.

Efegil, Ertan (2011), 'Analysis of the AKP government's policy toward the Kurdish issue', *Turkish Studies* 12: 1, 27–40.

Ekmekci, Faruk (2011), 'Understanding Kurdish ethno-nationalism in Turkey: socio-economy, religion, and politics', *Ethnic and Racial Studies* 34: 9, 1608–17.

Elicin, Yeseren (2014), 'Neoliberal transformation of the Turkish city through the Urban Transformation Act', *Habitat International* 41, 150–5.

Eraydin, Ayda and Tuna Taşan-Kok (2014), 'State response to contemporary urban movements in Turkey: a critical overview of state entrepreneurialism and authoritarian interventions', *Antipode* 46: 1, 110–29.

Ercan, Müge Akkar (2011), 'Challenges and conflicts in achieving sustainable communities in historic neighbourhoods of Istanbul', *Habitat International* 35, 295–306.

Eren, İmre Özbek (2014), 'What is the threshold in urban regeneration projects in the context of urban identity? The case of Turkey', *SPATIUM International Review* 31, 14–21.

Ergin, Murat (2014), 'The racialization of Kurdish identity in Turkey', *Ethnic and Racial Studies* 37: 2, 322–41.

Ergun, Nilgun (2004), 'Gentrification in Istanbul', *Cities* 21: 5, 391–405.

Eskander, Saad (2000), 'Britain's policy in southern Kurdistan: the formation and the termination of the first Kurdish government, 1918–1919', *British Journal of Middle Eastern Studies* 27: 2, 139–63.

Esposito, John L. (1993), *Islam and Politics*, third edition, New York: Syracuse University Press.

Farro, Antimo L. and Deniz Günce Demirhisar (2014), 'The Gezi Park movement:

a Turkish experience of the twenty-first-century collective movements', *International Review of Sociology: Revue Internationale de Sociologie* 24: 1, 176–89.

Fernandez, Sonya (2009), 'The crusade over the bodies of women', *Patterns of Prejudice* 43: 3, 269–86.

Findley, Vaughn C. (2005), *Turks in World History*, Oxford: Oxford University Press.

Florez-Morris, Mauricio (2007), 'Joining guerrilla groups in Colombia: individual motivations and processes for entering a violent organization', *Studies in Conflict and Terrorism* 30: 7, 615–34.

Foggo, Hacer (2007), 'The Sulukule affair: Roma against expropriation', *Roma Rights Quarterly* 4, 43–7.

Freitag, Markus and Marc Bühlmann (2009), 'Crafting trust: the role of political institutions in a comparative perspective', *Comparative Political Studies* 42: 12, 1537–66.

Galletti, Miralla (1999), 'The Kurdish issue in Turkey', *The International Spectator: Italian Journal of International Affairs* 34: 1, 123–34.

Gawrych, George W. (1983), 'Tolerant dimensions of cultural pluralism in the Ottoman Empire: the Albanian community, 1800–1912', *International Journal of Middle East Studies* 15: 4, 519–36.

Gellman, Mneesha (2013), 'Remembering violence: the role of apology and dialogue in Turkey's democratization process', *Democratization* 20: 4, 771–94.

Genç, Kaya (2014), 'Turkey's Twitter army', *Index on Censorship* 43: 1, 106–10.

Genel, Sema and Kerem Karaosmanolu (2006), 'A new Islamic individualism in Turkey: headscarved women in the city', *Turkish Studies* 7: 3, 473–88.

Gerhards, Jürgen and Silke Hans (2011), 'Why not Turkey? Attitudes towards Turkish membership in the EU among citizens in 27 European countries', *Journal of Common Market Studies* 49: 4, 741–66.

Gkarksel, Banu (2012), 'The intimate politics of secularism and the headscarf: the mall, the neighborhood, and the public square in Istanbul', *Gender, Place & Culture: a Journal of Feminist Geography* 19: 1, 1–20, p. 15.

Goffman, Daniel (2002), *The Ottoman Empire and Early Modern Europe*, Cambridge: Cambridge University Press.

Göl, Ayla (2009), 'The identity of Turkey: Muslim and secular', *Third World Quarterly* 30: 4, 795–811.

Gole, Nilüfer (1996), *The Forbidden Modern: Civilization and Veiling*, Ann Arbor, MI: University of Michigan Press.

Granovetter, Mark S. (1983), 'The strength of weak ties', *American Journal of Sociology* 78: 6, 1360–80.

Green, Andy, Germ Janmaat and Hele Cheng (2011), 'Social cohesion: converging and diverging trends', *National Institute Economic Review* 215: 1, R6–R22.

Gül, Murat, John Dee and Cahide Nur Cünük (2014), 'Istanbul's Taksim Square and Gezi Park: the place of protest and the ideology of place', *Journal of Architecture and Urbanism* 38: 1, 63–72.

Gulay, Erol N. (2007), 'The Gülen phenomenon: a neo-Sufi challenge to Turkey's rival elite?', *Critique: Critical Middle Eastern Studies* 16: 1, 37–61.

Gunay, Zeynep (2012), 'Historic landscapes of exclusion in Istanbul: right to the city?' Paper presented to the 15th International Planning History Society Conference, 'Cities, nations and regions in planning history', Sao Paulo, Brazil, 15–18 July.

Gunes, Cengiz (2012), 'Unblocking the impasse in Turkey's Kurdish question', *Peace Review: A Journal of Social Justice* 24: 4, 462–9.

Gunes, Cengiz (2013), 'Explaining the PKK's mobilization of the Kurds in Turkey: hegemony, myth and violence', *Ethnopolitics* 12: 3, 247–67.

Gunter, Michael M. (2000), 'The continuing Kurdish problem in Turkey after Öcalan's capture', *Third World Quarterly* 21: 5, 849–69.

Gunter, Michael M. (2008), *The Kurds Ascending*, New York: Palgrave Macmillan.

Gunter, Michael M. (2013), 'The Kurdish Spring', *Third World Quarterly* 34: 3, 441–57.

Gürcan Efe, Can and Efe Peker (2014), 'Turkey's Gezi Park demonstrations of 2013: a Marxian analysis of the political moment', *Socialism and Democracy* 28: 1, 70–89.

Gurses, Mehmet (2010), 'Partition, democracy, and Turkey's Kurdish minority', *Nationalism and Ethnic Politics* 16: 3–4, 337–53.

Hanioğlu, M. Sükrü (2008), *A Brief History of the Late Ottoman Empire*, Princeton, NJ: Princeton University Press.

Haynes, Jeffrey (2010), 'Politics, identity and religious nationalism in Turkey: from Atatürk to the AKP', *Australian Journal of International Affairs* 64: 3, 312–27.

Hendrick, Joshua (2013), *Gülen: the Ambiguous Politics of Market Islam in Turkey and the World*, New York: New York University Press.

Heper, Mettin (2007), *The State and Kurds in Turkey: the Question of Assimilation*, Basingstoke: Palgrave Macmillan.

Heper, Metin (2000), 'Political studies in Turkey', *Turkish Studies* 1: 2, 125–34.

Heper, Metin and Senem Yıldırım (2011), 'Revisiting civil society in Turkey', *Southeast European and Black Sea Studies* 11: 1, 1–18.

Hovannisian, Richard G. (ed.) (2003), *Confronting the Armenian Genocide: Looking Back, Looking Forward*, New Brunswick, NJ and London: Transaction.

Hürsoy, Siret (2012), 'The paradox of modernity in Turkey: issues in the transformation of a state', *India Quarterly* 68: 1, 49–67.

İçduygu, Ahmet, David Romano and Ibrahim Sirkeci (1999), 'The ethnic question in an environment of insecurity: the Kurds in Turkey', *Ethnic and Racial Studies* 22: 6, 991–1010.

İçduygu, Ahmet and B. Ali Soner (2006), 'Turkish minority rights regime: between difference and equality', *Middle Eastern Studies* 42: 3, 447–68.

Ince, Basak (2012), *Citizenship and Identity in Turkey: from Ataturk's Republic to the Present Day*, London and New York: I. B. Tauris.

Jacobs, Jane (1961), *The Death and Life of Great American Cities*, New York: Random House.

Jenkins, Gareth (2003), 'Muslim democrats in Turkey?' *International Institute for Strategic Studies* 45: 1, 45–66.

Jenkins, Gareth (2008), *Political Islam in Turkey: Running West, Heading East*, Basingstoke: Palgrave Macmillan.

Johansson-Nogués, Elizabeth and Ann-Kristin Jonasson (2011), 'Turkey, its changing national identity and EU accession: explaining the ups and downs in the Turkish democratization reforms', *Journal of Contemporary European Studies* 19: 1, 113–32.

Joppke, Christian (1996), 'Multiculturalism and immigration: a comparison of the United States, Germany, and Great Britain', *Theory and Society* 25: 4, 449–500.

Kalaycıoğlu, Ersin (2010), *Islam, Secularism, and Democracy: Insights from Turkish Politics*, Istanbul: Sabancı University.

Karakoç, Ekrem (2013), 'Ethnicity and trust in national and international institutions: Kurdish attitudes toward political institutions in Turkey', *Turkish Studies* 14: 1, 92–114.

Karaman, Ozan (2014), 'Resisting urban renewal in Istanbul', *Urban Geography* 35: 2, 290–310.

Karaman, Ozan and Tolga Islam (2012), 'On the dual nature of intra-urban borders: the case of a Romani neighbourhood in Istanbul', *Cities* 29: 4, 234–43.

Karasipahi, Sena (2009), *Muslims in Modern Turkey: Kemalism, Modernism and the Rise of the Islamic Intellectuals*, London and New York: I. B. Tauris.

Karasulu, Ahu (2014), '"If a leaf falls, they blame the tree": scattered notes on Gezi resistances, contention, and space', *International Review of Sociology: Revue Internationale de Sociologie* 24: 1, 164–75.

Karaveli, Halil M. (2010), 'An unfulfilled promise of enlightenment: Kemalism and its liberal critics', *Turkish Studies* 11: 1, 85–102.

Kasaba, Reşat (1997), 'Kemalist certainties and modern ambiguities', in *Modernity and National Identity in Turkey*, ed. R. Kasaba and S. Bozdoğan. Seattle and London: University of Washington Press, pp. 15–37.

Kavakçı, Merve (2010), *Headscarf Politics in Turkey: a Postcolonial Reading*, Basingstoke: Palgrave Macmillan.

Kaya, Nurcan and Clive Baldwin (2004), *Minorities in Turkey: Submission to the European Union and the Government of Turkey*, London: Minority Rights Group International.

Keele, Luke (2005), 'Macro measures and mechanics of social capital', *Political Analysis* 13: 2, 139–56.

Keyman, E. Fuat (2012), 'Rethinking the "Kurdish question" in Turkey: modernity, citizenship and democracy', *Philosophy and Social Criticism* 38: 4–5, 467–76.

Keyman, E. Fuat and Tuba Kanci (2011), 'A tale of ambiguity: citizenship, nationalism and democracy in Turkey', *Nations and Nationalism* 17: 2, 318–36.

Kirişci, Kemal (2011), 'The Kurdish issue in Turkey: limits of European Union reform', *South European Society and Politics* 16: 2, 335–49.

Kirişci, Kemal and Gareth M. Winrow (1997), *The Kurdish Question in Turkey: an Example of a Trans-state Ethnic Conflict*, London: Frank Cass.

Kocabas, Arzu (2006), 'Urban conservation in Istanbul: evaluation and re-conceptualisation', *Habitat International* 30, 107–26.

Kolukirik, Suat and Şule Toktaş (2007), 'Turkey's Roma: political participation and organization', *Middle Eastern Studies* 43: 5, 761–77.

Koopmans, Ruud and Paul Statham (1999), 'Challenging the liberal nation-state? Postnationalism, multiculturalism, and the collective claims-making of migrants and ethnic minorities in Britain and Germany', *American Journal of Sociology* 105: 3, 652–96.

Köse, Talha (2011), *Alevi Opening and the Democratization Initiative in Turkey*, SETA Foundation for Political Economic and Social Research: Ankara.

Koyuncu-Lorasdaği, Berrin (2010), 'The prospects and pitfalls of the religious nationalist movement in Turkey: the case of the Gülen movement, *Middle Eastern Studies* 46: 2, 221–34.

Kuru, Ahmet T. and Alfred Stepan (2012), *Democracy, Islam, and Secularism in*

Turkey Series: Religion, Culture, and Public Life, New York: Columbia University Press.

Kuymulu, Mehmet Barİş (2013), 'Reclaiming the right to the city: reflections on the urban uprisings in Turkey', *City: Analysis of Urban Trends, Culture, Theory, Policy, Action* 17: 3, 274–8.

Kuzu, Durukan (2016), 'The politics of identity, recognition and multiculturalism: the Kurds in Turkey', *Nations and Nationalism* 22: 1, 123–42.

Laçiner, Sedat and Ihsan Bal (2004), 'The ideological and historical roots of the Kurdist movements in Turkey: ethnicity, demography, and politics', *Nationalism and Ethnic Politics* 10: 3, 473–504.

Lelandais, Gülçin Erdi (2014), 'Space and identity in resistance against neoliberal urban planning in Turkey', *International Journal of Urban and Regional Research* 38: 5, 1785–806.

Lewis, Bernard (1968), *The Emergence of Modern Turkey*, Oxford: Oxford University Press.

Li, Yaojun, Andrew Pickles and Mike Savage (2005), 'Social capital and social trust in Britain', *European Sociological Review* 21: 2, 109–23.

Loizides, Neophytos G. (2010), 'State ideology and the Kurds in Turkey', *Middle Eastern Studies* 46: 4, 513–27.

Maksudyan, Nazan (2005), 'The *Turkish Review of Anthropology* and the racist face of Turkish nationalism', *Cultural Dynamics* 17: 3, 291–322.

Mango, Andrew (1999), 'Atatürk and the Kurds', *Middle Eastern Studies* 35: 4, 1–25.

Marcus, Aliza (2007), *Blood and Belief: the PKK and the Kurdish Fight for Independence*, New York: New York University Press.

Mardin, Şerif (1962), *The Genesis of Young Ottoman Thought: a Study in the Modernization of Turkish Political Ideas*, Princeton, NJ: Princeton University Press.

Mardin, Şerif (1973), 'Center-Periphery Relations: a Key to Turkish Politics?', *Post-Traditional Societies* 102: 1, 169–90.

Mardin, Şerif (2005), 'Turkish Islamic exceptionalism yesterday and today: continuity, rupture and reconstruction in operational codes', *Turkish Studies* 6: 2, 145–65.

Mateescu, Dragoş C. (2006), 'Kemalism in the era of totalitarianism: a conceptual analysis', *Turkish Studies* 7: 2, 225–41.

May, Asena (2013), 'Twelve sycamore trees have set the limits on Turkish PM Erdoğan's Power', *American Foreign Policy Interests: the Journal of the National Committee on American Foreign Policy* 35: 5, 298–302.

Michael, Michális S. (2008), 'Navigating through the Bosphorus: relocating Turkey's European/Western fault line', *Global Change, Peace and Security: formerly Pacifica Review* 20: 1, 71–85.

Miles, Robert and Annie Phizaklea (1980), *Labour and Racism*, London: Routledge and Kegan Paul.

Moudouros, Nikos (2014), 'Rethinking Islamic hegemony in Turkey through Gezi Park', *Journal of Balkan and Near Eastern Studies* 16: 2, 181–95.

Mousseau, Demet Yalcin (2006), 'Democracy, human rights and market development in Turkey: are they related?' *Government and Opposition* 41: 2, 298–326.

Mousseau, Demet Yalcin (2012), 'An inquiry into the linkage among nationalizing policies, democratization, and ethno-nationalist conflict: the Kurdish case in Turkey', *Nationalities Papers* 40: 1, 45–62.

Müftüler-Baç, Meltem (2000), 'The impact of the European Union on Turkish Politics', *East European Quarterly* 34: 2, 159–79.

Mutlu, Servet (1995), 'Population of Turkey by ethnic groups and provinces', *New Perspectives on Turkey* 12, 33–60.

Newton, Ken (2001), 'Trust, social capital, civil society, and democracy', *International Political Science Review* 22: 2, 201–14.

Newton, Ken (2006), 'Political support: social capital, civil society and political and economic performance', *Political Studies* 54: 4, 846–64.

Norris, Pippa (2002), *Democratic Phoenix: Political Activism World Wide*, Cambridge: Cambridge University Press.

Öktem, Kerem (2004), 'Incorporating the time and space of the ethnic "other": nationalism and space in Southeast Turkey in the nineteenth and twentieth centuries', *Nations and Nationalism* 10: 4, 559–78.

Onar, Nora Fisher and Meltem Müftüler-Baç (2011), 'The adultery and headscarf debates in Turkey: Fusing "EU-niversal" and "alternative" modernities?', *Women's Studies International Forum* 34, 378–89.

Öncü, Ahmet (2003), 'Dictatorship plus hegemony: a Gramscian analysis of the Turkish state', *Science and Society* 67: 3, 303–28.

Öncü, Ahmet (2013), 'Turkish capitalist modernity and the Gezi revolt', *Historical Sociology* 27: 2, 151–76.

Öniş, Ziya (2012), 'The triumph of conservative globalism: the political economy of the AKP era', *Turkish Studies* 13: 2, 135–52.

Ontas, Ozlem Cankurtaran, Sema Buz and Burcu Hatiboglu (2011), 'Youth and political participation: case in Turkey', *European Journal of Social Work* 16: 2, 249–62.

Örs, İ. R. (2014), 'Genie in the bottle: Gezi Park, Taksim Square, and the realignment of democracy and space in Turkey', *Philosophy and Social Criticism* 40: 4–5, 489–98.

Özbudun, Ergun (2014), 'AKP at the crossroads: Erdoğan's majoritarian drift', *South European Society and Politics* 19: 2, 155–67.

Özcan, Ali Kemal (2006), *Turkey's Kurds: a Theoretical Analysis of the PKK and Abdullah Öcalan*, London and New York: Routledge.

Ozgulu, Tarik H. (2008), 'Middle Easternization of Turkey's foreign policy: does Turkey disassociate the West?', *Turkish Studies* 9: 1, 3–20.

Ozkirimli, Umut (2013), 'Vigilance and apprehension: multiculturalism, democracy, and the "Kurdish Question" in Turkey', *Middle East Critique* 22: 1, 25–43.

Ozkirimli, Umut (2014), 'Multiculturalism, recognition and the "Kurdish question" in Turkey: the outline of a normative framework', *Democratization* 21: 6, 1055–73.

Özler, Ş. Ilgü and Ani Sarkissian (2011), 'Stalemate and stagnation in Turkish democratization: the role of civil society and political parties', *Journal of Civil Society* 7: 4, 363–84.

Özoğlu, Hakan (2004), *Kurdish Notables and the Ottoman State: Evolving Identities, Competing Loyalties, Shifting Boundaries*, New York: State University of New York Press.

Özyürek, Esra, (ed.) (2007), *The Politics of Public Memory in Turkey*, Syracuse, NY: Syracuse University Press.

Park, Bill (2012), *Modern Turkey: People, State and Foreign Policy in a Globalised World*, London and New York: Routledge.

Pettifer, James (1998), *The Turkish Labyrinth*, London: Penguin.

Pichler, Florian and Claire Wallace (2007), 'Patterns of formal and informal social capital in Europe', *European Sociological Review* 23: 4, 423–35.

Putnam, Robert (2000), *Bowling Alone: the Collapse and Revival of American Community*. New York: Simon and Schuster.

Radnitz, Scott, Jonathan Wheatley and Christoph Zürcher (2009), 'The origins of social capital: evidence from a survey of post-Soviet Central Asia', *Comparative Political Studies* 42: 6, 707–32.

Reşat, Kasaba (1997), 'Kemalist certainties and modern ambiguities', in *Rethinking Modernity and National Identity in Turkey*, eds Reşat Kasaba and Sibel Bozdogan, Seattle and London: University of Washington Press, pp. 15–36.

Rex, John and Sally Tomlinson (1979), *Colonial Immigrants in a British City*, London: Routledge and Kegan Paul.

Rodrik, Dani (2013), 'The wrath of Erdoğan', *Juncture* 20: 2, 129–30.

Romano, David (2006), *The Kurdish Nationalist Movement*, Cambridge: Cambridge University Press.

Rosen, Lawrence (2005), 'Theorizing from within: Ibn Khaldun and his political culture', *Contemporary Sociology* 34: 6, 596–9.

Saatchi, Mustafa (2002), 'Nation-states and ethnic boundaries: modern Turkish identity and the Turkish–Kurdish conflict', *Nations and Nationalisms* 8: 4, 549–64.

Saktanber, Ayşe (2006), 'Women and the iconography of fear: Islamicization in post-Islamist Turkey', *Signs: Journal of Women in Culture and Society* 32: 1, 21–31.

Saktanber, Ayşe (2007), 'Cultural dilemmas of Muslim youth: negotiating Muslim identities and being young in Turkey, *Turkish Studies* 8: 3, 417–34.

Saktanber, Ayşe and Gül Çorbaciolu (2008), 'Veiling and headscarf-skepticism in Turkey', *Social Politics: International Studies in Gender, State and Society* 15: 4, 514–38.

Sandıkcı, Özlem (2013), 'Strolling through Istanbul's Beyoğlu: in-between difference and containment', *Space and Culture*, 18: 2, 198–211.

Saraçoğlu, Cenk (2009), '"Exclusive recognition": the new dimensions of the question of ethnicity and nationalism in Turkey', *Ethnic and Racial Studies* 32: 4, 640–58.

Sarfati, Yusuf (2015), 'Dynamics of mobilization during Gezi Park protests in Turkey', in *The Whole World is Texting: Youth Protest in the Information Age*, ed. Irving Epstein, Pittsburgh, PA: Sense Publishers, pp. 25–43.

Sarigil, Zeki (2010), 'Curbing Kurdish ethno-nationalism in Turkey: an empirical assessment of pro-Islamic and socio-economic approaches', *Ethnic and Racial Studies* 33: 3, 533–53.

Satana, Nil S. (2012), 'The Kurdish issue in June 2011 elections: continuity or change in Turkey's democratization?', *Turkish Studies* 13: 2, 169–89.

Seckinelgin, Hakan (2006), 'Civil society between the state and society: Turkish women with Muslim headscarves?' *Critical Social Policy* 26: 4, 748–69.

Secor, Anna J. and John O'Loughlin (2005), 'Social and political trust in Istanbul and Moscow: a comparative analysis of individual and neighbourhood effects', *Transactions of the Institute of British Geographers* 30: 1, 66–82.

Senay, Banu (2008), 'How do the youth perceive and experience Turkish citizenship?' *Middle Eastern Studies* 44: 6, 963–76.

Şentürk, Recep (2010), *Açık Medeniyet Çok Medeniyetli Dünya ve Topluma Doğru*, Istanbul: Timaş Yayınları.

Sezgin, Dilara and Melissa A. Wall (2005), 'Constructing the Kurds in the Turkish press: a case study of *Hürriyet* newspaper', *Media, Culture and Society* 27: 5, 787–98.

Sezgin, Ibrahim Can (2013), 'The link between the foreign policy of states and escalating political violence: Turkey and the PKK', *Critical Studies on Terrorism* 6: 1, 167–88.

Shah, Tabish (2010), 'Securitized identities and less secure western multi-ethnic states: a critical geopolitics of the East–West discourse – Turkey and beyond', *Nationalities Papers* 38: 3, 393–412.

Smith, Heather J. and Tom Tyler (1997), 'Choosing the right pond: the influence of the status and power of one's group and one's status in that group on self-esteem and group-oriented behavior', *Journal of Experimental Social Psychology* 33: 2, 146–70.

Smith, Stephen Samuel and Jessica Kulynych (2002), 'It may be social, but why is it capital? The social construction of social capital and the politics of language', *Politics and Society* 30: 1, 149–86.

Smith, Thomas W. (2005), 'Civic nationalism and ethnocultural Justice in Turkey', *Human Rights Quarterly* 27: 2, 436–70.

Smooha, Sammy (2008), 'Types of democracy and modes of conflict management in ethnically divided societies', *Nations and Nationalism* 8: 4, 423–31.

Somer, Murat (2002), 'Ethnic Kurds, endogenous identities, and Turkey's democratization and integration with Europe', *The Global Review of Ethnopolitics* 1: 4, 74–93.

Somer, Murat (2005), 'Resurgence and remaking of identity: civil beliefs, domestic and external dynamics, and the Turkish mainstream discourse on Kurds', *Comparative Political Studies* 38: 6, 591–622.

Somer, Murat (2011), 'Does it take democrats to democratize? Lessons from Islamic and secular elite values in Turkey', *Comparative Political Studies* 44: 5, 511–45.

Somer, Murat (2012), 'Moderation of religious and secular politics, a country's "centre" and democratization', *Democratization* 21: 2, 244–67.

Sözalan, Özden (2013), 'A few remarks on the lessons of Gezi uprising', *The International Journal of Badiou Studies* 2: 1, 146–51.

Suter, Brigitte (2013), 'Perceptions, contestations and negotiations on race, ethnicity and gender: the case of sub-Saharan African migrants in Istanbul', *SBF Dergisi* 68: 1, 59–81.

Suvari, Çakir Ceyhan (2010), 'A brief review of ethnicity studies in Turkey', *Iran and the Caucasus* 14: 2, 407–18.

Tezcan, Baki (2012), 'Ethnicity, race, religion and social class: Ottoman markers of difference', in *The Ottoman World*, ed. Christine Woodhead, London and New York: Routledge, pp. 159–70.

Tittensor, David (2012), 'The Gülen movement and the case of a secret agenda: putting the debate in perspective', *Islam and Christian–Muslim Relations* 23: 2, 163–79.

Tok, Evren and Melis Oğuz (2013), 'Manifestations of neoliberal urbanisation: the case of Sulukule/Istanbul', *Planlama* 3: 2, 57–66.

Toktaş, Şule (2005), 'The conduct of citizenship in the case of turkey's Jewish minority: legal status, identity and civic virtue aspects', *Comparative Studies of South Asia, Africa and the Middle East* 26: 1, 121–33.

Toprak, Metin, Nasuh Uslu and Judd D. King (2009), 'Transformation of Turkish politics: socio-political, economic and ethnic peculiarities', *Bilig, Journal of Social Sciences of the Turkish World* 50, 199–232.

Travis, Hannibal (2013), 'Did the Armenian genocide inspire Hitler? Turkey, past and future', *Middle East Quarterly* 20: 1, 27–35.

Tuğal, Cihan (2014), '"Resistance everywhere": The Gezi revolt in global perspective', *New Perspectives on Turkey* 49, 157–72.

Turam, Berna (2015), *Gaining Freedoms: Claiming Space in Istanbul and Berlin*, Stanford, CA: Stanford University Press.

Turunç, Hasan (2011), 'The post-westernisation of EU–Turkey relations', *Journal of Contemporary European Studies* 19: 4, 535–46.

Ulker, Erol (2005), 'Contextualising "Turkification": nation-building in the late Ottoman Empire, 1908–18', *Nations and Nationalism* 11: 4, 613–36.

Ulusoy, Kivanç (2011), 'The European impact on state–religion relations in Turkey: political Islam, Alevis and non-Muslim minorities', *Australian Journal of Political Science* 46: 3, 407–23.

Üngör, Uğur Ümit (2011), *The Making of Modern Turkey: Nation and State in Eastern Anatolia 1913–1950*, Oxford: Oxford University Press.

Uslu, Emrullah (2007), 'Turkey's Kurdish problem: steps toward a solution', *Studies in Conflict and Terrorism* 30: 2, 157–72.

Uzer, Umut (2011), 'The genealogy of Turkish nationalism: from civic and ethnic to conservative nationalism in Turkey', in *Symbiotic Antagonisms: Competing Nationalisms in Turkey*, eds Ayşe Kadıoğlu and E. Fuat Keyman, Salt Lake City: University of Utah Press, pp. 103–32.

Vahide, Şükran (2005), *Islam in Modern Turkey: an Intellectual Biography of Bediuzzaman Said Nursi*, New York: State University of New York Press.

Varnali, Kaan and Vehbi Gorgulu (2014), 'A social influence perspective on expressive political participation in Twitter: the case of #OccupyGezi', *Information, Communication & Society*, 18: 1, 1–16: DOI: 10.1080/1369 118X.2014.923480.

Walby, Sylvia (2013), 'Violence and society: introduction to an emerging field of sociology', *Current Sociology* 61: 2, 95–111.

Weller, Peter and Ihsan Yilmaz (2012), *European Muslims, Civility and Public Life: Perspectives On and From the Gülen Movement*, London and New York: Continuum.

White, Jenny B. (2002), *Islamist Mobilization in Turkey: a Study in Vernacular Politics*, London: University of Washington Press.

White, Jenny B. (2012), *Muslim Nationalism and the New Turks*, Princeton, NJ: Princeton University Press.

Yavuz, M. Hakan (1998), 'A preamble to the Kurdish question: the politics of Kurdish identity', *Journal of Muslim Minority Affairs* 18: 1, 9–18.

Yavuz, M. Hakan (2001), 'Five stages of the construction of Kurdish nationalism in Turkey', *Nationalism and Ethnic Politics* 7: 3, 1–24.

Yavuz, M. Hakan (2003), *Islamic Political Identity in Turkey*, New York: Oxford University Press.

Yavuz, M. Hakan (2009), *Secularism and Muslim Democracy in Turkey*, Cambridge: Cambridge University Press.

Yavuz, M. Hakun (2013), *Toward an Islamic Enlightenment: the Gülen Movement*, New York: Oxford University Press.

Yeğen, Mesut (2007), 'Turkish nationalism and the Kurdish question', *Ethnic and Racial Studies* 30: 1, 119–51.

Yel, Ali Murat and Alparslan Nas (2013), 'After Gezi: moving towards post-hegemonic imagination in Turkey', *Insight Turkey* 15: 4, 177–90.

Yel, Ali Murat and Alparslan Nas (2014), 'Insight Islamophobia: governing the public visibility of Islamic lifestyle in Turkey', *European Journal of Cultural Studies* 17: 5, 567–84.

Yildiz, Ali Aslan and Maykel Verkuyten (2012), '"We are not terrorists": Turkish Muslim organizations and the construction of a moral identity', *Ethnicities* 13: 3, 359–81.

Yildiz, Kerim and Georgina Fryer (2004), *The Kurds: Culture and Language Rights*, London: Kurdish Human Rights Project.

You, Jong-sung (2012), 'Social trust: fairness matters more than homogeneity', *Political Psychology* 33: 5, 701–21.

Yüksel, Metin (2006), 'The encounter of Kurdish women with nationalism in Turkey', *Middle Eastern Studies* 42: 5, 777–802.

Zan, Srabac, Ola Listhaug and Tor Georg Jakobsen (2012), 'Patterns of ethnic intolerance in Europe', *Journal of International Migration and Integration* 13: 4, 459–79.

Index

Note: the letter t following a page number indicates a table; page numbers in *italics* indicate illustrations